# RESISTANCE, CHAOS AND CONTROL IN CHINA

*Also by Robert P. Weller*

POWER AND PROTEST IN THE COUNTRYSIDE
Studies in Rural Unrest in Asia, Europe, and Latin America
(*co-editor with Scott E. Guggenheim*)

UNITIES AND DIVERSITIES IN CHINESE RELIGION

# Resistance, Chaos and Control in China

## Taiping Rebels, Taiwanese Ghosts and Tiananmen

Robert P. Weller

University of Washington Press
Seattle

Library of Congress Cataloging-in-Publication Data
Weller, Robert P. (Robert Paul), 1953–
Resistance, chaos and control in China : Taiping rebels,
Taiwanese ghosts and Tiananmen / Robert P. Weller.
p.   cm.
Includes bibliographical references and index.
ISBN 0–295–97285–8
1. China—History—Taiping Rebellion, 1850–1864.   2. China–
–History—Tiananmen Square Incident, 1989.   3. Ghosts—Taiwan.
I. Title.
DS759.W455   1994
951'.035—dc20                                    93–20037
                                                      CIP

Published simultaneously in Great Britain by
The Macmillan Press Ltd

Printed in Hong Kong

# Contents

*Acknowledgements*

PART I    INTERPRETING RESISTANCE AND RESISTING
          INTERPRETATION

1   Resistance                                                        3

2   Saturation and Potentials                                        16

PART II   TAIPING REBELLION

3   Jesus's Brother and the Chinese Periphery                        33

4   Saturating the Movement: God Gets Power                          50

5   Too Many Voices                                                  69

6   Precipitation and Institution: The Taiping Rises Up              86

PART III   TAIWANESE GHOSTS

7   Hot and Noisy Religion                                          113

8   Saturated Ghosts and Social Change in Taiwan                    129

9   Failed Precipitations                                           154

10  The Limits to Cultural Domination                               169

PART IV   CONCLUSION: TIANANMEN AND BEYOND

11  Institutions of Control, Institutions Beyond Control            187

12  Irony, Cynicism, and Potential Resistance                       205

# Contents

| | |
|---|---|
| *Notes* | 225 |
| *Character List* | 231 |
| *Bibliography* | 236 |
| *Index* | 249 |

# Acknowledgements

The research for this book owes a great deal to many people, too many for me to mention more than just a few. Most of the work on the Taiping Heavenly Kingdom took place at Nanjing University in 1984–1985. I am grateful to the History Department for providing me with an intellectual home there, and especially to Professors Cai Shaoqing and Mao Jiaqi, both of whom provided friendship and advice. Both helped shape my understanding of the Taiping movement, and both also opened doors that would probably have remained closed to me without their help. Liang Ken was a wonderful companion as well as an invaluable help during my time in Guangxi. I am especially indebted to the authorities of Guiping County, and particularly to Li Yulin and the staff of the history museum, all of whom put their interest in the topic above the excitement and trepidation of a rare and exotic visit from a foreigner.

In Taiwan, I am grateful first of all to Liu Bingzhen, who took me on my initial visit to the Eighteen Lords temple. My thanks also go to Hsin-Huang Michael Hsiao and others at the Institute of Ethnology of the Academia Sinica, my hosts and colleagues in Taiwan on many occasions. Finally, Wei An and Marianne Fritz provided valuable assistance gathering data on the campaigns that followed Tiananmen.

I have presented various parts of the argument to Anthropology Department seminars at the University of North Carolina, the University of Chicago, and Harvard University; to the MIT faculty seminar sponsored by Anthropology/Archaeology and the Center for International Studies; at the International Conference on Cultural Change in Post-War Taiwan sponsored by the University of Washington and National Taiwan University; to the Modern China Seminar at Columbia University; to the Anthropologists in Boston studying China (with a special thanks to the Watsons for hosting it); and to my colleagues in the Boston University Anthropology Department and the Institute for the Study of Economic Culture. All helped me think more clearly about the argument – a few challenging questions are worth a great deal.

The idea for the book itself first began to form at the Conference on Communities in Question, held in Hoa Hin, Thailand. I am grateful to the sponsors for organizing such a rewarding (and pleasant) conference, and especially to Jean Comaroff, whose comments started me thinking about resistance and meaning. Finally, the book has benefited a great deal from discussion with friends and from comments on the manuscript itself. Above all, I am grateful for the generous and thoughtful help of Peter Berger, Myron Cohen, Paul Cohen, Stevan Harrell, Robert Hefner, Alice Ingerson, Susan Naquin, and Rubie Watson.

ROBERT P. WELLER

# Part I

## INTERPRETING RESISTANCE AND RESISTING INTERPRETATION

# 1

# Resistance

A new literature on cultural resistance has enormously expanded our view of how people challenge the systems in which they live. While in the 1960s and 1970s we concentrated on armed peasant rebellion, recent years have turned us instead to devil worship in South America (Taussig, 1980), Mexican–American sexual humor (Limón, 1989), Chinese social networks (Yang, 1989), and safety pins in British ears as aspects of a subversive cultural resistance. While this may reflect in part the political changes of the 1980s, it also forces us to ask about the relation between the two kinds of resistance. Armed peasant rebellion and quiet cultural subversion seem quite different, and we tend to use different theoretical approaches for them. Yet each kind of resistance implies a relation to the other, with armed rebellion having clear cultural roots, and cultural resistance having at least the possibility of coming out of the closet as an actual political movement.

This book explores the problem of these different kinds of resistance, arguing that we need a single approach, which sees the shared processes involved in open rebellion, in tacit cultural resistance, and in the cooptation of resistance. The cases I discuss are all Chinese, and all fairly modern, but otherwise as diverse as they can be. The Taiping rebellion in the middle of the nineteenth century was resistance by any definition. It saw massive armies, many millions of casualties, and a radically egalitarian ideology. The rebels, self-proclaimed Christians led by Jesus's younger brother, captured and held the economic core of China for a decade, and very nearly toppled the regime.

The second case lies at the other end of the spectrum of resistance, if it can be called resistance at all. Ghost worship, especially at a few unusual temples, became extremely popular in Taiwan in the late 1980s. Vaguely associated with the underworld, gamblers, and ill-gotten gains generally, the great popularity of ghosts in Taiwan strongly suggests parallels with Taussig's analysis of devil worship in Colombia as a critique of capitalism (Taussig, 1980). Yet if this is resistance, it appears to be very different from

3

the Taiping rebellion – tacit instead of explicit, and embedded in everyday life instead of strongly institutionalized as a new state. Indeed, one could easily argue that it is not resistance at all, but just a kind of play with the system, or even a celebration of capitalism. It is the kind of situation that forces us to question what "resistance" really is. We tend to think of the Taiping rebels and the Taiwanese ghosts as quite different kinds of phenomena. Yet if both are resistance in any sense, we need a common explanation that still does justice to the differences.

These two cases suggest new lines of analysis for a third, which I will address more briefly in the concluding chapters: the Tiananmen Square demonstrations in May and June 1989, and the aftermath of the tragedy as the state reasserted ideological control. Tiananmen deserves attention not just for the events in the square – explicitly political like the Taiping rebellion, but without its strong institutional structure to shape the movement – but because the campaigns that followed force us to ask about future possibilities for resistance. Even as the state powerfully exerts its control over all external channels to express alternate views, people create new ways to deflect and defuse official cultural domination.

In exploring these cases, I will argue that they illustrate important shared processes, in spite of their apparent diversity. As part of a broader theory of change, a theory of resistance needs to address both the cultural antecedents to a movement like the Taiping, and to uncover the mechanisms through which tacit, everyday cultural "resistance" might develop into such movements. All three movements, in spite of their great differences, in fact shared important early features. Yet all three played out the relation between interpretation and institution in very different ways.

This chapter and the next take up some of the theoretical problems of resistance, from the question of what actually qualifies as resistance, to the relation between institution and interpretation. We often speak too loosely of resistance and thus fail to make some theoretically useful distinctions. I will argue in particular that some occasions and actions nourish a rich surfeit of multivocalic meaning which opens up many interpretive possibilities. These can include a strong potential for resistance, but only as one possibility among many. Alternative interpretations are not themselves political resistance. Specific social processes shape the possible realizations of that potential, only occasionally fostering explicit and active resistance movements. After that I will move to the specific cases, taking up the rich possibilities of their early stages, and the mutual relationships between specific interpretations and changing social institutions as active resistance developed or simply remained an implicit possibility.

## TWO PUZZLES

My concern with these issues began with my first long-term research in Taiwan in the late 1970s, even though I was looking into rather different topics. Any period of fieldwork raises unexpected questions at the same time as it begins to answer old ones. Even when they do not seem to concern the topic at hand, the specters of these new puzzles may continue to haunt one in the years that follow. This book stems from two such images, both based in popular religious experience.

The first puzzle has no immediate relation to resistance. It began with my initial systematic questioning about religion, and never ended. Informants who were quite voluble and friendly on most topics simply had nothing to say about religion. These were people who constructed elaborate rituals on a regular basis, and some of them made ritual offerings of incense every day. Yet I often felt that I knew the meanings of their religion, based on the secondary anthropological literature, better than they did.

My first regular line of questioning concerned the Earth God (Tho Te Kong). Every neighborhood has its own Earth God and a temple to house him, and in many cases elsewhere in China there are reports of local worthies said to have become Earth Gods after death. The story of the Earth God seemed like an easy place to begin As it turned out, every family did indeed worship the Earth God, but no one had anything at all useful to say about who he was. The best I ever got was, "Go ask Old Ong, he likes those old stories." Old Ong, as it turned out, had nothing to say either, but did recommend a movie he had seen about the deity a few years earlier.

The explanation, I thought (rightly), was that legends about gods were far less important than actual ritual dealings with them, at least in this community. The problem only got worse, however, when I moved to explanation of ritual. People who burn incense every day, for example, usually offer one stick to the ancestors on their domestic altar, another stick to the gods ensconced in the house, and a third stick just outside the door. This had already been explicated in several important studies of Chinese religion (e.g., Feuchtwang, 1974; Wolf, 1974) as being for the three main categories of beings – ancestors, gods and ghosts, seen as a kind of supernatural parallel for kin, bureaucrats and strangers. The incense for ancestors and gods seemed clear enough when I spoke to people, but that outside stick became a problem. I began to see the look that anthropologists dread, the uncomfortable stare that starts when our questions stop making sense, and people wonder if they really have to answer. In this case, at least, I was able to get answers with a minimum of pushing, but the answers were inconsistent from one person to the next. Some people said "ghosts," the answer I expected, but others told me the other major being worshipped outdoors – the Emperor of Heaven, highest of all the deities and as far as one can get from the lowly ghosts. Still others just ducked the question. My uneasy feeling was that people had no ready answer, but looked for parallels in beings typically worshipped outside, and gave me the first that came to mind.

Things only got worse when my questions moved from simple daily ritual to more elaborate and unusual events. To give just one more example, the Emperor of Heaven receives an offering of a whole pig at annual rituals in honor of the birthday of a major community deity. A great deal of ritual attention surrounds the pig, but one of the most striking things is the large cleaver thrust into the animal's skull and left standing starkly in its head throughout the offering. I could only get two explanations for this, neither very satisfying to an anthropologist in search of interpretive abundance. The first ran along the lines of "We're Chinese; this is how we do things." The second was even more frustrating: "It looks pretty that way," I heard over and over about this and many other ritual details. I took this to mean that it would not look right any other way, but it was hardly up to the standards of rich explication that one would expect from, for instance, the Zambian Ndembu whom Victor Turner described (Turner, 1967).

I had come to Taiwan as a graduate student versed in interpretive anthropology, including Turner and especially Clifford Geertz, who had put the problem of meaning at the center of his influential definition of religion (Geertz, 1973b:98–108). In the same essay he defined a symbol as "any object, act, event, quality, or relation which serves as a vehicle for a conception" (Geertz, 1973b:91). There were vehicles galore in Taiwan, but the conceptions seemed hard to find.

This is not to argue that our own constructions have no value unless they directly echo the explicit interpretations of our informants. I was bothered simply by the lack of a good way to deal with people's strikingly insouciant attitude toward explicit interpretation. The relative lack of interest in such efforts constitutes an ethnographic fact whose significance has tended to disappear under our own ability to construct interpretations.

Let me turn to the second puzzle, which relates to a specific incident, again involving those pigs offered on the birthday of a major community god. In Sanxia township, the area where I worked, the birthday of their god Co Su Kong is the most important ritual event of the year. The temple plaza only has room to display a dozen pigs, and the temple will display the twelve largest in the community. Families of the area vie to raise the most obese animals – pigs too fat to stand up and walk around, even too fat to roll over if you are very lucky. The day of the birthday is filled with offerings, both at home and in the temple. Onlookers, people selling goods to the crowd, and the occasional dragon or lion dance totally block traffic. The highlight comes when people promenade their pigs individually into the temple plaza, accompanied by bands and more dragon and lion dances. Each pig, slaughtered, shaved (except for the top of the head), neatly marked with rows of government meat inspection stamps, with a pineapple in its teeth, entrails, a duck and a live fish hanging from its mouth, and a cleaver in its head, straddles a kind of scaffold that makes it look even more enormous than it already is. The entire conglomeration sits in the middle of a plywood tower, gaudily painted in the brightest colors with historical tales and complex decorations. The scene borders on chaos with the pigs trying to push through the packed throng of happy spectators in the plaza.

All of this had been described in some detail by Emily Martin [Ahern] (and published a few years later, Ahern, 1981b). Arguing broadly that pigs stand in for people in the ritual, she made the specific case that the pigs represent Taiwanese, as opposed to mainland Chinese, and that the ritual itself is an affirmation of Taiwanese ethnicity.[1] I do not want to retrace the details of Ahern's analysis here; suffice it to say that I found (and continue to find) her argument that the ritual implies a kind of quiet political resistance convincing. Moreover, the consistent pressure from the government to reduce the scale and especially the expense of such rituals seemed to strengthen the case. In a situation where people could not speak openly about such issues, ritual provided a safe way of marking off Taiwanese identity and resisting mainlander control of public discourse.

All of which brings me to the 1979 performance of the ritual in Sanxia. The birthday took place just a few weeks after the United States had officially broken diplomatic relations with Republic of China government in Taiwan in favor of the People's Republic of China. People worried that Taiwan's economy would collapse, or even that the Red Army would come pouring across the Taiwan Strait. The government asked for donations to buy jet fighters. While the temple in Sanxia rejected suggestions that their birthday ritual be canceled entirely, they did volunteer to cut down on expenses and donate the proceeds to the government. While the temple had paid a great deal of lip service (while giving almost no real support) to government economizing campaigns in the past, this time they made a powerful statement through the ritual itself. As a way of saving money, the towers housing the pigs were left completely undecorated, painted solid white. Far more than a simple statement about austerity, those white towers added a vision of death to one of the happiest events of the year – white is the color of mourning in China.

I have argued elsewhere that people in Taiwan sometimes maintained their rituals in the face of government pressure through a kind of cynical ritual disguise (Weller, 1987b). They have sometimes claimed, for example, that raising obese pigs for the gods is in fact a useful agricultural competition. Yet this case was completely different. The dominant feeling I got was in no sense cynical; it was a rallying around the flag.

The somber mood and reduced scale of the ceremony quite strongly supported the mainlander-dominated government that the ritual was supposed to be resisting. Had the interpretation as ethnic resistance been wrong from the beginning? If not, how had something apparently so central to the ritual been so suddenly transformed, without much changing the structure of the ritual itself? At the heart of the problem lay the question of whether we could ever argue for a kind of tacit form of everyday resistance. These cases imply that we can never read such a clear and unified intrinsic meaning into the formal elements of any ritual.

Both of these ethnographic problems – the general lack of interest in religious explication and the resistance turned to patriotism – question the relation between ritual and interpretation. While the need for an adequate theory of change prompted social scientists and historians to look for patterns of everyday resistance, such a theory will also have to deal with interpretive silences and with apparent resistance suddenly turned to collaboration. If people do not speak directly of resistance, at what point can we properly impose such a reading? While some have claimed that we can and should identify such tacit resistance, others claim just as strongly that powerful hegemonic structures undercut apparent resistance, making it superficial or simply illusory. I will argue that both schools share problematic assumptions about meaning, and that an approach tying meaning more closely to socially organized interpretation leads to interesting new directions for analysis.

WHAT IS RESISTANCE?

Let me begin with the booming literature that looks for tacit resistance, and then turn to the opposed literature that instead sees only cultural domination. The two approaches together create a false argument, an apparent contradiction based on the over-interpretation of inherently multiple meaning. Neither extreme adequately roots interpretation in actual history and social organization. The argument for a counter-hegemonic discourse has roots in Antonio Gramsci's search to find and organize the voice of the Italian working class before World War II. Gramsci identified the seed of a revolutionary consciousness in the working class, even while recognizing the power of the dominant ideology. Speaking of the "man-in-the-mass," he wrote that:

> One might almost say that he has two theoretical consciousnesses (or one contradictory consciousness): one which is implicit in his activity and which in reality unites him with all his fellow-workers in the practical transformation of the real world; and one, superficially explicit or verbal, which he has inherited from the past and uncritically absorbed . . . Critical understanding of self takes place therefore through a struggle of political "hegemonies" and of opposing directions (Gramsci 1971:333).

For Gramsci, daily experience thus created the seed of a counter-hegemony, one that could grow explicit in class struggle.

Drawing at least in part on Gramsci's insights, a more recent literature has turned to the analysis of how peasant culture or working–class culture differs systematically from the dominant ideology. One important approach identifies a shared body of traditional expectations within the class, which will lead to resistance if violated, for instance as part of the transition to a market-based economy. Writing about eighteenth–century English riots, for instance, E. P. Thompson argues that

> these grievances operated within a popular consensus as to what were legitimate and what were illegitimate practices in marketing, milling, baking, etc. This in its turn was grounded upon a consistent traditional view of social norms and obligations, of the proper economic functions of several parties within the community, which, taken together, can be said to constitute the moral economy of the poor (Thompson, 1971:78).

James Scott has developed a similar case for Southeast Asia in his influential *The Moral Economy of the Peasant* (Scott, 1976). Both authors make a somewhat stronger case than Gramsci, arguing in essence for a class culture in its own right, rather than the contradictory consciousness of Gramsci. Resistance here lies just below the surface – a constant class friction ready to burst into flames when the moral economy is violated. The existence of a moral economy of the poor implies a kind of permanent implicit resistance, an alternative view of the world already developed beneath the dominant ideology.

Other authors have come at the idea of a submerged peasant culture from other directions. Carlo Ginzburg (1980), for example, has given us the story of Menocchio, a sixteenth-century miller and accused heretic. Idiosyncratic product of a fascinating combination of influences, Menocchio was good evidence of Gramsci's claim that everyone is in some sense a philosopher. Ginzburg pulls at the various threads that wove Menocchio's thought, from a world made of wormy cheese to a critique of Latin. The underlying warp of this fabric is again a hidden peasant tradition: "The crucial element is a common store of traditions, myths, and aspirations handed down orally over generations. In both cases [namely Menocchio and an earlier heretic named Scolio], it was contact with written culture through their schooling, that permitted this deeply rooted deposit of oral culture to emerge" (Ginzburg, 1980:117). For Ginzburg this peasant alternative remained deeply hidden, emerging into the historical record only rarely.

The existence of such alternatives to a dominant culture opens the door for the analysis of unspoken forms of resistance, and for the search for evidence that gives life to these alternatives even when they have no voice. Scott's more recent work, for example, has dealt with the "ordinary weapons of relatively powerless groups: foot dragging, dissimulation, false compliance, pilfering, feigned ignorance, slander, arson, sabotage, and so forth" (Scott, 1985:29). He sees such implicit resistance typifying even an area without active class struggle, and without strongly drawn class boundaries.

In quite another part of the world, Michael Taussig has analyzed the baptism of money by Colombian plantation workers (Taussig, 1980). I have already alluded to this study for its apparent striking similarity to the Taiwanese ghosts, and I will take it up again later when I discuss that case. Taussig's informants told of people who substituted a peso bill for a baby during a baptismal rite. The switch doomed the soul of the baby, but the bill gained the property of self-increase. Every time the bill was spent, it returned to its owner, taking along all the money in its vicinity. Taussig drew a strong parallel with capitalist commodity fetishism, where an investment appears to return with a profit, as if by magic. The Colombians, however, were not simply drawing a supernatural analogy with the market – they were also damning it as evil. For Taussig, a peasant use-value culture provided the germ of a critical consciousness of capitalism and exchange-value culture. Resistance again lies very close to the surface, even in everyday religion.

Perhaps most influential of all in recent years has been Mikhail Bakhtin writing on Rabelais and peasant Carnival traditions (Bakhtin, 1984). Living at the juncture between the Middle Ages and the Renaissance, Bakhtin's Rabelais helped shatter the medieval official language of order by drawing on the popular language of the marketplace and popular traditions of Carnival. Here again a peasant voice always existed, even while it was generally submerged beneath the official language. That voice became loud in moments of transition, and Bakhtin saw it as an important factor in the origins of the Renaissance. The reversals of Carnival, where a fool reigns as king, have now made commonplace analyses that see Carnival as a fertile area for resistance.

In fact, this entire literature on alternative cultures has encouraged us to see resistance in everything from rap music to ignoring a stop sign. While I do not wish to oversimplify often complex and insightful analyses, we can at least characterize a line of argument justifying the use of "resistance" for many of the acts of everyday life: working classes maintain their own alternative views of the world in the face of pressure from a hegemonic discourse. According to this theoretical approach, these alternatives constitute genuine resistance both in their refusal to accede to the hegemony and in their ability to generate new social forms in the right circumstances. The opposition generally remains unspoken because the broader social forces allow it no voice. At most times it remains a safe resistance, which works through metaphor and irony, and never resists directly.

**Another View**

In spite of the great popularity of the search for resistance in everyday life, others have offered an alternative far more pessimistic about the possibility of counter-hegemonies and daily resistance. The literature on Carnival provides a convenient summary of the arguments. For Bakhtin Carnival was an incubator for an alternative view of the world that played a major role in ending the official discourse of the Middle Ages. Others have treated it comparably as an expressive tool, helping to forge a unity of the working classes in the class struggle (Gilmore, 1984:96–125). Yet from quite a different theoretical angle, Carnival simply reiterates the dominant social structure. Umberto Eco (1984), for example, notes the systematic structural reversals of Carnival – the world stood on its head – and argues that the reversals work primarily to emphasize the structure itself. Turning everything upside down really changes nothing, except perhaps by drawing attention to the thing itself. Everyone involved is quite clear that after playing with the social hierarchy in reverse one day, all will return to live in it right side up the next day. More recently still, Stanley Brandes has written that "it is reasonable to assume that the periodic expression of chaos in [Mexican] fiestas reassures people about the stability of their social order. If deviant behavior can occur openly and publicly, without seriously harmful consequences, then society demonstrates its resilience" (Brandes, 1988:169). Such arguments have been familiar to anthropologists at least since Gluckman analyzed the functions of rituals of rebellion in maintaining order in southeast Africa (Gluckman, 1960).

Far from being a focal point for resistance, Carnival thus becomes either a sociological safety valve or a new reiteration of the social hierarchy. These approaches imply a powerful unity in any society through an omnipotent discourse or a very basic shared structure. If such analysts are right that, for example, fundamental ideas about hierarchy are basic to Indian (Dumont, 1980) or Chinese (Sangren, 1987) society, one would expect apparent resistance in fact to share notions of that hierarchy. Whatever such "resistance" appears to oppose, it in fact simply recreates its society. Such an analysis would not be at all surprised by pig offerings suddenly turned to patriotism; it would have questioned the ethnic resistance interpretation from the beginning. Similarly, it would be less interested in the Taiping rebels' radical ideology, and more in how their actual social organization recreated much of the imperial hierarchy. Taiping law required monogamy, but Taiping leaders came to have large numbers of wives and concubines; Taiping ideology was radically egalitarian, but its leaders lived lives of imperial luxury. Rap music may at first appear to be cultural resistance, but it ends up as a McDonald's jingle.

## Interpretation and Resistance

If resistance thus appears to be everywhere for some, it is nowhere for others, a chimerical vision that disappears under a cold stare. While this sound-bite summary may simplify the sophistication of many actual arguments, it does, I think, capture at least the ideal type of two approaches to the material. These two types of explanation appear to contradict each other; no room remains for a diplomatic reconciliation. How can we choose between them? How are we to interpret the significance of Taiwanese ghosts or even Tiananmen? As long as we insist on pulling a single "true" reading out of events and symbols – whether as clear opposition or clear acquiescence – we remain trapped between the Scylla of an inevitable but unspoken resistance and the Charybdis of an irresistible hegemony.

As a result, many authors have grown wary of the idea of resistance, even as they feel the need to address it. People looking at resistance have begun to speak with caution of the "romance of resistance" (Abu-Lughod, 1990), or of substituting "subversion" for "resistance" (Yang, 1989). They recognize the problems inherent in theories that see such a powerful structural or hegemonic unity that internal change seems impossible and human agency irrelevant. On the other hand, they are uncomfortable with resistances that do not resist.

Neither the resistance nor the hegemony view is subject to easy disproof. Both require us to look beneath the surface of what people say and do to find an underlying order, and both thus leave room for contradictory interpretations of agreed-upon facts. The two arguments appear impossible to reconcile and impossible to choose between. In fact, I will argue that the problem does not lie so much in these specific answers, but rather in the questions that both ask. Both arguments share a faulty semiotic that attempts to read a single meaning from a text, ritual, or action. Both fail to deal with the multiplicity of voices and styles in their "texts," with the possibilities of varying readings in different contexts or by different people, or with the possibility that such multivocality simply remains unresolved. Meaning lies not just in the text, but in socially and historically grounded processes of interpretation.

Even when these theories ground meaning in social life, they pull out clear interpretations only by greatly simplifying experience. James Scott, for example, who clearly recognizes this problem, argues that one can choose between the hegemonic and resistance explanations on empirical grounds (Scott, 1985:39–41). By making this argument, he quite properly places interpretation in a broader social context. Nevertheless, he draws a far more consistent picture of regular resistance than would be possible for many cases, and certainly for Taiwan. Scott would argue that, unlike Taiwan, class divisions in Sedaka are fairly clear and increasing, class struggle lies just below the surface, and empirical evidence for a resistance interpretation is thus more available than in many cases of so-called cultural resistance. On the other hand, critics accuse such theories of oversimplifying class relations and ignoring other kinds of social solidarities.[2] Hegemony theories tend just as much to a simple view of society as a unified entity, without effective class or other lines of struggle. Both downplay the real problems of cross-cutting solidarities and changing divisions, further pushing their theories away from the real problems of ambiguity and shifting interpretation.

Both the ethnic pigs who suddenly turned Nationalist and the general interpretive silence about religion in Taiwan demand a focus on the active, social processes of interpretation. An insistence that every text has its single reading will miss the point, drawing us back into the same old argument. The most ironic statements, after all, have literal readings that subvert their own subversion, just as literal statements have ironic readings. The key question in asking about tacit resistance is how to sort these things out in relation to actual social and historical processes. Even the tendency to read political implications from all religion, which typifies all the literature I have discussed so far, risks pushing inherent meaning too far. Political meaning as both resistance and accommodation lies below the surface, but so do many other possible readings. This book thus concentrates on the social possibilities of making one line of interpretation explicit and broadly accepted, at the expense of all the other possibilities.

Each of the cases I discuss features a central ritual or activity that is particularly rife with possible interpretations. Rather than trying to pull out an illusory single correct reading, I will concentrate on the interplay of possibilities, asking when and how particular interpretations come to dominate. Rather than decoding culture, I will be examining the social organization of meaning, the intimate ties between institution and interpretation. Rather than seeing resistance everywhere or nowhere, I will view it as one of many potential lines of interpretation. Looking at the problem in this way preserves the richness of the interpretive possibilities, and also clarifies how resistance can actually come to dominate in the competition to impose an interpretation. It allows us to see tacit everyday resistance in the same theoretical light as open struggle, and clarifies the successes and failures of various interest groups vying to dominate interpretation.

# 2

# Saturation and Potentials

Throughout this book I will be interested especially in situations that are overloaded with a glut of possible meanings, but where no single line of interpretation has yet come to dominate. This view has precursors in various critiques of the decodable meanings of structuralism, from Victor Turner's discussions of multivocal symbols (1967), to the sociolinguistic turn away from structures of *langue* to the contextual meanings of *parole*, to post-structuralism in literary criticism. Each of these approaches pushes us away from structure alone, and toward a more complex view of indeterminate and ambiguous interpretation. While I will go on to argue that the ambiguities are resolved in certain social circumstances, comparable to the kinds of institutionalized rationalization that Max Weber saw in the Protestant sects (Weber, 1946), let me begin here with the argument for inherently indeterminate interpretation.

Such a view challenges claims that a structure of symbols encodes a structure of meaning in a fairly straightforward way, as if a machine could simply read them off. Nevertheless, the master structuralist, Claude Lévi-Strauss, evoked one of the clearest examples of what I mean. In his works on Amazonian myths, Lévi-Strauss often mentioned Richard Wagner's *Tristan and Isolde*, especially when he discussed mediators – mythical themes that inseparably combine structural oppositions. He addressed particularly two such mediators, opossums and rainbows. Just as rainbows bridge opposite sides of the sky and opposite ends of the spectrum, opossums cross categories as givers of both life and death. Both differ from nearly everything else he discussed by being impossible to reduce to one or the other binary pole of culture/nature or life/death. Along the same lines, the love philter/death philter in *Tristan* also fulfills an "opossum function" (Lévi-Strauss, 1970:281).

Lévi-Strauss called this phenomenon "chromaticism," music based on a continuous range of small intervals, rather than the larger intervals associated with the key signatures of tonal music

16

(Lévi-Strauss, 1970:256–281). Here he again referred implicitly to Wagner, this time to the overture to *Tristan*. The overture is famous among musicologists for the "Tristan chord" which forms its heart. The Tristan chord in a sense marks the culmination of tonal music, and by the same token its demise in the twentieth-century move to chromatic music. Like any good mediator, the chord constantly shifts its ground without ever establishing a key, creating a remarkable sense of unease in listeners. Over and over again it develops the tension that precedes a resolution into a tonic chord, and each time it somehow shifts into something else. Wagner never establishes a key for the movement, or perhaps it is better to say that he has written in too many keys at once. This is not the silly but shocking effect of leaving the last chord off a Beethoven symphony, where the key has long been clearly established and cutting the final resolution is just a kind of frustrating joke. Instead Wagner creates a vertigo of too many possibilities, a surplus of significations and signatures, constantly teasing about revealing its true nature, but in fact irresolvable.

The entire idea of mediators is a critical point in structuralism, for it is exactly the point where a simple structuralist reduction to decodable meanings breaks down. Mediators occupy inherently ambiguous, irresolvable positions in the structure, unlike proper structuralist signs whose position in a set of contrasts encoded a clear and unitary meaning. Signs that contrast with themselves, like chords in too many keys, cracked open the doors through which the critics of structuralism would later pour, seeing all signs reverberating far beyond their proper set of contrasts, carrying multiple sets of meanings, overloading the structure until it finally shattered.

Each of the cases of resistance I will discuss also has an overture based on the Tristan chord, overloaded with possible lines of interpretation. Such surfeits of hyperactive meaning occur over and over, not as exceptions to structural regularity, but as basic processes of interpretation. The heart of Bakhtin's discussion of Rabelais, in fact, concerns just this overabundance of meaning. His point about the language of the marketplace or Carnival does not simply argue for structural reversals, or for an independent peasant language as structured as the official discourse. At the core of such language, for Bakhtin, lies a permanently unresolved sense of becoming, where opposites unite and the possibilities are endless. Speaking about one of Rabelais' favorite images, for example, Bakhtin writes:

Thus, in the image of tripe life and death, birth, excrement, and food are all drawn together and tied in one grotesque knot; this is the center of bodily topography in which the upper and lower stratum penetrate each other. This grotesque image was a favorite expression of the ambivalence of the material bodily lower stratum, which destroys and generates, swallows and is swallowed (Bakhtin, 1984:163).

This great melting pot of meaning, where the possible ramifications far outweigh the neat categories of official thought, typifies situations that teem with too many possibilities. Bakhtin speaks of verbal play in the book "as if words had been released from the shackles of sense, to enjoy a play period of complete freedom and establish unusual relationships among themselves . . . The brief coexistence of these words, expressions, and objects outside the usual logical conditions discloses their inherent ambivalence" (Bakhtin, 1984:423). Structuralist systems of signs have left their meanings far behind, and we can begin to see how Chinese can enjoy their elaborate rituals without worrying too much about specific interpretations.

Even the words "Rabelaisian" and "gargantuan" have come to indicate an overwhelming surfeit, an overflow of thick meanings. This is not the simple excess of overeating; it is a flood of superfluity, sizes and quantities ranging from the unmanageable to the impossible. The characters themselves are ludicrously large, and their appetites are larger still. The writing itself reinforces this, from Panurge's introducing himself in thirteen languages (three of them imaginary) (Rabelais, 1955:197–201), to his addressing Friar John as one hundred sixty-six different kinds of ball-bags, finally ending with "my waggling ball-bag, my dear friend" (Rabelais, 1955:360–361). Friar John reciprocates a few pages later with his own equally long and entirely new list of ball-bags. This grotesque overabundance, itself superimposed on the absurd combination of insult and friendly greeting, overwhelms any search for simple meanings, just as the language of the marketplace or Carnival holds power through the impossibility of reducing its excesses to any kind of official discourse.

Roland Barthes makes a similar point in a very different context, during his essay on taking one's pleasure in texts. He asks us to imagine someone "who abolishes within himself all barriers, all classes, all exclusions . . .; who mixes every language, even those said to be incompatible; who silently accepts every charge of illogicality, of incongruity . . . Now this anti-hero exists: he is the reader of the text at the moment he takes his pleasure" (Barthes, 1975:3). Here again any neat decodings of meaning have fled in the face of overwhelming excess.

While I will return to the problem of how any interpretation ever comes to be agreed on, all of this sheds new light on Taiwanese interpretive silences about ritual, their apparent overabundance of symbolic vehicles without the articulated conceptions to go along with them. A surfeit of interpretive possibilities saturates such rituals, and by the same token insists on no single interpretation. Most Chinese, after all, are neither literary critics nor anthropologists, and feel no compulsion to pull out the "true" interpretation. There are other reasons to participate in rituals – curing diseases, remembering the ancestors, impressing the neighbors, having a good time – and it is enough to believe that some expert somewhere knows what the symbols mean.

While I was living in Sanxia, I asked my next-door neighbor about those pig offerings I discussed in the last chapter. He had raised a pig all year to offer at the god's birthday, and I had been with him when he presented the pig with great excitement in front of the temple just a few days earlier. He got into a small argument with another friend who had joined us; the friend was a very minor ritual expert who knew about proper mourning dress. My neighbor said the whole business with the cleaver, the guts, the fish and everything else was just for aesthetics; it simply had no wider meaning. The ritual would be equally proper without all those things; it just would not look as nice. The friend, however, took issue with him, arguing that everything must be somehow significant. Neither one either knew or much cared what that significance might be. The argument was only over whether the whole elaborate performance had any significance to anyone at all. The superfluity of possible interpretations means that one can stop with no interpretations, just as the overabundance of possible key signatures in the Tristan chord leaves one in no key at all.

This approach also begins to clarify the way pig sacrifices could speak one year to Taiwanese ethnic identity against the mainlanders, and the next year to patriotic support for the mainlander-dominated government. Like much ritual, this one contains a multiplicity of possible interpretations, but insists on none. No reading is ever fully closed, and reinterpretation constantly remains possible. Even such radically different interpretations as ethnic resistance and patriotic collaboration coexist easily in the ritual.

Pierre Bourdieu wrote that "It is because subjects do not, strictly speaking, know what they are doing that what they do has more meaning than they know" (Bourdieu, 1977:79). Explicit interpretation in fact limits significance, while leaving ritual or any other behavior uninterpreted keeps all the possibilities open. Bourdieu reminds us that the uninterpreted world extends everywhere; it is not just an odd feature of ludic peasant markets and Carnival. Doing things without interpreting them forms the broad base of experience, and the process of creating orthodox interpretations is itself problematic.

Active, political resistance, for Bourdieu, lies in the transformation from "what goes without saying and what cannot be said for lack of an available discourse" (doxa, in his terms) into the explicit, authorized language of orthodoxy or heterodoxy (Bourdieu, 1977:170). Taken for granted experiences "undergo nothing less than a *change of state* when they recognize themselves in the *public objectivity* of an already constituted discourse . . .: 'Words wreck havoc', says Sartre, 'when they find a name for what had up to then been lived namelessly'" (Bourdieu 1977:170, emphasis in original). Such transformations, for Bourdieu, tend to occur in times of crisis, when changing experiences force people to question who they are. They create the possibility of political resistance. Each of my cases concerns just this interplay between indeterminate practice and explicit discourse, and each really spells out one of Bourdieu's three terms. The Taiping successfully created a heterodox discourse, the Taiwanese ghosts remained a taken for granted doxa in spite of many attempts, and the aftermath of Tiananmen concerns promotion of an orthodoxy.

## INTERPRETIVE COMMUNITIES AND POTENTIALS FOR RESISTANCE

I have been loosely following various post-structural trends in literary theory to argue that many rituals contain lots of possibilities, but no single core of meaning. "Texts" do not directly determine meaning, and there is always another reading. This approach overcomes the insoluble arguments between resistance and hegemony which I discussed in the previous chapter. Carnival nourishes the seeds of both resistance and hegemony, but reduces to neither. Yet this approach it also brings along its own problems: is every text open to any reading, with each new reader really writing from scratch, as more extreme post-structuralists contend? Are all rituals buried in an overabundance of indeterminate possibility? If we examine real action in real social contexts, the answer must clearly be no. At least in some circumstances, people agree on shared interpretations, no matter how fuzzy the "text" may be in the abstract. The indecipherables of pure texts sometimes become lucidly clear in a social context.

This is by now a standard criticism of post-structuralist literary theory. The critics suggest a kind of reductio ad absurdum – if meaning lies completely in the eye of the beholder, how can all those post-structuralists understand each other's texts so well? In fact, how can any of us communicate? If I ask my class to close the door, usually the door gets closed. Many other interpretations were available – I might have been giving an example of a particular syntactic structure, or imitating someone, or trying to embarrass a student who just walked in late. Yet in practice, in this specific context, both my students and I easily share a single interpretation. How does this reconcile with the kind of open-endedness I have been arguing for?

Stanley Fish, perhaps because he is one of the most radical of the post-structuralists and has thus had to face this problem squarely, has pointed in a promising direction. He steered attention out of texts and into social relations by recognizing that "interpretive communities" limit the interpretations actually possible in any real context (Fish, 1980:303–321). We pre-read texts, in effect, by reading them within a socially established context of interpretation. Having been socialized into particular lines of interpretation, we favor them. Real texts in real contexts are thus not so very flexible after all. This discovery, of course, echoes earlier anthropological critics of structural meaning, like Geertz's (1973b) insistence that thought is public.

Fish has, if anything, gone too far in socializing meaning, so that it is difficult to see how people ever create new interpretations. Nor is any room left for practice that remains uninterpreted, although perhaps such a bias toward explicit language is understandable in literary studies. The idea of interpretive communities, as it stands, implies an unproblematic social structure, without the contradictions and conflicts of real life. Fish's approach leaves both the real social organization of interpretive communities, and the actual relations between interpretation and institution, relatively undeveloped.

Yet Fish has pointed in a very useful direction, leading us out of the hermeneutics of meaning and into the social organization of interpretation. He pushes us to ask how interpretive communities are structured, how they change, and how they impose or develop interpretations. Texts or rituals can determine meanings after all (at least in the etymological sense of determination as setting boundaries), but only within particular social contexts and structures. Our attention moves from the texts and rituals themselves to the relation between institution and interpretation, out of literary theory and into anthropology and history. The post-structuralist emphasis on inherently open-ended interpretation offers new ways of dealing with interpretive complexity, but also risks becoming an ivory tower virtuosity that ignores the effects of social organization.

Fish does not explicitly leave room for the kinds of interpretive silence I have been discussing, but the idea of interpretive communities promises to help with the problem. It allows us to suggest that the social relations of interpretation may be stronger or weaker, with some cases of very strongly developed institutions that clearly insist on a single interpretation, and others with little or no socialization into any particular interpretation. The most heavily overloaded situations thus occur where the social organization of interpretation has broken down or where no effective mechanism of interpretive socialization exists.

When Barthes (1975) argued that some texts are more pleasurable than others, he similarly contrasted the pleasureless texts of ostensibly literal language with the blissful breakdown of interpretive convention in which he takes his pleasure. And much the same is true for Bakhtin's contrast between the strongly institutionalized official language of the medieval elites and the peasant language of market and Carnival, where there is little institutional structure to impose an interpretation. The critical contrast is between areas where established institutions socialize or impose particular interpretations, and those where the lack of a strong social organization of meaning allows interpretive silence or free play with interpretive possibilities. Rather than assuming a systematic structure of meaning as the rule, I take such structures to be active creations that occur only under certain social circumstances.

Put in these terms, the problem harks back to Max Weber's work on rationalization – the process of consciously systematizing all aspects of life toward socially defined goals, instead of blindly following the shreds and patches of tradition. While Weber discusses this transformation primarily in individual terms in his best-known work on the Protestant ethic in Europe (Weber, 1958), much of his other work links rationalization directly to new institutions, both when he discusses American Protestant sects (Weber, 1946) and the rationalization of traditional and charismatic authority. Rationalization as a specific form of explicit and shared interpretation rests on particular kinds of institutional structures. The problem of institution and interpretation had always been at the core of Weber's work.

Yet the theoretical case for the inherent instability and multiplicity of interpretation that I have been developing helps to resolve some problems in Weber's formulation, just as Weber helps supply them with a needed institutional base. Weber's earlier works in particular seemed to imply an inevitable evolution toward rationality, because rational systems work more efficiently. The inherent ambiguity of meaning, however, clarifies how rational systems may be undermined, as new interpretations inevitably challenge the dominant rationality. The evidence from all three cases I will discuss indicates that rationalities can be undone, and that the processes of complicating, overloading and deflecting interpretation can in fact serve a critically important function in social transformation.

Saturation in chemistry offers a convenient metaphor for this process. Saturated solutions stand just on the verge of precipitating.[3] They are as full as they can get, having dissolved everything put in them, just as a ritual may dissolve all attempts at interpretation. Yet just one little push can change the entire character of the solution by precipitating out a solid when there was only liquid before. Under the right conditions saturated solutions, shifting and cloudy, can precipitate into new and tangible compounds. If saturated events are thick, overflowing with dissolved possibilities, precipitated interpretations are thin and easier to analyze. We recognize them easily through their thoroughly worked-out interpretations that we hear consistently and uniformly, and through the social structures that support them – all quite unlike those Taiwanese pigs. Only at this point of explicit interpretation can we speak clearly of political resistance or accommodation. The metaphor also brings out the energy that must be invested to cause a precipitation: imposing a dominant interpretation requires work. There is nothing inevitable or irreversible about this process; every society contains pressures both toward more explicit and institutionally grounded interpretation, and toward an indeterminate chaos of potential meanings.

Each case I discuss begins with a high degree of saturation, but they vary greatly in how much a unified interpretation ever comes to dominate. Explaining the differences requires a close look at the history and social organization of meaning. While academics often show a Weberian preference for the rationalizing processes of precipitation, one of the points these Chinese cases establish is the tremendous power and broad appeal of leaving meaning messy, as well as the concrete institutional difficulties and sacrifices of drawing out explicit, agreed-upon interpretations.

It should be clear by now that I do not see resistance as something inherent to all cases where meaning remains relatively open-ended. Insisting on such a reading simply recreates the arguments between resistance and hegemony that I have already discussed. Instead, politically significant resistance is only one possible line of pre-cipitation, which lies nascent in a saturated solution along with many other kinds of possibilities. We need to understand when people realize the potential for resistance, how that one reading can come to triumph over all the other possibilities. This will require following out the various possible interpretive communities that an indeterminate interpretation can mobilize, and examining the struggle to create and institutionalize new such communities.

Not all resistance, of course, lies either in saturated potentials or in major political movements. Many acts of day-to-day resistance have clear interpretations to all involved. Whatever its other connotations, sneaking cigarettes in the high school bathroom constitutes resistance against the school authorities. Yet here the social organization of interpretation has been defined by the authorities. It differs from the kinds of cases I explore here, where saturation allows a complex interplay between daily practice, established authority, and the germs of new interpretive institutions. Unlike bathroom cigarettes, the resistance I examine here threatens real political change, if it is ever realized.

The story never ends when a new and distinct interpretation comes to dominate as the only true meaning. There is, after all, always another reading. Every seizure of control over meaning opens itself to a new disintegration as alternative interpretations open up. Powerfully controlled meanings constantly threaten to dissolve back into solution, just as indeterminate meaning undergoes constant pressures toward a single interpretation. The inherent openness of meaning allows no closure here. Precipitation and dissolution are processes in constant tension, not absolute categories.

My basic approach is thus to pull out the various potentials inherent in any saturated situation, identify the social and historical processes that sometimes allow one potential to precipitate out, and look again for the tensions and potentials in the new system. This search for potentials may seem odd. We tend to sneer, after all, at counterfactual arguments in history. History happened the way it happened, and there is little point in analyzing the imaginary. Yet such an argument suggests that the past somehow differs fundamentally from the present, with the past developing along its clear lines of cause and effect, while the present is filled with possibilities among which we actively choose. Any historical explanation in fact implies that events would have been different had a certain action not taken place (Aron, 1977:168–170).[4] Bringing the same analytical tools to the past as to the present requires examining and differentiating among potentials.

Those Taiwanese pigs held the potential for both the ethnicity and the patriotic readings all along. Neither one had to be realized at any given time, but either could appear. By the same token, no explicit interpretation at all necessarily had to surface. While I will not squeeze those pigs any further here, the interesting questions do not so much involve the underlying meanings of the ritual performance alone, but rather the circumstances under which various explicit and widespread interpretations have managed to prevail. Much the same argument, of course, goes for Carnival. Le Roy Ladurie's *Carnival in Romans* (1979) shows clearly the various potentials dormant within the Romans Carnival, when several factions attempted to use the same Carnival performance for both repression and resistance.

## FREE SPACE AND PROBLEMS OF PRECIPITATION

Unlike many studies of resistance, I am thus not willing to read resistance into every saturated ritual. Difference alone is not resistance, certainly not politically significant resistance. One could argue, of course, for a broader definition of resistance that includes these overloaded situations: difference resists by not fully following the official line. Yet such a broad definition loses sight of other potential interpretations (like accommodation), and will never find the processes that can lead to politically important transformations. Rather than decoding resistance from complex and ambiguous ritual, I will look at the social relations and historical struggles that accompany the creation of actual resistance. While the best studies of resistance have done this anyway (e.g., Scott, 1985; Comaroff, 1985), making the approach theoretically explicit allows us to respect our informants' interpretive silences, where no particular interpretation is drawn out, and to understand how apparent resistance can suddenly take a very conservative turn. Both Taiping rebels and Taiwanese ghosts become open to the same theoretical tools.

Resistance is not everywhere. I will argue, however, that the indeterminate meaning that thrives in the absence of rigorous institutions of interpretive control typically indicates a strong potential for resistance, as one among many possible readings. From the point of view of official discourse, the thick and slippery overwhelming of structured meaning is perverse, no matter how harmless the intent of the participants on any one occasion. Victor Turner developed this point more fully when he discussed communitas, a clear example of what I am calling saturation. Communitas offers a blend of

> lowliness and sacredness, of homogeneity and comradeship. We are presented, in such rites, with a "moment in and out of time," and in and out of secular social structure, which reveals, however fleetingly, some recognition . . . of a generalized social bond that has ceased to be and has simultaneously yet to be fragmented into a multiplicity of ties (Turner, 1969:96).

Official powers always try to control communitas because it "is essentially opposed to structure, as antimatter is hypothetically opposed to matter. Thus, even when communitas becomes normative its religious expressions become closely hedged about by rules and interdictions – which act like the lead container of a dangerous radioactive isotope" (Turner 1974:243).

This is far different from arguing that all communitas or all indefinite interpretation is resistance, and Turner does not make this argument. It does help to clarify, however, why the proponents of official discourse and precipitated interpretations generally feel uncomfortable faced with saturation. Really thick rituals accept no reduction to a single thin reading; they bubble with alternatives, even if they offer no specifics. Yet in itself this is still not resistance, because there are many other possibilities, and because an explicit interpretation as resistance may never be drawn out. In addition, understanding actual social movements requires the ability to focus theoretically on the point where a movement forms, that is, when the potential resistance becomes actual.

This approach has several implications that I will develop in the chapters that follow. First, it suggests the tremendous difficulty of creating and maintaining a single, definitive interpretation. Perhaps because those of us who usually do these analyses are intellectuals ourselves – professional precipitators of meaning – we tend to think that agreed-upon, explicit interpretations convince through the power of the ideas alone (see also Worsley, 1968:xxv). The theoretical material I have drawn on so far suggests just the opposite: convincing interpretations require social organization, the active creation of new communities of interpretation. The move from indeterminate meaning to definitive interpretation involves a social transformation where one group successfully develops and promotes its interpretation above all others. The empirical material that follows shows just how difficult this transformation can be.

The second implication of all this is that certain areas offer a relatively free space for resistance, even if that resistance remains only one potential among many.[5] The difficulty of institutionalizing an interpretation implies that most saturated events will simply remain saturated. Just as a resistance reading will be very hard to forge and enforce successfully, so will a reading that serves the official structure of power. Areas that teem with overabundant significance never fully socialize meaning, and their interpretive communities are not well established. As a result, they are very easy to penetrate from all angles, but very difficult to control from any direction. They tend to dissolve attempts at domination of meaning as black holes suck in all objects, but give off nothing, not even light. While precipitation is not impossible given an adequate social organization, it is difficult. I will discuss several cases where the state and others try to impose unified interpretations, but consistently fail. That potential for resistance remains amid the kaleidoscopic array of possible readings, making saturated areas one fruitful place to look for the germ of resistance movements. Chinese religion, with its typical use of condensed symbols and complex ritual, and in the absence of any strong social institutions of interpretation, provides one of the free spaces for potential resistance in Chinese history.

Finally, like Turner on communitas, I will be concerned to show the positive functions of saturation. Unlike Turner, I will also be primarily concerned with how and when indefinite and multivocal meaning can transform into resistance. The processes of saturation and precipitation create a constant push and pull. New institutions can combine with new interpretations to create shared, definitive understandings. Yet this new interpretation is in turn subject to reinterpretations, making a general push toward a further dissolution that must be contested by controlling interpretation. The transitions back and forth imply important social transformations, and will require a close look at the relations between ideas and social change.

I take up each case of resistance in roughly chronological order. All three begin with complex and indeterminate meaning, but each illustrates a very different possible development. The early period of the Taiping rebellion showed the great power of saturated ritual to attract followers and create new ideas, along with its severe limitations for social organization. The Taiping successfully managed to create and enforce a single interpretation, enshrining its new interpretive community as one piece of a new state structure. Yet the new Taiping orthodoxy had important costs even as it solved the earlier organizational problems. The case addresses both the social organization of meaning as one interpretation comes to dominate, and the grave difficulties of maintaining such an interpretation.

The Taiwanese ghosts provide an example of overloaded ritual that just stays saturated in spite of numerous attempts to dictate a single version, from a television soap opera to a fake temple. They again illustrate the difficulty of imposing an interpretation, along with the free space for potential resistance that religion offers in China. Most of all, they clarify the need for an analysis of potential instead of inherent meanings.

Tiananmen was another event where the possibilities of interpretation far outran the shared meaning. In this case, however, the state already possessed an extraordinarily powerful mechanism for imposing a thin interpretation. More than the events in the square itself, I will be concerned with the government's efforts to impose its own interpretation on the demonstrations through its massive apparatus of ideological control. Using the evidence from the other cases on the difficulty of dictating an authoritative interpretation and on the inherent weaknesses of such thinned-out meaning, I will argue against the long-term success of efforts like this, and for the existence of free space for resistance under socialism as under other systems.

# Part II

## TAIPING REBELLION

# 3

# Jesus's Brother and the Chinese Periphery

The Taiping Heavenly Kingdom generated one of the most cata-clysmic rebellions in history. It rose from a tiny upstart religious sect in an inaccessible backwater to capture the economic core of China and nearly topple the Qing Dynasty. From a few hundred adherents calling themselves God Worshipers (*Bai Shangdi Ren*) in 1845, the movement had thousands of followers by 1851 when it named itself the Taiping Heavenly Kingdom and founded a new dynasty.[6] It had an army of over a million when it captured Nanjing in 1853 and proclaimed the city its new Heavenly Capital, Tianjing (Michael, 1966–71, I:70). The dead far exceeded 10 million.

For all its huge scale and enormous bloodshed, however, much of the Taiping Heavenly Kingdom's historical significance lies instead in its ideas, which both Nationalist and Communist revolutionaries in the twentieth century would see as precursors. The rebels proposed, for example, to communalize much of the economy. Early followers liquidated their wealth into a communal "holy treasury" (*sheng ku*), and the leadership later proposed (but did not systematically carry out) a radical land reform in which the state would own all land, parcelling it out in equal shares to everyone.[7] Constantly proclaiming the brotherhood of all as children of God, Taiping ideology was radically egalitarian.

While the land reform, radical as it was, had some antecedents in China, Taiping gender relations took a very new turn. During the early stages of the movement, adults lived in gender-segregated camps and the leadership strictly forbade sexual relations, even among married couples. Both genders had specific economic responsibilities. The women primarily produced things like clothes, but the Taiping also had detachments of women soldiers. Women could also expect to receive equal shares of land with their husbands in the land reform. In addition, Taiping law demanded monogamy and forbade foot binding.

33

Yet Taiping religious beliefs provided perhaps the greatest surprise of all in the Chinese context. Arguments about how "Christian" the movement was are as old as the rebellion, especially among Westerners at the time trying to decide if it merited support or was just blasphemy.[8] Taiping ideas about the Trinity or the Holy Ghost, for example, were clearly quite fuzzy, and the leader's claim to be Jesus's younger brother won no friends among Western observers. Yet properly Christian or not, many of the ideas were very new to China. The Taiping believed in one God instead of many, and that Jesus had died for their sins. They performed baptisms, said Christian prayers, and printed Christian texts including both testaments of the Bible (along with their own third testament). They destroyed huge numbers of non-Christian idols. In a country where intensive missionary activity throughout the nineteenth century had only a tiny effect, and in a region of Guangxi so cut off it would not see its first missionaries for several decades, Taiping Christianity was new and radically different.

While the historical documents do not allow a clear and detailed view of the social processes that first made such ideas convincing and then set the rebellion off in rural Guangxi, they do provide some very suggestive glimpses. One of the most striking is the missionary Theodore Hamberg's retelling of the eyewitness account he got from Hong Rengan, cousin and first convert of the Taiping leader, Hong Xiuquan.[9] As Hamberg relates it, while Hong Xiuquan was away from the base area in Guangxi:

> some very remarkable occurrences had taken place in the congregation of God worshippers, which had brought disorder and dissension among the brethren. It sometimes happened that while they were kneeling down engaged in prayer, the one or the other of those present was seized by a sudden fit, so that he fell down to the ground, and his whole body was covered with perspiration. In such a state of ecstasy, moved by the spirit, he uttered words of exhortation, reproof, prophecy, &tc. Often the words were unintelligible, and generally delivered in rhythm (Hamberg, 1854:45).

The chaos was so great that the congregation, apparently fearing for its survival, asked Hong to separate the divine from the satanic possessions when he returned (Hamberg, 1854:46). Significantly, as I will discuss, this period also saw a massive increase in the movement's following.

Too many voices spoke at once. Each had unquestionable authority as God, Jesus or some other spirit, but they spoke with no harmony. This is a key aspect of the multiplying meaning that provides the focus of the next few chapters, a small window into how the people of Guangxi made Hong's Christianity their own and how cultural alternatives became armed conflagration.

I will argue that dissolving Hong's original Christianity into local Guangxi culture through spirit possession and other means, overloading his ideas with multiple and inconsistent local interpretations, won the early God Worshipers much of their following and shaped much of their future. Conditions in this part of Guangxi had created a free space for resistance both socially and in local cultural practice. Hong's ideas became entangled in local specifics, briefly creating the extraordinarily rich and complex scenes to which Hamberg alludes. In the absence of strong interpretive communities, the newly saturated God Worshipers saw a burst of creative energy, a great surge in the size of the congregation, and a general breakdown of control. This was a sort of dissolution of interpretive authority that transformed the movement and created an enormous potential for resistance. I take up this transformation in Chapter 4.

While overloading Hong's original ideas with local possibilities may have created the movement, Hamberg's reference to disorder and dissension reveals the organizational limits to saturated solutions and irrational authority. Ordered political action required thinning meaning back out, precipitating an ideology out of the solution and institutionalizing the interpretive community to go with it. Much of the early history of the God Worshipers plays off indeterminate meanings and popular enthusiasm on the one hand, and interpretive control and state power on the other. The creation of a new Taiping ideology occurred simultaneously with state formation, and clarifies both the social difficulty of precipitating out ideas, and the new problems that can result, as I discuss in Chapter 6.

The rest of this chapter examines the precursors to that process of piling on too much meaning. I begin with Hong's development of his initial, idiosyncratic version of Christianity based on a dream vision, and then move to structural features in central Guangxi that weakened local interpretive communities, helping to create a privileged social space for the rebels.

## HONG XIUQUAN'S VISION

Hong Xiuquan was born into an ambitious Hakka farm family in Hua County, only about thirty kilometers north of Canton. As usual for a Chinese family at the time, their ambitions for Hong centered around his educational achievements and the hopes that their bright son could achieve the wealth and power of political office by passing the official examinations. He was a promising child and apparently breezed through the county exams, the entry level which conferred no degree.[10]

The examination system in China created formidable competition at every level; only a tiny percentage of the candidates passed. Most Chinese intellectuals resigned themselves to repeated failures, often making a living as local teachers. While Hong's career as a prophet was to be truly extraordinary, his career as a traditional scholar was absolutely typical. He first travelled to Canton for the prefectural exams in 1827, at the remarkable age of thirteen; not so remarkably, he failed. By 1830 he was teaching in his native village.

The next stab at the exams was in 1836. He failed again, but had an interesting adventure in the process. On the streets of Canton he met Liang A-fa, arguably the first Chinese Christian evangelist. Liang gave Hong a copy of *Good Words to Admonish the Age* (*Quanshi Liangyan*), a compilation he had made of selected translations from the Bible and from missionary sermons and writings (Jian 1958:1693). Liang apparently hoped to attract just such failed intellectuals as Hong Xiuquan. Yet Hong did not read the book, and just put it on his shelf when he got home.

Hong took another shot at the examinations the next year, with the usual result. This time, however, the nervous pressure and the agony of defeat apparently overwhelmed him, leading to an experience that will sound very familiar to anyone versed in the origins of millenial prophets everywhere. He fell ill for several days during which he had a strange vision.[11] In the vision he felt like he was dying, and a group of heavenly attendants lifted him to heaven with great pomp. On arrival an old woman (his Heavenly Mother in a later version) washed off the filth he had picked up by associating with earthly people, and old men slit him open and replaced his internal organs with fresh ones. He met various relatives, including an elder brother and a father, very dignified in his black dragon robe and huge golden beard. The old man lamented the state of the world:

What man on earth did I not cause to be born and reared? Who does not eat my food and wear my clothing? . . . Have they not the slightest thought of awe or respect for me? They have been greatly deluded and misled by evil demons, and they waste those things which I have bestowed upon them as offerings to these evil demons, as if the demons had given birth to them and nourished them (*Taiping Tianri* in Michael, 1966–1971, II:54).

The old man and others taught Hong many verses, whose meaning was mysterious at the time. Hong also fought extensive battles with imps and demons contesting the old man's authority, finally discovering the demonic leanings of Confucius himself. Toward the end, the old man presented Hong with a sword and a seal of office, sending him reluctantly down to earth to cleanse the world of demons and idol worship.

Here was a saturated world indeed, which like any good dream offered no single line of interpretation, but instead a cornucopia of suggestive but confusing detail, from the color of the old man's beard to the details of the poetry. The condensed dream-world symbolism offered Hong a host of possibilities, but he chose to take none of them, just as many Taiwanese do not interpret cleavers in pigs' heads. He apparently chalked the vision up as a weird experience, and simply let it sit without much interpretation.

Psychoanalysts, fortune-tellers and prophets live to draw definitive interpretations out of such thick visions, but for the moment Hong simply remained a school teacher and failed scholar. He tried the exams one last time in 1843, once again reaping only disappointment. On returning home this time, for some reason, he decided to read Liang A-fa's tract, which had now been gathering dust on his bookshelf for seven years. The experience moved the dream from saturation to precipitation, and Hong from school teacher to prophet.

Hong understood at last that the old man was God, and his elder brother was Jesus. As Jesus's younger brother, he was on earth to bring Christianity back to China, whose Christian beginnings and devotion to God were long forgotten, but now revealed to Hong in his vision. Following the instructions in *Good Words to Admonish the Age* he baptized himself, his cousin Hong Rengan, and his friend Feng Yunshan and their families in the local river. Obedient to the starkly iconoclastic principles they would maintain in the years to come, they also removed the god images from their domestic altars (Jian, 1958:1659).

Many of the early Protestant missionaries in China were evangelical fundamentalists, who shared far more with the Bible-thumping revivals of the Great Awakening than with the mainline Christian missions that came to dominate the China field by the twentieth century (Wagner, 1982:11–17). Liang A-fa was one of the first in what they hoped would be a wave of native evangelical preachers that would sweep over China, and his tract emphasized the particular Christianity of these radicals – an omnipotent, stern and jealous God who was more Old Testament than New, the strictest morality as a sign of salvation, and a quickly looming Day of Judgment. Jesus was important for having saved the world from its sins, but this Christianity put far less stress on Jesus as the apostle of love or God as all-forgiving mercy (Wagner, 1982:16; Jian, 1958:1669–1695).

Hong now set about understanding as much as he could about Christianity, initially through the study of Liang's text as it meshed with his vision and with his general knowledge as a Chinese intellectual. He gained a certain amount of interpretive flexibility through the mysterious language of some of these first attempts at Chinese translations. In addition to radically new concepts, the Chinese itself often became bizarre or even incomprehensible in places, perhaps allowing Hong to see it as part of the Chinese tradition of equally opaque prophetic texts (Jian, 1958:1667). Working with what he had, followed by his tiny handful of faithful in Hua County, Hong forged a new Christianity out of his saturated dream and Liang's murky text. God had sent a second son to earth to revive the Christian message.

Hong appeared to harbor no rebellious intent during these years. He may have been angry at the system that spurned him, but he continued to teach school, feeding a new generation into the system. Removing the graven images from his home surely struck the villagers as eccentric, but hardly revolutionary. No one is required to have such images, after all. Hong instead hoped to fill his missionary goals, replacing idolatry with Christianity.[12]

Hong and his followers, however, did engage in enough iconoclasm to anger the village elders.[13] They removed the Confucian tablets from school rooms in which they taught, unwilling to work in an idolatrous environment. As a result, they themselves were removed from their jobs, and Hong Rengan took a beating from his older brother (Hamberg, 1854:24). Without any real base of support – their evangelism apparently had little effect and the group remained tiny – they felt compelled to leave the village. Perhaps their Christianity seemed too Western in Hua County. After all, the smoke had just cleared from the Opium War, and the main battles had not been far away.

Probably more importantly, however, this was part of a regional core area of China, where the mechanisms of interpretive control functioned well. Destroying Confucian tablets may have intended no political rebellion, but it insulted proper orthodoxy and the local village authorities could not approve. Hamberg reports additional evidence that the local powers were ideologically queasy with Hong. A local *xiucai*, holder of the degree Hong never achieved and therefore a very important man locally, had offered to correct the errors in Hong's new religious books. Hong spurned him, of course (Hamberg, 1854:22). A bit later, the village elders exchanged argumentative verses with the two Christian Hong cousins concerning their refusal to help prepare a major festival. Hamberg reports that afterwards the elders "never asked the assistance of the younger Hongs in their idolatrous practices" (Hamberg, 1854:26). That is, the elders apparently banned them from major religious festivals, which were, among other things, important signs of community membership and solidarity. Hong's ideas were too radical for Hua County. Unwelcome at home, probably with Biblical ideas of prophets wandering in the wilderness in mind, Hong Xiuquan and Feng Yunshan headed toward wild and peripheral Guangxi in 1844, where they would fare far better.

Hong's new ideas were not resistance in any direct political sense. While his removal of Confucian tablets certainly reflected his frustration with the system, his continuing to teach the classics for the next several years shows that he had not rejected it. While he opposed accepted canons of religious interpretation, he had created no significant interpretive community of his own, beyond his very few followers. The village powers isolated his ideas long before they showed any political inclination. Theorists of cultural resistance would include his new ideas as a form of tacit resistance; Hong's Christianity certainly challenged some of the cultural underpinnings of the status quo. Yet Hong had no chance of building the institutions of interpretation that a move to direct resistance would require as long as he stayed in Hua County. We can thus identify a potential for resistance, but it was still socially insignificant before 1844.

While Hong's idiosyncratic ideology stands unique, the general process typifies the experience of prophetic leaders elsewhere. Hong

Xiuquan fits very neatly into Anthony Wallace's description of the experience of leaders of revitalization movements, who almost always begin from a vivid vision where a supernatural being blames problems on a violation of rules and promises salvation for new behavior (Wallace, 1956). Quite typically, the vision comes as part of an illness after a great disappointment, and includes the kind of death and rebirth symbolism that Hong also experienced.

Intellectuals with blocked ambitions also occur over and over as leaders of such movements. From the Zambian Watchtower movement in the early twentieth century (Fields, 1982:335), to the Maori Hau Hau rebellion (Adas, 1979:109), to the Taiping Heavenly Kingdom, frustrated intellectuals seem especially good at precipitating new ideologies for new movements. New movements offer them the social mobility and leadership positions they had not achieved through normal channels. In turn, they offer their skills as intellectuals in constructing systems of thought, galvanizing new ideas out of old materials, precipitating new interpretations that can form the seed of the new movement.

Hong's new Christianity would provide just such a seed for the Taiping rebellion. Yet by themselves, these ideas explain none of the movement. As he left for Guangxi, Hong had built no institutions and had almost no following. While I have described his development as a case of saturation and precipitation, the process took place at an individual level only, far from the social transformations I really hope to address. Hong in 1844 could easily have remained an eccentric with an idiosyncratic ideology, largely ignored and without broader social significance. The critical process was yet to come, as Hong moved into the relatively free social and cultural space of east–central Guangxi, and quickly found his new system of thought dissolved and remade by the local people.

## FREE SPACE AND RURAL UNREST

The cauldron that brewed the Taiping rebellion was Xunzhou Prefecture, a mountainous backwater on the periphery of the Cantonese-speaking part of China, known for its poverty, ignorance and violence. It may have been internal to China, but functioned in many ways as a wild frontier. Like other such peripheral areas of China in the mid-nineteenth century, it had sizable populations of non-Han Chinese ethnic groups, poor transportation, and relatively weak penetration by the state. The God Worshipers would develop base areas in close communication with each other in three of the prefecture's four counties (Gui, Guiping, and Pingnan). The most important of these was at Thistle Mountain (Zijing Shan). Even today Thistle Mountain remains remote, inaccessible and poor. The trip when I went in 1985 began in Guiping town, a quiet rustic town that houses the county government, as it did a century ago. No bridges span the rivers in the area, and the journey thus began with a ferry ride, followed by a drive of several hours. The drive ended abruptly when deep mud made the dirt road impassible. The local historians and officials who accompanied me decided to abandon our car where it was stuck; there was no other traffic to worry about. We walked the rest of the way to another river, where the car would have been left anyway. The next ferry might have held a dozen people on a calm day, but certainly not a car. No large vehicle could be transported across that river, and there are thus still no cars or trucks at Thistle Mountain. About a mile walk past the ferry dock stood the settlement at Thistle Mountain.[14] Even the feast they served us showed how rural the area was, featuring hill country delicacies like fox, mountain toad and pangolin.

In the 1840s the area was more inaccessible by far, and as the local pirate population well knew, water transport held the key to controlling access. This was a world of silver miners, indigo workers, and charcoal burners, of Yao tribesmen, sinicized Zhuangs and immigrant Hakkas, of pirates, bandits, and strongmen. If Hong had left the comforts of the Cantonese core looking for the untamed wilds, he must have been satisfied with his new home.

I will save a detailed discussion of religious interpretive communities in the area for the next chapter. Here I want to sketch the broad outlines of the major changes transforming Xunzhou in the 1840s, which led to a general breakdown of interpretive communities and control of all kinds. Local elders and literati had acted quickly and effectively in Hua County to isolate Hong's ideas, putting him in a kind of ideological quarantine. The changes in peripheral Guangxi, however, left such people in a much weaker position. Along with other typical sources of control, from local landlords to august magistrates, they found it impossible to slow the movement.

Theories of rural unrest often identify two major sources for this kind of institutional breakdown: the economic displacements that accompany the powerful entry of capitalist markets and production (e.g., Wolf, 1969; Paige, 1975), and the social problems that stem from changes in the state (e.g., Skocpol, 1979; Tilly, 1982). While east–central Guangxi in the 1840s was hardly a center of capitalist development, it did experience important indirect effects from the expanding world system. And while the state was never strong there, it lost even more control during this period. These processes helped question established interpretive communities, setting up free social space for an expansion of uncontrolled interpretation.

Increased land concentration and increased demands for cash typically accompanied expanding world capitalism in the nineteenth century (Migdal, 1982), and these processes apparently occurred in the Xunzhou area in the 1840s. Landlords, in need of cash to buy new products, may have increasingly asked for rents in cash (Li *et al.*, 1982:150–151). Some evidence also points toward increasing rents at the same time (Lu, 1982:6), and tax rates in the area also seem to have been disproportionately high (Li *et al.*, 1982:152; Liu, 1963). At the same time, quick internal population growth and massive immigration added to pressure on the land.[15] These are exactly the kinds of changes that theories of economic transformation and rebellion see threatening cultural standards and thus leading to rural unrest.

Price deflation exacerbated these trends. China had a bimetallic currency system; peasants primarily had access to small copper coins, which they could exchange for silver in order to pay taxes or rent. China's favorable balance of trade for much of the eighteenth century had reversed by about 1820, due in large part to opium imports from the British, and silver began to flow out of the country (Myers, 1980:85). As a result, peasants needed more copper to buy the necessary silver, increasing the hardships of greater demands for cash. While the evidence is quite incomplete, there appears to be a case for increasing land concentration in Xunzhou in the 1840s, as peasants could not meet their debts.[16] There was a major anti-rent movement shortly after the Taiping uprising left the area. Xunzhou also seemed to have an extraordinarily high number of pawn shops at the time (Liu, 1963).

Peasants in rural Xunzhou prefecture relied on the market to supplement inadequate farm income by selling mountain crops. Charcoal and indigo were the most important. Charcoal could be made in small, low technology kilns in the villages and sold to the plains where wood was in short supply. They could also process indigo dye locally, growing the crop on marginal mountain land and extracting the dye in large cauldrons still visible today. Both commodities required very low capital inputs, but neither one was very profitable. They tended to allow marginal people to squeak by, but little more. At Thistle Mountain, perhaps 10 percent of income came from charcoal and 20–30 percent from indigo (Guangxi . . ., 1962:26).

Other changes on the eve of the Taiping stand out more clearly. The new shortage of silver had led to the reopening of some played-out silver mines during the Daoguang reign (1820–1850) in northern Gui County, very near the God Worshipers' base areas (Liang, 1981). Much of the mining was done by small, independent miners after larger commercial miners found it unprofitable. The county gazetteer described the miners as

> rootless crowds that arrived in great confusion. After only a year or two, the deepest mountains and farthest valleys filled with vagrants. The men are strong and tough, without family ties . . . They form secret societies and engage in all kinds of illegal activity, but investigators do not dare enter (*Guixian Zhi*, 1893, juan 1:12).

Several thousand of these miners would join the rebellion (*Guixian Zhi*, 1893, juan 1:13).

Indirectly, the Opium War, which ended in 1842, had weakened social order in the area even more. The treaty ending the Opium War forcibly opened new ports in distant parts of the country to British shipping; Canton had been the only port open to foreigners until then. As a result of the competition from new ports and continuing Chinese reluctance to allow foreign travelers good access to Canton city, large numbers of Chinese inland transport workers, who had carried trade goods between Canton and the rest of China, lost their jobs. At the same time, bandits and pirates of the Canton core area found their opportunities for plunder reduced. Many of these rootless people entered Guangxi in the 1840s (Xie, 1950; Wakeman, 1966:126), joining the already troublesome silver miners.

The local gazetteers record a startling increase in bandit activity at the time, often claiming that the area had been relatively quiet before then. Bandits active near the God Worshipers' bases in

Xunzhou in the late 1840s included Big-head Goat (aka Zhang Zhao), Big Carp (aka Tian Fang), Wild Boar Arrow (aka Chen Awu), Zhang Jiaxiang, Su Sanxiang, and many, many others (*Xunzhou Fuzhi*, 1897, juan 55; *Pingnan Xianzhi*, 1883, juan 18). Their gangs ranged from the dozens to the hundreds or more. One discouraged contemporary source even suggested that 30–40 percent of Guangxi's population was bandits in 1854 (Yan, 1962). An increase in river piracy particularly weakened state control of Xunzhou.[17] The rivers were the only viable means of communication with the area, and the very weak Qing navy lost all control over river traffic. Every local gazetteer and nearly every contemporary observer included a long section on the depredations of these groups, marking their clear increase in the 1840s. While the economy may have grown strained, the usual mechanisms of social control were breaking down completely.

Big-head Goat provides a particularly useful example, especially because he flirted briefly with the God Worshipers. Like many of the pirates, he came originally from Guangdong Province, where he had first worked as a boat hand (Su, 1889a, juan 1). With the loss of river traffic, he turned his professional knowledge to piracy. He began his depredations in Guangdong, and worked his way up river into Guangxi. By 1850, when the God Worshiping rebels began to gather an armed force in the village of Jintian, he and several other pirates controlled the nearby rivers. They provided "protection" for the river trade, looting those who did not pay their fees. He was bold enough to launch several major attacks on towns around 1851, using dozens of boats and over a thousand pirate followers (*Pingnan Xianzhi*, 1883, juan 18:27).

The flirtation with the God Worshipers came when he and seven other bandit chiefs joined the movement in 1850. Only one of them (Luo Dagang) would last more than a brief time. All eight were Triad Society leaders, as were many bandits. The Triads formed the major secret society network of southern China, very loosely organized as sworn brotherhoods with secret signs and initiation ceremonies.[18] Their rituals and networks provided an alternative to above-ground social relations, and they sometimes espoused anti-Qing Dynasty messages, as did the Taiping. They offer further evidence for the weakening of normal ties and the creation of alternatives. Yet rather than breaking with much Chinese tradition like the God Worshipers, they drew heavily on a current of Chinese values that emphasized loyalty, brotherhood and righteous resistance against illegitimate power. They wanted to restore the Ming Dynasty, not found a new Christian one.

In fact, just these ideological differences made the alliance with the God Worshipers short-lived. Stories about why Big-head Goat left vary, but all imply his unwillingness to submit to the stern moral discipline of Hong's religion. As Hamberg tells it, the God Worshipers sent sixteen men to teach Christianity to the bandits. The bandits paid for the service, and fifteen of the teachers contributed their earnings quite properly to the common treasury. One greedy man, however, kept his money, and the God Worshipers cut off his head when they found out. Big-head Goat and the others thought this was extreme, and left the movement (Hamberg, 1854:55).[19] Taiping official documents are rather different, saying that the pirate had "pretended to worship God, while along river banks he caused disturbances and destruction, acting very much without restraint." Some of the God Worshipers were led astray: "Going along with the current and the muck, they followed Ta-t'ou-yao [Big-head Demon, the Taiping authors changed a character to be more pejorative] in seeking material wealth" (*Tianqing Daolishu* in Michael, 1966-1971:375). Fortunately, Jesus had warned the leaders through spirit possession, and when Big-head Goat rebelled, they crushed him. The particular version of the story does not matter. It illustrates both the prevalence of illegitimate power in the area, and the radical difference of the God Worshipers' ideas.

This process of breakdown of central authority also occurred in the relation between local elites and the government. Normally local magistrates, who were always outsiders by imperial policy, relied heavily on cooperation from local literati and large landholders. While this was a source of strength for both locals and magistrates, it was also a source of conflict and compromise. The government always had to face down pressures for greater local autonomy, and it was clearly losing the battle in east–central Guangxi in the 1840s.

Some of the local powers in Guangxi during this period developed into a new kind of strongman, known locally as rice lords (*mifan zhu*) (Zhong, 1984a; Xie, 1950:32–35). Although the term appears unique to Guangxi, the phenomenon represents another case of the strongman pattern that has developed in other frontier areas of China (Meskill, 1979:88–91). Usually wealthy and well-connected to begin with, wielding their privately paid forces of armed braves, such strongmen were both plunderers and patrons. While preying fiercely on their enemies, they also contributed to local shrines and managed local institutions. Urban and political elites may have feared these local powers, but such official leaders also relied on their cooperation (Meskill, 1979:90).

Guangxi's rice lords were wealthy locals, usually from large and powerful families, who maintained close ties to local criminals. They partly protected their clients and partly profited off banditry toward others. References to them begin in the 1840s, exactly the period when economic turbulence, banditry and rapid immigration weakened central authority in the area (Zhong, 1984a:4). They were powerful and independent enough that the authors of local gazetteers lamented their presence. The strongest of the rice lords ran their areas like satrapies – monopolizing armed force and controlling wealth; they effectively replaced civil government in some areas. Zhong (1984a) has tentatively identified fifteen rice lords in Guangxi between the 1840s and the 1860s. Clearly, these strongmen provided local threats to state power, which the state was unable to suppress. The God Worshipers benefited from the support of one of these local strongmen – Hu Yiguang, who acted as patron to Hong and Feng, helped them raise an armed force, and became one of the Taiping kings (*Xunzhou Fuzhi*, 1897, juan 56).

Finally, the complex ethnic relations in the area added fuel to the fires of the 1840s. The specific details of the ethnic composition of the population remain very fuzzy. The Yao, with their distinctive dress, language, and slash-and-burn cultivation, were a relatively small minority who lived in the less accessible areas of the region. A much larger portion of the population was Zhuang. By the mid-nineteenth century the Zhuang had been largely sinicized, farming and dressing as Chinese, and often bilingual in Zhuang and the local dialect of Cantonese. The local gazetteers stress that they were just like Chinese by this time, except for language, and for the odious (to the Chinese) practice of male and female Zhuangs singing paired songs to each other. An apparently small number of Cantonese-speaking Chinese also lived there. These may well have been the descendants of earlier northern Chinese immigrants (Guangxi had been an anti-Qing redoubt in the seventeenth century), although they could also have been fully sinicized Zhuangs. The area also had a large population of nineteenth-century immigrant Hakkas. Hakkas were unusual among Chinese groups for their adaptation to mountain agriculture in marginal areas, and because Hakka women worked in the fields and did not bind their feet. As late immigrants, they tended to live in scattered households.

Local documents often speak of conflict between local (*tu*) and immigrant (*lai*) groups, and one of the largest of these conflicts netted the God Worshipers about 3,000 armed Hakkas fleeing from a more powerful native force. The exact ethnic significance of these terms, however, remains unclear. In general, the "immigrants" were Hakka and the "natives" were sinicized Zhuang, although they may also have included non-Hakka Chinese who had a long history in the area.

The famous immigrant/native feuds that characterized the area by the 1840s have led scholars to emphasize the distinctiveness of the various local ethnic groups (e.g., Kuhn, 1977; Kojima, 1983). Yet the region clearly also saw extensive contact among the groups. Bilingualism was common (Hakkas and Zhuangs communicated in Cantonese, *Xunzhou Fuzhi*, 1897, juan 54:77), and intermarriage occurred, although we have no way to judge its frequency. Shi Dakai, a local miner who became one of the Taiping kings, apparently had a Hakka father and a Zhuang mother (Liang, 1981:53, Guangxisheng . . ., 1956:74).

Important religious interconnections also tied the groups together to some extent. My interviews with current residents of Xunzhou about religion and ethnicity in their youth (in the 1920s and 1930s) revealed significant shared use of temples and some shared use of religious experts. This evidence comes from well after the Taiping period, but there is no documentary evidence that the religious traditions of the ethnic groups were more isolated from each other during the mid-nineteenth century. Ethnic feuding preceding the Taiping period need not imply ethnic isolation. In fact, evidence from other parts of China indicates the ease with which religious influences passed between Chinese and aboriginal ethnic groups, even when relations were tense and sometimes violent (e.g., Shepherd, 1984).

Few of the major temples in the area, for example, had specific ethnic identifications. Some clearly had Yao origins. The many local Pangu temples, for example, originally honored a heroic dog who (at least according to Han Chinese stories) became the founding ancestor of the Yao.[20] Other temples, like the Liuwu temple in Sigu, Gui County, had stories tied to the paired singing that the authors of the gazetteers so disliked. As Hamberg (1854:38) put it, the pair sang "licentious" couplets and "indulged in illicit intercourse" for seven days before dying. Yet all ethnic groups shared these and other temples in the early twentieth century, and probably in the mid-nineteenth century as well. People worshiped because a temple was efficacious more than because it conformed to their ethnic identification.

My interviews also suggested extensive sharing of religious experts, particularly in the use of Yao mediums by other ethnic groups. While there is some risk in reading these modern oral recollections of the early twentieth century back to the 1840s, there is little evidence against such contact among ethnic groups. This kind of contact is consistent with similar situations of ethnic competition elsewhere in China and in other societies. Such cultural exchange occurs frequently in peripheral areas, where marginalized ethnic groups are thought to have hidden powers.[21] Ethnicity in the area was an uncomfortable combination of cultural exchange and deadly competition, undoubtedly exacerbated by the recent economic problems and the influx of many new Hakka migrants. An apparent earlier pax sinica in the area had faltered in the 1840s, along with many other aspects of social control.

Many of the details of life in the mountains of Xunzhou Prefecture remain hazy, but certain basic patterns of change in the 1840s nevertheless emerge clearly. Marginal commercial occupations became an important part of the economy with the reopening of the silver mines and supplemental agricultural production of indigo and charcoal. The position of tenants may have been worsening, throwing them increasingly at the mercy of the market. Internal population growth and immigration added further pressures and worsened ethnic tensions. At the same time, the large influx of displaced Guangdong bandits and pirates weakened already flimsy local social control. The usual social institutions of control, from the political machinery of the magistrate to the informal controls of local landlords and literati, were disintegrating.

All of this opened a free space for the God Worshipers, a fertile field where established interpretive communities of all kinds held less and less sway, and where Hong's new ideas could grow with far less interference than in his home community. Yet Hong's text-based Christianity hardly seemed to fit with the wild frontier atmosphere in Guangxi when he arrived in 1844. Sternly moralistic in a land of strongman politics, insistently monotheistic in a cosmos of many gods, and egalitarian in a world at home with hierarchy, how did Hong's ideas thrive? I will argue that the answer lies in the transformation of his ideas in local hands, a new saturation of Hong's Christianity that would shape the rest of the movement.

This newly conglomerated religion gave the movement tremendous appeal and power, even as its inherent dissolution of authority created new problems.

# 4

# Saturating the Movement: God Gets Power

Hong Xiuquan and Feng Yunshan arrived in east–central Guangxi in 1844, and the fortunes of their ideas began to change very rapidly in the new conditions there. Hong wandered back to his home county in 1845; there was nothing yet to hold him in Guangxi. During this period he also spent a brief spell in Canton with the Southern Baptist missionary Issachar Roberts, who refused to baptize him (Hamberg, 1854:32). Feng, however, settled at Thistle Mountain, preaching Hong's doctrine with remarkable success. When Hong returned to the area in 1847, he must have been astonished to find a large and increasingly bold following of God Worshipers. The numbers of converts grew at an astonishing rate, clearly reaching 2,000 or 3,000 followers in 1848, and perhaps 10,000 by the time of the first armed camp at Jintian in 1850.

The great success in recruitment stemmed in part from a relative loss of control by the original movement leaders. Especially in Hong's absence, his neatly codified ideas merged into Guangxi popular culture, creating a new and explosive mix of complex possibilities. The localization and pulling apart of his Christian ideology fell into two broad stages. During the first stage, from about 1845 to the end of 1847, Hong's God appeared increasingly as a kind of primus inter pares of local gods, rather than the one and only God. He proved his relative power through traditional means – curing and contests of strength with other gods. The second stage began in 1847, and continued to the beginnings of the armed movement in 1850. Attacks on other gods ended, to be replaced by the charismatic power of spirit possession. This change helped create an entirely new group of local leaders, and greatly increased the following. Significantly, Hong himself was absent for most of both stages, and Feng was gone for most of the second.

Given the absence of the original leaders and the powerfully privileged place of religion in Guangxi at the time, something very new had developed by 1848 and 1849. Much of the clarity of Hong's original vision had been lost, but a new and uniquely local mixture had taken it over. Both the ideas and the social relations of the new God Worshipers were chaotic, but filled with possibilities and excitement. This chapter will follow the early saturation of the God Worshipers, from the particular features of Guangxi religious space which made God sensible there, to God's claims to power within the local set of practices. Chapter 5 will follow the story to the anarchic scenes of spirit possession that preceded the final crystallization of the movement into an armed rebellion with a new state structure.

## ODD GODS AND FREE RELIGIOUS SPACE

Just as the changes of the 1840s had made east–central Guangxi an especially favorable site for a new movement, the particularities of religion there created an even more powerfully free space. Even in the most developed core areas, religion in China experienced only loose controls, leaving it open to the kinds of interpretive silences or alternative interpretations I discussed in Chapter 1. With the weak state and rapid changes in Guangxi, local religion developed some marked peculiarities even by the fairly relaxed standards of Chinese elsewhere.

The great majority of Chinese popular gods are said to be the spirits of humans whose outstanding moral worth allowed them to continue helping people from the spirit world. Guan Gong, for example, remains one of the most popular gods all across China. He was one of the major figures in the historical novel *Romance of the Three Kingdoms*, a warrior known as much for his righteousness and unshakeable loyalty to his sworn brothers, as for his martial prowess. Tian Hou (called Ma Co in Taiwan; Mandarin Mazu), one of the most popular deities in coastal areas, illustrates the same principles through a very different kind of life. She was an unmarried woman who rescued seafarers in distress through supernatural means. She died young, but the continued miracles from her spirit led to her increasing popularity (Watson, 1985:296).

Gods act in some ways like bureaucrats and in some ways like parents. The bureaucratic metaphor is very powerfully developed (Wolf, 1974). Many informants in Taiwan today will spell it out quite explicitly, explaining that the lowest gods are like policemen, higher gods like governors, and the Emperor of Heaven like the old emperor or the modern president. All the available ritual media reinforce the point. God images usually wear the robes of official earthly office, and sit augustly with their legs apart and hands on their knees, gazing majestically out at their supplicants. Temples themselves reproduce the architecture of a magistrate's official quarters, including especially the curved eaves, which sumptuary laws limited to degree holders, as all magistrates were. People say that when praying to the god, you have to give your exact name, address and birth date, otherwise the god will not be able to find your file. Ritual specialists further strengthen the image by filling out pre-printed petition forms, modeled after imperial legal documents, for even the simplest rituals. And worshipers always burn paper spirit money for the gods, just as any official dealings with bureaucrats required payments.

Yet gods also have a parental aspect, as did magistrates in theory, if not always in practice. Like parents, gods will intercede for their children, even as they expect proper morality and respect from them. The goddesses in particular can be very nurturing, although any god feels a responsibility toward his or her charges. Quite unlike bureaucrats, anyone can develop a personal relationship with a god. Emily Martin [Ahern] writes of informants who compare gods to parents instead of officials. One person, for example, denying that offerings to the gods were like cash gifts to petty officials, argued that "Offering things to the gods is just like taking a gift to one's host. A stranger won't necessarily help you no matter how nice a gift you bring, and a good friend will help even if you bring nothing at all" (Ahern, 1981a:99). Another, making the same point, said "It is only necessary to do good deeds and burn three sticks of incense and they will be enormously happy. A god is a being with a very upright heart. He is fair and just, rewarding without favoritism" (Ahern, 1981a:99). The combination of bureaucrat and parent is not odd in China, where magistrates were "father–mother officials" (*fumu guan*). It is simply a utopian idealization of how things ought to be.

Anyone can worship any gods on their domestic altars, and anyone can develop a minor god temple. The important god temples, however, all have powerful associations with communities. Every neighborhood houses an Earth God (called She Gong in the Guangxi area).[22] The neighborhood takes joint responsibility for worshiping the Earth God and keeping up his shrine. If a family moves, they will worship a new Earth God. At a higher level, larger social communities typically share a single primary deity and temple. These temples can branch out over regions, or even nation-wide, but locally the deity presides over just the one area. Major annual rituals take place on behalf of the community, and can be funded by a household tax in addition to voluntary contributions. Major community temples hold the greatest of such rituals, the *jiao*, at intervals of several years. These rituals renew the cosmic mandate of the entire community and reinforce the position of the temple as the symbolic center of the community.

### Loose Interpretive Communities

None of this means that the interpretation of gods throughout China was clear and unambiguous, a definitive version shared by one and all. The boundaries of religious interpretation in China were very loosely guarded. While nearly everyone might share the most basic picture of popular gods as idealized parent–bureaucrats, specific gods often received radically differing interpretations. Even very different versions of what constituted a god were available, for example in Buddhism's version of popular gods as beings still trapped in the world of reincarnations, and thus grossly inferior to Buddhas and Bodhisattvas (Weller, 1987c:110–117).

A casual observer can still often see small Chinese children, sticks of incense thrust into their fists, learning the characteristic gestures of god worship at their parents' hands. This is their first introduc-tion to the iconography and ritual treatment that shows gods as kind bureaucrats. They will also hear tales of famous gods like Guan Gong, and especially of miracles performed by their local god. If they become educated, they will read stories of the deification of various gods, and everyone would hear these stories in outdoor operas and from professional story tellers.

Beyond this very loose collection of information, however, very little in the society fostered more specific or unified interpretations. At least before Christianity, no Chinese child memorized catechisms in order to be admitted to the Church, no priest reinforced proper belief through the confessional, and no church sermons demanded weekly attendance to doctrine.[23] In general, Chinese clergy have no congregations, and Chinese popular temples have no clergy. Buddhist and Daoist clergy either lived in special temples of their own, or practiced as individuals out of their homes, doing rituals for a fee. Communities ran their own temples by committee, and hired clergy on an ad hoc basis when a specific ritual required them. In great contrast to the Western religious tradition, therefore, no one took official responsibility to ensure orthodox religious interpretation, and enormous variations occurred frequently. The general lack of a priestly hierarchy and of religious institutions that could control interpretation meant a great latitude for overloading the gods with inconsistent interpretations. The meaning of a complex and colorful ritual was always up for grabs, as it was for those pig offerings for the Taiwanese god that I have already discussed.

The lack of any strong interpretive community for Chinese religion did not stop various people from trying to influence interpretation in their favor. It just made it extraordinarily difficult for them to succeed. One of the most important such attempts came from the state, which always hoped to sort what it considered orthodoxy from heterodoxy. Unlike the medieval European state, however, Chinese officials had no direct institutional control over religion, and no such institutions even existed. Their manipulations thus took the more subtle and far less effective forms of offering an alternative cult and trying to coopt popular gods.

Their alternative, the official state cult, sponsored altars in all capital cities from the counties to the nation as a whole, and required officials to perform periodic rituals there (Feuchtwang, 1977; Weller, 1987c:130–134). In so far as it intended to influence popular belief, it failed in large part because dignified Confucian officials were so reluctant to let the rabble attend their elegant rituals.[24] Rather more successful over the centuries was an attempt to coopt appropriate local gods by having the emperor grant them official titles. Local magistrates might then contribute to rituals at such temples, or build new temples to them. Both Guan Gong and Mazu fall into this category. Hansen documents the beginnings of this procedure in the twelfth century, when local elites began to champion the causes of their regional gods, and the government recognized them with titles (Hansen, 1990).

Watson traces this process very clearly for Mazu, whose final official title was the Empress of Heaven (Tian Hou). Yet the constant lack of any institutions of interpretive control doomed this effort, too. If Mazu conveyed imperial pacification and "approved" culture to the officials who promoted her cult, she meant independence to Taiwanese (who avoided the officially built temples and even the official designation as Empress), coastal pacification to large lineage elites in the Canton delta, fertility to their wives, and so on (Watson,

1985). This possibility of state deification served many purposes: it allowed local elites to promote their communities, and succeeded in fostering broader regional cults in place of (or sometimes in addition to) strictly local gods. It did not particularly succeed, however, in changing or unifying interpretation. Local interpretation remained rich in possibilities, and official deification added no powerful interpretive community that might have left things less indeterminate.

Local elites occupied a somewhat better position to exercise interpretive control. Like the state officials, they controlled no institutions of interpretation. Unlike the state, however, they often could influence what temples were built and what rituals funded. They managed this most successfully in the powerful lineage villages of parts of southeast China, where an exceptionally strong and unified local elite controlled both kinship and economic power. These same people usually also managed major community temples, and collected temple "contributions" through their armed self-defense corps (Watson, 1985:314–315).

This relatively strong control, at least by Chinese standards, led to a general thinning out of otherwise thick and complex ritual (Watson, 1985:318). Yet even with all this power, the local elites of the Canton delta area had little control over interpretation, as Watson shows in detail – the men of the dominant lineages saw Mazu very differently from their wives, and members of subordinate lineages had still other interpretations. With no direct control, and no real interpretive community, even these elites could only partially dampen the multiple voices of saturated gods.

In most areas of China elites had still less influence, because they were a less united and often less powerful force. When I did fieldwork in Taiwan's Sanxia Township, for example, the temple management constantly tried to influence ritual performance, and constantly failed. As usual, the managers were members of the local elite, but in an area with a far less unified elite group than the dominant lineage villages of the New Territories, they represented only one of the local factions. Like Watson's case, they tried to simplify and thin out ritual performance and interpretation. Having far less real control, however, the Sanxia temple managers had very little success. Grass roots' opposition, for example, watered down an attempt to simplify offerings at the annual ghost festival, and the people finally ignored the attempt completely when they actually made their offerings (Weller, 1987c:56–59). The broad lack of institutionalized interpretation allowed the coexistence of many interpretations of this ritual, as I have discussed at length elsewhere (Weller, 1987c).

All of this suggests that interpretive communities involving gods and their rituals in China remained extremely loose, in spite of pressure from officials and local elites. Even strongly controlled areas like the Canton delta had only very limited interpretive authority. Religion everywhere in the world is broadly saturated – the condensation and multivocality of religious symbols grant them power even as they make interpretive control difficult. Yet religious interpretive communities were particularly loose in China compared to other complex societies, where a much tighter tie between religion and state often made for stronger institutions of interpretation. If there was vague agreement in China that gods were somehow moral beings tied to hierarchy and community, there was strikingly wide variation in how people understood particular gods, and even in what constituted morality, hierarchy and community. The powerful ability of popular religion in China to weather attempts at interpretive control created a relatively free space for resistance, even if that resistance remained only one possibility of many.

## Odd Gods on the Periphery

The gods of Xunzhou Prefecture rang some remarkable changes on the already wide range of possibilities typical elsewhere in China. Religious interpretive communities may have been weak everywhere, but they waned to almost nothing in east–central Guangxi during the 1840s. The combination of the weak state and ethnic mixing that characterized the Chinese periphery, along with the general weakening of institutions of social order in the 1840s, allowed religion in the area to become a potent brew of potential interpretations. Already thick with extraordinary possibilities by Chinese standards, the area could incorporate Hong's new ideas far more easily than his home village, located in a developed area and dominated by a single lineage.

The most important community temples in the Xunzhou area honored the Three Generations (Sanjie), a reference to three members of the Feng family. Each of these Fengs had achieved Daoist perfection, the most recent during the seventeenth century. The people of Gui County built the first temple to them shortly after that, and branch temples spread throughout the region (*Guiping Xianzhi*, 1920, juan 15:10). My informants at Thistle Mountain remembered six of these temples in the area, and many more existed throughout the Xunzhou region.[25] The three Fengs represented that older tradition of Chinese temples dedicated to entirely local saints and worthies, independent of any national religious pantheon.[26] In other ways, however, these were fairly typical community temples, sponsoring *jiao* festivals every few years and probably controlled by local community leaders. When the local elite created one of the early self-defense militias in the area to fight the unrest building in the 1840s, they put the headquarters in the Three Generations temple in Daxuanxu (also called Xinxu), a major market town near Thistle Mountain (Guangxi Shifan Xueyuan . . ., 1981:272).

If the Three Generations temples fit the pattern I have been discussing fairly well, all of the other important ones threatened instead to break the mold. The next most important temples in the Thistle Mountain area enthroned King Gan (Gan Wang), a god with a very different history. The King Gan cult centered in Xiangzhou, just to the north of Thistle Mountain. Local gazetteers listed at least five temples to him, including one near Sanjiang, a major river port for Thistle Mountain people. King Gan became a high official while among the living, and thus seems like proper material for deification. Yet he achieved his position through the most immoral means. A geomancer identified an excellent burial site that promised high office, but it had to be used right away. Wasting no time, King Gan murdered his mother, buried her in the right spot, and became a successful official.

If the core Chinese temples we know most about tacitly supported the secular government by reproducing it in Heaven as a kindly bureaucracy, King Gan implied a tacit criticism by offering a reading of the government as a corrupt body of criminals. Like the local rice lords, King Gan kept even local officials under his thumb. According to legend, he once possessed a boy while a magistrate was passing by the temple in his sedan chair. Speaking through the boy, King Gan demanded that the magistrate go inside and worship, and that he contribute a set of official robes (an extremely generous gift) to the temple. The official obeyed. At least according to the Taiping, the temple was also guilty of inspiring people to sing obscene songs, probably a reference to Zhuang style paired singing of love songs. (The *Taiping Tianri* relates these stories in detail, see Michael, 1966–1971:73–76; see also Hong Rengan's confession in Michael, 1966–1971:1519, and Hamberg, 1854:36–37.) The King Gan temple near Sanjiang was quite large, and lay along an especially dangerous mountain route, riddled with bandits during the 1840s. King Gan must have had very complex associations. On the one hand, the temple had been placed there to protect people from danger and particularly to shield travelers from the dangerous ghosts of the many people who died there. Yet on the other hand, King Gan was much like a bandit himself. Similar meanings must have attached to his use against epidemics by being carried around the area (*Xunzhou Fuzhi*, 1897, juan 54:87).

The multiplicity of possible associations typifies the kind of indeterminate interpretation I am looking at. This temple was important enough to be rebuilt even after the Chinese Revolution of 1949. In contrast, the local Three Generations temple remains an empty shell with just three incense pots.[27] King Gan temples also had periodic *jiao* festivals. The local gazetteer only mentions King Gan and the Three Generations as having this major community ritual (*Xunzhou Fuzhi*, 1897, juan 54:67).

Other temples are less shockingly aberrant, but still seem odd. The entire area brims with temples dedicated to Pangu (also called Panhu or Panwang), with at least five in the Thistle Mountain region. As I mentioned in Chapter 3, these temples have close associations with Yao origin myths, but my informants claimed that everyone took part in rituals there. Pangu is well known throughout China as a legendary figure whose body parts formed various features of the world. Yet a different Pangu tradition exists in southwest China, including especially Guangxi. The Guangxi Pangu is actually a confusion of names with Panhu, a legendary dog described in the *Hou Han Shu* (Lü, 1982:1–7). Frustrated in his attempts to crush a bandit, a Han Dynasty emperor offered a generous reward, including the hand of his daughter in marriage, to anyone who could bring him the head of the bandit general. To everyone's amazement, the emperor's dog Panhu showed up one day with the head in his jaws. The daughter insisted on completing the bargain, and the odd couple went up to the mountains where they had six sons and six daughters, founding a new tribe.

This tale sounds like typical Han Chinese aspersions on "barbarian" ethnic groups, but Pangu/Panhu is quite clearly a pivotal Yao deity. While the Yao I spoke with did not argue with the story when it was repeated to me by a Han informant, recorded Yao stories about Panhu emphasize instead the god's helping the tribe on its migrations through southern China, and they told me such stories on Thistle Mountain. They also showed me several ritual texts with references to Pangu/Panhu.[28] Pangu temples throughout the area thus spoke to very different kinds of traditions from most gods in core areas of China, even though Han Chinese worshiped there alongside Yao and Zhuang. They further thickened the saturated soup of Guangxi religion with dog worship, totemic ancestors, and the confusion with the more officially acceptable Pangu tradition.

Many other major temples also tied to strictly local legends and often to minority ethnic traditions. The important Qiansa temple in Caicun, Guiping County, for instance, commemorated a vagrant who created a walkway over a river by throwing in cow dung that magically became rocks.[29] This was another case of a strictly local legendary figure whose morality was vague at best, and certainly not any reflection of officially sanctioned cultural values.

I have already mentioned how the Liuwu temple at Sigu provided a popular site for Zhuang-style paired singing. It honored illicit lovers who may have been suicides. According to local oral history, one was a failed degree-holder, and the other a woman singing on Liuwu Mountain. They sang together for seven days and nights, and then died. Ants covered their bodies with earth, and the local people said they had become immortals. Like King Gan, this temple could demand worship, and people said anything from stomach ailments to snake attacks could come from ignoring it (Guangxi . . ., 1962:49). Here again a number of different strands interweave with the usual idea of gods, from local Zhuang traditions to a kind of menace that typical gods elsewhere never threaten.

Similar but smaller temples included the Lang (or Langguang) temple and the Grandaunt Liu (Liu Dagupuo) temple, both at Thistle Mountain. The Lang temple stood at Sanjiang, on the river toward the main market, where many people had drowned. A little like the local King Gan temple, this temple appeased nearby ghosts. Grandaunt Liu represented the spirit of a girl who had died young, but did many good works both before and after death.[30] This temple resembled *guniang* temples in Taiwan that honor girls who died young, or for that matter the origin story of Mazu (Wolf, 1974:49–50). Unlike the Taiwan temples, however, this one had a major local following, and unlike Mazu, it had absolutely no state recognition.

Indeed, odd gods existed throughout late imperial China (like temples to accidentally disinterred bones, or to prematurely dead girls in Taiwan, or to fox fairies in north China), but in the core areas that are ethnographically best described, such temples rarely developed into the major community temples they were in more peripheral Guangxi. Just as rice lords competed successfully for secular power with proper Confucian bureaucrats, King Gan and the others competed successfully for divine power with more standard gods.

The potential for odd gods existed everywhere in Chinese religion, but even the weakly institutionalized interpretive communities of more developed areas managed to limit them to hidden corners. The conditions in Guangxi, however, with their ethnic interactions, weak state, economic upsets, rice lords, bandits and all the rest, allowed this undercurrent to rise boldly to the surface. The relative saturation of Chinese gods everywhere grew extreme in Guangxi in the 1840s, with all kinds of potential readings that ran the gamut from officially approved values (King Gan as an official, Pangu as the legendary world creator), to metaphors for local independence from the state (nearly every deity had strictly local roots), to representations of banditry (the threat of the Liuwu temple, the murderous tale of King Gan), to references to ethnicity (Pangu, the various associations with paired singing). Here was an especially free space for resistance, even if that resistance still remained only one potential on the eve of the Taiping uprising. A wild array of possible precipitations lay waiting in those god temples, and the social deterioration of the 1840s kept everything in motion, decreasing the institutional ability to impose any authoritative reading on the situation. The Taiping's God would finally unify the multivocalic possibilities of Guangxi's gods, but not before God Himself underwent some transformations.

GOD MEETS THE GODS

In an area used to worshiping mother killers, dung tossers and illicit lovers, God did not seem as odd as he must have in Hong's home village in Hua County. This openness to odd gods was one of the reasons behind the local acceptance of Hong's new God. Chinese gods remain popular as long as they grant people's wishes, and even an efficacious stone may soon gather a large clientele. Hong's

God became popular in Xunzhou in part because His oddness did not upset the local people, but also because He soon proved to be especially efficacious and powerful. This proof did not reside within Hong's original ideology, but grew from God's ability to cure illness and to humiliate other gods without retaliation. In other words, God's power came to be defined within the highly charged terms of the local popular religion, rather than in Hong's terms.

This process of hijacking Hong's Christianity began in the mid-1840s, as the movement claimed conventional religious power by humiliating other gods. They typically destroyed popular temples and desecrated the god images, often by tearing off their beards. While Hong and Feng may well have seen this as a bold blow at the heart of popular idolatry and superstition, god destruction was in fact always a perfectly plausible option within popular religious practice. Like family relationships or bureaucratic power in China, ties to gods required a mutual responsibility. A worshiper owed the father–bureaucrat respect and obedience, but rightfully expected protection and benevolence in return. Gods could lose their mandate in the same way that dynasties could lose their right to rule – by evading their responsibilities. The very weak institutions of control made gods, of course, far easier to overthrow than dynasties. Impotent deities might be broken to bits, burnt, or set floating down the river by angry crowds. Such carnage did not occur very often, but everyone knew it was a possibility. Gods can also defeat other gods, as when the Empress of Heaven "ate" a more strictly local deity in the New Territories (Watson, 1985:310).

Hong Xiuquan and Feng Yunshan had already attacked tablets to Confucius in the schools of Hua County. They apparently kept this up after they began teaching in Xunzhou. Yet they often covered up their own attacks, sometimes rewriting tablets they had just destroyed. One of the oral histories also speaks of Feng secretly destroying Earth God images at night (Guangxi . . ., 1962:53–54). Such attacks may have reflected their personal anger over educational failures, the anti-Confucian element of Hong's dream, and the hope for a more systematic attack on idolatry. Yet the efforts remained personal and secret, avoiding any popular reinterpretation but by the same token useless for recruitment.

The first more public attack apparently began in 1844, when Hong wrote a poem denouncing the immoral couple deified in the Liuwu temple, and wrote how "the lasciviousness in Kwangsi [Guangxi], men and women making proposals to each other and conduct worse than that of animals, all came from such evil demons" (*Taiping Tianri* in Michael, 1966–1971:67). From Hong's point of view, the poem probably attacked only this specific case of immorality; it was another isolated case. In addition, a poem falls far short of a physical attack. Yet the God Worshipers had a stroke of luck:

> Because of these verses the people were irritated against Siu-tshuen [Hong Xiuquan], and wished that the idols might display their power in killing him, but after some time the white ants came into the temple . . . and destroyed the building as well as the wooden images (Hamberg, 1854:38).

Suddenly the die was cast, and God was competing directly with the gods. Rather than allowing the idols to kill Hong, the new God won the battle, greatly enhancing His reputation and the size of the following. By taking advantage of this situation, however, the God Worshipers had put their deity squarely in the context of Guangxi's unusual popular gods, just one more competitor in a dog-eat-dog world.[31]

Direct attacks on temples became an open part of the God Worshiper strategy in 1846, when Feng led at least two attacks against his usual targets – an Earth God temple and a Confucian Wenchang temple (*Xunzhou Fuzhi*, 1897, juan 56:13). The attacks became far more common in 1847, the year that Hong returned to the area. Earth God temples provided common and easy victims at first (Guangxisheng . . ., 1956:35–36, 48; *Wuxuan xianzhi*, 1914:23–24). These shrines were small, physically vulnerable with no one usually attending them, and based only in small communities. The numbers of offended people at any attack would be small.

Yet they soon expanded to attack a King Gan temple, Pangu temples, a Thunder God (Leigong) temple, the Lang temple, and the Nine Demons temple (*Xunzhou Fuzhi*, 1897, juan 27:55, Guangxisheng . . ., 1956:35-36; Guangxi . . ., 1962:62–63). The Three Generations temple is notable by its absence from this list, which includes instead nearly every temple that did not fit the more broadly and officially sanctioned version of a god. Hong and Feng may have been anti-Confucian, but they still harbored many Confucian values. In every case they described, the movement's motives were not an all-embracing Christian iconoclasm, but a specific attack on what they saw as immorality. The God Worshipers attacked these gods because they were real, powerful, and corrupting. Their God was better, more upright and more powerful, but still part of the same system.

The most important attack from this list was their destruction of the central King Gan temple in Xiangzhou (*Taiping Tianri* in Michael, 1966–1971:73–76; Hamberg, 1854:36–37). After telling how King Gan had humiliated a magistrate, the Taiping version of the event celebrates their retaliation, as Hong ordered four followers to "dig out the eyes of the demon, cut off its beard, trample its hat, tear its embroidered dragon gown to shreds, turn its body upside down, and break off its arms" (*Taiping Tianri* in Michael, 1966–1971:73). Hamberg describes the consequences of this first attack on a genuinely major temple:

> As soon as this deed was known in the neighborhood, the people of the district offered a reward of one hundred dollars for the apprehension of the perpetrators. The demon, however, again possessed a young boy and said, "These men are sincere, you are not able to hurt them, you must only repair my image again, and then it will be all right." After this the people withdrew their proclamation. This event served to advance the reputation of Siu-tshuen [Hong Xiuquan], and the number of his followers rapidly increased (Hamberg, 1854:37–38).

This passage reveals what must have been a common dynamic during this period. Followers of the destroyed deities were dismayed and unhappy, yet the clear success of the attacks also impressed some of them greatly. The entire episode left King Gan intact and rebuilt. God had by no means proved to these people that King Gan was a fake and the He was the only God; they kept King Gan while recognizing that God was even more powerful. Hong and Feng may have seen all this as an affirmation of Christianity in opposition to popular religion, or of morality instead of depravity, but to the local people it was an affirmation of God's power within their own religious traditions.

This process of transforming Hong's God into an especially powerful spirit, but one not too radically different from the local tradition, also occurred in some ritual procedures that were clearly borrowed directly from Chinese popular tradition. These included use of a standard Chinese altar with candles, incense, three glasses of wine, meat offerings, and so on (Jian, 1958:1720; Hamberg, 1854:40). At least by Hong's return to Xunzhou in 1847, after he had spent some months with the missionary Roberts in Canton, he was aware that this was not standard procedure for Christians. Yet he was unable to affect any reform, just as he was unable to stop any of the other changes that the local followers were working in his movement. Recruiting success had encouraged the leadership to allow God to join the uncontrolled mix of interpretations that percolated in Guangxi, but having begun the process they could no longer control it.

The results were mixed. Clearly, proving God's power had gained many followers for the movement, yet it also alienated some of the people whose gods provided the victims. In addition, the increasing size of the movement began to make the local elite nervous, and the rampage of temple destruction in 1847 gave them an excuse to arrest Feng at the end of the year. Although Feng later gained his freedom, the arrest seems clearly to have caused the God Worshipers to move away from this strategy, either out of fear of politicizing the movement at that time, or because they felt they were undermining their own popular support. There are no further reports of temple destruction until 1850, almost three years later.

CURING AND POWER

While God was proving himself against the local deities, several leaders of the movement established their own power and prestige through magical curing. Curing very often forms a core part of religious movements, from Christian Pentecostal sects to Japanese New Religions (Martin, 1990:165–171; Davis, 1980). Curing works, at least in some sense. I have watched tears of gratitude from patients cured by possessed healers at a cult in Taiwan, along with the emotional thrill that runs through bystanders.[32] Sunday morning television evangelists in the West often offer the same thing. It is difficult to imagine a more immediate and effective demonstration of real power.

China has a number of traditions of curing, many of which the God Worshipers borrowed. Most respectable was traditional Chinese medicine's combination of theoretical analysis of the forces acting in and on the body with long practical experience of particular herbal and other therapies. That system required an educated understanding of the basic forces of the universe, their interactions, and the ways to manipulate them. It was scientific in the sense that it involved a predictable manipulation of natural energies; it needed neither spirits nor a charismatic healer.

As an educated man, Hong Xiuquan may have had some knowledge of traditional Chinese medicine, but in practice the more magical systems of curing were far more important to the God Worshipers. After all, mastery of medical technique came from learning the system, which anyone might do; other forms of curing, however, could demonstrate the genuine power of God in terms both powerful and familiar to the people of Guangxi. All of these more religious curing systems in China involve rhetorical control over spirits rather than mechanical control over nature. Daoist priests, for example, can write curing or protective charms that ward off evil influences. For larger problems, they perform elaborate exorcisms. In either case, they use the authority vested in them by very high gods to oust more lowly demons. Other kinds of more minor cures could come directly from gods in temples. For example, a god might allow use of incense ash from a temple as a protective amulet, or to be brewed into a curing infusion. For more important problems, the gods may show up in person, possessing a medium, diagnosing the problem and prescribing the solution to the participants in charismatic performances. All of these techniques imply a proof of spiritual power in the ability to see invisible causes of illness and to root out the perpetrators.

While such curing techniques occurred all over China, rural Guangxi apparently had them to excess, or at least so it seemed to the elite authors of local gazetteers. Every gazetteer lamented the local people's preference for religious curers over traditional Chinese doctors (e.g., *Pingnan Xianzhi*, 1883, juan 8:3, 7; *Guangxi Tongzhi*, 1891, juan 87:7):

> When people are sick they do not take medicine but instead invite Daoists to worship the peck measure and pray to the stars [a Daoist ritual], or they call in a sorcerer who wears flowers, waves a sword and dances with plates. They call this jumping demons (*tiao gui*). There are also sorceresses locally called devil-women (*guipuo*) (*Xunzhou Fuzhi*, 1897, juan 54:67).

The gazetteers seem baffled by people's disregard for medical healing.[33]

The God Worshipers placed themselves squarely within this tradition. Curing had not been part of Hong's original vision, or part of what Christianity he had picked up. Instead the movement again found itself becoming part of a powerful local tradition in a way that greatly enhanced their leaders' power and authority, while compromising their ideological independence.

One observer who was in Xunzhou at the time later described Hong's mastery of the sorcerer's arts: "The rebel Hong regularly forecast rain or clear weather, and drew magic charms to cure disease. He had some real efficacy, and the country people called him Master Hong, honoring him like a god" (Banwo, 1874). More recent oral traditions in Xunzhou also recall Hong as a curer who made important converts by writing charms in God's name, and often showing God's superior ability to local gods. In one case Hong's landlady had made offerings to her local Earth God to cure her disease, but to no avail. Hong threw the image in the water, curing the disease and winning new friends (Guangxisheng . . ., 1956:35–36). Another case involved Shi Dakai, who would become one of the movement's leading generals:

> Shi Dakai's mother fell gravely ill, and Dakai sent someone to get a Maoshan Daoist to exorcize the demon . . . This person ran into Hong Xiuquan on the way, who asked what he was doing. The man told Xiuquan, and Xiuquan replied, "Do not get some Daoist. I will write some efficacious charms for you to take back and put on the wall, and all will be well" (Guangxisheng . . ., 1956:45).

The mother was cured, and Shi was won over.

Hong Rengan's confession provides similar evidence, saying that his cousin had "the power of causing the dumb to speak, and when people who were afflicted with leprosy and strange illnesses were cured by reason of the faith that they had in him, it caused a still greater number of people to come to him" (in Michael, 1966–1971:1520). While these sources are not strictly reliable – none involve eyewitnesses – they do indicate the popular image that the God Worshipers created. People saw them as tremendously powerful in standard religious terms, whether or not Hong actually performed such cures.

While Hong personally established some reputation as a curer, a new and local leader eclipsed him in this area as he would in others. Yang Xiuqing rose to dominance during this period of religious adaptation and became one of the crucial shapers of the developing ideology. One reason for the vigor of healing in religious movements is its ability to prove real successes, and thus to empower individuals who are otherwise powerless. Yang Xiuqing was just such a case – a local poor farmer, charcoal burner, and sometime transport worker, typical of many of the young men who shaped local life at the time (Michael, 1966–1971:35–36; Zhong, 1984b:115–118). The evidence for his cures is clear and unambiguous (Jian, 1958:1880):

> Many sick persons had been cured in a wonderful manner by prayer to God, and Yang was said to possess the gift to cure sicknesses by intercession for the sick. From the description it would almost seem as if Yang had willingly submitted and prayed to have the sickness of the other conferred upon himself, and that he for a short while had borne his sufferings, whereby he redeemed the disease of the other, and was afterwards himself released from the consequences of his own intercession (Hamberg, 1854:46).

A later Taiping document told a similar tale, and appeared to associate Yang's curing with spirit possession by God, beginning in 1848 (*Tianqing Daoli Shu* in Michael, 1966–1971:374–375). An anti-Taiping source described the same thing: "Thus he hopes to fool the masses, and indeed the masses are fooled. Alas!" ("Yueni Jilüe", n.d.:34–35). The final result was the valorization of Yang as the Redeemer of Sickness, who saved others by taking on their diseases, just as Christ had saved them by taking on their sins.

Hong and Feng had entered the Xunzhou region with a radical religious alternative, but soon found themselves claiming power squarely within the terms of local popular religious practice. Whether these original leaders liked it or not, many local people saw God as another claimant on local spiritual authority, Who stood out from the crowd because of His great successes, rather than because He promised a radically new religion.

With the very weak institutional control over religious interpretation in the area, and the thick and multivocalic mix of interpretations that already existed, the God Worshipers chose not to maintain their ideological purity, in contrast to the Western missionaries. Instead, they soon found themselves thrown into the vat along with everything else, adding further to the complexity of the local brew, but losing some of their original identity. The result by 1848 was a highly charged mixture of potential interpretations, within which the God Worshipers had successfully shown their own power. At the same time, however, their heavy-handed techniques had made enemies and ended in the arrest of Feng. With Feng off the scene for a while, and Hong only recently returned (and soon to leave again to try to rescue Feng), the original leadership continued to lose ideological control of the movement. 1848 brought a new step in the fermentation of the movement, as local traditions of spirit possession added to the multiplicity of voices and further expanded the possibilities.

# 5
# Too Many Voices

By allowing God to become just one more god, the new movement brought all the inherently complex possibilities of local popular religion into play. God became enmeshed in the ethnic, localist, and above all political (both pro- and anti-government) potentials of the local religious mixture. When the first God Worshiper became possessed, the movement took another gigantic step into its own dissolution into local popular practice, even as it transformed that practice. The first possessions probably began in late 1847, just as the temple destruction movement was losing its power, and as Feng Yunshan was removed from the scene. The first medium may have been someone called Yang Qingxiu.[34] As Hong Rengan later described the episode:

> Yang Ch'ing-hsiu [Qingxiu] was able to ascend to heaven, and in the sky there was the sound of drums and music. An angelic boy also descended to announce Hung's [Hong's] name and say: "Three eight two one; grain is food of jade; a man sits over all the land to be the guide of the people." Each time when there was a proclamation, an angelic boy would come down and speak (in Michael, 1966–1971:4–5).

The "angelic boy" undoubtedly described a possessed medium. Chinese terms for mediums often include the term "boy" (e.g., *jitong, luotong*), no matter what the age of the medium.

The text of the medium's message also illustrates the high "coefficient of weirdness" (Malinowski, 1935:218–233) that communications with gods often show; it makes no more immediate sense in Chinese than it does in English. The apparent impenetrability of the message added to the general sense of overwhelming possibilities that I have been discussing, and strengthened the feeling that the Lord had blessed the movement with these special messages that went beyond the limitations of everyday language. As always, however, other readings waited beneath the surface. In this case, the Chinese characters can be read for their shapes rather than their meanings. The combination of the characters for "three," "eight," "two," and "one" makes Hong, "grain" and "is" make Xiu, and "man" written over "one" ("all" in Michael's translation) and "land" makes Quan, thus spelling out the leader's name. This kind of language game recalls Bakhtin again on language play in Rabelais, but also resonates with numerous connotations in Chinese tradition. One form of fortune telling, for instance, dissected characters into their component parts. In addition, the Triad societies liked to use such secret encodings for various characters important in their rituals and beliefs. Here was a message, therefore, that indicated heavenly mystery to some, secret affirmation of Hong's authority to others, and recognition of strong Triad links (at a time when the God Worshipers had ties to various Triad bandit groups) to still others.

Whatever the date and details of the first possession, by 1848 the God Worshipers had entered a period dominated by spirit possession. Taiping documents indicate about two hundred cases of spirit possession, and these surely represent only a small part of what actually occurred.[35] The published Taiping sources described only the incidents that the leaders later approved; we know the others primarily through Hamberg and especially through denunciations of other mediums in surviving documents. The passage from Hamberg I quoted earlier clearly shows the importance of multiple possessions to the movement in 1848 and 1849, as various members of the congregation entered a "state of ecstasy" and exhorted, reprimanded and prophesied to the group (Hamberg, 1854:45).

## LOCAL TRADITIONS

This immersion in spirit possession pushed the God Worshipers even deeper into local religious practice. Spirit mediumship through possession occurred commonly throughout south China, but it seemed unusual in both quantity and quality in the Xunzhou region, at least compared to better studied parts of China. Even today, possessed spirit mediums continue to play an important role in the area, patronized by people at all levels of society. Twice when I was in Guiping town, local cadres pulled me aside, knowing I was interested in spirit possession, to tell me their personal experiences. In both cases, they made sure no one else was in earshot, and began by explaining how they were good Communists and educated men, and did not believe any of this.

Nevertheless, one of them explained how he could no longer identify his mother's grave, because he had not been able to worship there during the Cultural Revolution. The medium he consulted described the exact location of the grave, even down to details like a tree root that had grown through the coffin. The other cadre had been to a medium who correctly predicted several details of his future. Both proclaimed their disbelief, but both wanted to be sure that I understood how accurate this knowledge was, and how impossible to obtain through secular means. This part of Guangxi clearly maintains spirit medium traditions much more powerfully than many other areas of China, due partly to its very peripheral position and partly to the strength of the local tradition.

The Xunzhou region was as much a relative hotbed of possession in the 1840s as it appears to be now. Those gazetteers that bewailed the local fondness for religious curing instead of traditional Chinese medicine usually cited spirit mediums as the heart of the problem. The Guangxi area shared with Taiwan and many other parts of China possession in which a spirit spoke through the body of a medium. By entering such an altered state of consciousness, professional mediums performed divination, cured patients, and so on. The medium would usually take on the personality characteristics of the possessing god, solemn and intimidating in some cases, brandishing martial weapons in others, or jumping impishly about in still others. The medium's voice would also change, often becoming harder to understand as the power and difference of the god manifested itself through the medium. In some cases, the god would not speak, but instead wrote characters with a brush. Such characters were highly saturated – a wild scribble with many possible readings, as far from ordinary writing as the god was from the ordinary being he or she possessed.

A second form of mediumship apparently also thrived in the area, although it is rarely reported in other parts of China. In this form the medium, again in an altered state of consciousness, journeys to the supernatural world where he or she can examine objects and speak to the spirits. In one common variation, the medium can examine a tree that represents every person, diagnosing health from the health of the plant, divining numbers of children from the number of buds, and so on (*Xunzhou Fuzhi*, 1897, juan 54:67).[36] In other cases, mediums might speak directly with spirits. Experts can induce this kind of trance in their clients, sending regular people on spirit journeys.

This form of possession may have been so common in the Xunzhou area because of its relation to Yao spirit journeys that still form part of their initiation ritual. The Yao informants I interviewed in Guangxi described how Yao masters lead all initiates on elaborate first journeys to the spirit world, introducing them to what they will need to know there. Afterwards the initiates may be able to undertake their own journeys.[37] One of the Yao I spoke with agreed to act out a possession episode in spite of the presence of various local officials. He seemed clearly able to perform as a medium on his own.

The imperial government had to tolerate possession, especially given its powerlessness in Xunzhou in the 1840s. Yet like the current government, it discouraged the practice whenever possible. It could not approve a practice that allowed for divinely sanctioned messages completely beyond its control. As direct messages from the gods, inherently uncontrollable by any interpretive institution, possessions were potentially subversive. As I have argued elsewhere, it was this potential for subversion, rather than any necessarily subversive content, that led to government suppression of possession cults in many cases (Weller, 1984).

## THE POWER OF POSSESSION

The very local tradition of spirit journeys must have made Hong's vision easier to accept in Xunzhou than it had been in his native county, which apparently lacked such a strong tradition. Hong's dream, after all, must have sounded exactly like one of those medium-led trips to the supernatural world that characterized the area. Hong's divine revelation may well have been simply a bizarre dream to the inhabitants of relatively sophisticated Hua County, but it was quite plausibly a real spirit trip to Heaven for the people of Xunzhou.

This initial reinterpretation of Hong's vision became far more powerful when the God Worshipers entered deeply into local possession traditions. Adherents of the movement made massive use of both the local possession traditions. Hamberg seems to describe the form most common in south China, where the spirit descends into the body of a medium and speaks directly through him or her. Most of the officially recorded possessions in Taiping documents also follow this pattern. Yet the God Worshipers clearly also drew heavily on the much less commonly described tradition of sending souls on spirit journeys to the underworld. Taiping sources, for example, describe several cases where the medium Xiao Chaogui (soon to be one of the top leaders), as Jesus, led his audience one at a time up into Heaven. Late in 1849, for instance, "the Heavenly Elder Brother [Xiao as Jesus] called together the mass of little ones, choosing each one and admonishing cautious speech, and individually raised them up, lofting each to Heaven" (*Tianxiong Shengzhi* in Wang, 1985:209). He even led his human self up to Heaven at least once, when Jesus suggested that Xiao Chaogui return with Him for an hour or so when he ascended (*Tianxiong Shengzhi* in Wang, 1985:209)

Hong Xiuquan must have had mixed feelings about all of this. In earlier, simpler days, he had clearly opposed many practices of popular religion. In a poem written around 1845, he had warned that:

The fifth kind of wrong is witchcraft;
By the evil arts of deceiving the multitude, Heaven's
   penalty is incurred.
Death and life, calamity and sickness, all are determined
   by Heaven;
Why then deceive the people by the useless manufacture
   of charms?
Incantations to procure luck, vows to the demons, services
   to the devils,
Fastings and processions, all are of no avail
                    (*Yuandao Jiushi Ge* in Michael, 1966–1971:29).

Yet now Hong found that the immersion of his original ideology in just these practices was creating the enormous following he had dreamed about.

The ebbing of Hong's staunch monotheism in favor of a God who competed as an equal with other gods, which had begun with the temple destructions a few years earlier, had reached an extreme by the time of the spirit possession in 1848. The new opening quickly created new local leaders. The mediums Yang Xiuqing (possessed by God; also a curer as I discussed in Chapter 4) and Xiao Chaogui (possessed by Jesus), nearly unknown until this time, soon joined the very highest leadership of the movement. At the same time, the new dominance of local leaders and local customs brought thousands of people into the fold.

Spirit possession by the mass of followers threatened to remove interpretive authority within the God Worshiping community completely away from the control of the original leaders. Hong himself, of course, did not need to be possessed to occupy a special position – he was already God's son. Yet any possessed adherent immediately earned equal authority, just by being believably possessed by a spirit of equal stature to Hong. A medium could even overrule Hong by speaking the words of Jesus or God directly, both of whom outranked Hong as his older brother or father. Both Yang Xiuqing and Xiao Chaogui posed just this dilemma for Hong, and both took pains to assert their privileged authority from the very first day.[38] Both entered the fray in 1848, Yang/God in the spring and Xiao/Jesus later in the fall.

At His first visit, we only know that God displayed "innumerable miracles and powers" (Michael, 1966–1971:98). Jesus, however, immediately spoke to dissension within the ranks: "I have descended into the golden mouth of the Western King [Xiao Chaogui] in order to explain in detail to the Heavenly King [Hong], because Xiao Chaolong [probably a lineage cousin of Xiao Chaogui] has offended me: I am Jesus" (*Tianxiong Shengzhi* in Wang, 1985:192). Mediumship had clearly joined the struggle for control in 1848. Jesus often also took pains to stress his superiority to his little brother Hong. Just a month later, for instance, "The Heavenly Elder Brother Christ addressed the Heavenly King, saying 'Hong Xiuquan, Younger Brother, do you recognize me?' The Heavenly King responded 'Your small little brother does recognize you'" (*Tianxiong Shengzhi* in Wang, 1985:192). Both Yang and Xiao would often demand that Hong acknowledge their higher status while they were possessed.

To make matters worse, all kinds of other spirits also appeared, from local star spirits to various beings the later Taiping would describe as imps and devils. In addition to Hamberg's description of many people getting possessed and causing enormous dissension, we also have records of God and Jesus attacking other mediums. Hamberg records a sort of excommunication that resulted in one case: "One of the Wang clan had spoken against the doctrine of Jesus, and led many astray, but he was excluded from the congregation, and his words declared false, being spoken under the influence of a corrupt spirit" (Hamberg, 1854:46). Such demons plagued the movement all the way up to its transformation into an armed rebellion in 1850. Leaders asked Jesus for help controlling star spirits in 1849, imp constellations later that year, and devils in early 1850. As late as the summer of 1850, Jesus demanded the investigation and arrest of a rival medium within the movement, a man named Li who was threatened with execution if he ever spoke again (Wang, 1985:201). I will save the leaders' attempts to create order out of this chaos for Chapter 6. Here I want only to establish that the voices of many other mediums still echo between the lines determined much later by the established Taiping leadership, which validated only the voices of Yang and Xiao.

Possession could thus offer a kind of epitome of saturation, where every voice had equal authority, and no interpretive institution could stand against the direct instructions of the gods. This ultimate overload of meaning, however, constantly pushed toward a single interpretation. Indeed, every possessed proclamation constituted a mini-precipitate, since it required an explicit statement that often contradicted others. Many of the God Worshipers' possessions of 1848 and 1849 seemed to address the growth of mutually incompatible interpretations, especially in the challenges to the authority of other mediums and the constant worry about a lack of unity in the movement. Interpretive silence no longer remained possible, but the mediums fought over whose meaning would finally dominate.

The records reveal frustratingly little detail about how all of this actually took place. They are thin descriptions that highlight only those voices that finally won the fight. Mass possession movements elsewhere in the world, however, show regular enough features that we can get a good idea of what that period of rich multivocality and endless possibility might have been like for the God Worshipers. The sections that follow will cite comparative material in some detail, as a way of suggesting how the dynamics of that early community of God Worshipers might have worked.

## The Emotional and Aesthetic Power of Trance

Uncontrolled possession cults are saturated by their very nature, as the inherent authority of each medium allows new interpretations to thrive without effective interference. This plethora of possible meanings itself contains a tremendous appeal to new followers. It typically offers the excitement and charisma of personal experience with powers beyond the normal world, along with the heady experience of constantly innovative and responsive interpretations with irreproachable claims to supernatural validity.

Institutional control of interpretation is much easier for some forms of religious action than for others. Control is easiest when the leaders can lay claim to more orthodox interpretations through their greater knowledge, and enforce those claims through established interpretive communities, as with the tremendous erudition and institutions controlled by the medieval Catholic Church. Yet it can be very difficult when anyone at all has direct access to divine knowledge, as in the case of uncontrolled spirit possession.

The option for anyone to speak with divine authority, for the masses to overload the field with their own unassailable interpretations, makes any kind of control difficult because people direct their own interpretations. There is a continuum from more to less self-interpreting religious practice, which generally creates a continuum of thicker to thinner religion. At one extreme, mass spirit possession is almost impossible to control. The spirit will tell you exactly what it means, and if you get it wrong, the spirit can come back again to correct you. This is direct communication with the divine world, and it leaves little room for the state or any other religious intermediary. Possession can break through even accepted canons of interpretation with relative impunity. Visions and visionary dreams are a little easier to control. They may seem to contain clear messages, but they are private (unlike most possession) and can be subject to reinterpretation by authorities as mere metaphors. Signs and omens offer the potential for still more control, as they often require religious experts to interpret their apparently opaque messages. Finally, texts and rituals often form the lifeblood of thin interpretation, especially where people are illiterate. Institutionalized religion thrives on texts and rituals, whose correct interpretation only the leaders themselves can determine. While any religious form can end up saturated if the interpretive community fails – after all, texts do have multiple readings – the reverse is not true. The very nature of mass possession makes institutional control and the dominance of a single precipitated interpretation almost impossible.

Weak as it may be for developing strong institutions, uncontrolled possession offers a powerful charisma that greatly benefits recruitment. Such cults owe a great deal of their mass appeal to the emotional and aesthetic power of trance performances (Thrupp, 1962:26–27). No one sleeps through the service when possessed

Holy Ghost people in the West Virginia mountains begin to pass rattlesnakes around.

Other forms of communication with the gods in China are cold and dull by comparison – the god speaks only haltingly through the fall of divination sticks, through the inscrutable verses tied to Yijing hexagrams, or at best through a muddled dream subject to many interpretations. Possession, in contrast, brings the spirit directly to the people. Taking over its human medium, the spirit actually speaks, answers questions, preaches and exhorts. The mediums' voices may become shrill, fast, and strangely accented with the gods' voices, much as Hamberg described for the possessed God Worshipers speaking in rhythm and often unintelligibly. Their human personalities disappear, transformed into the particular presence of the god. Indeed, the whole arena seems transformed out of ordinary life with the thrill of the arrival of extraordinary beings.

This is especially true of cults that feature mass possession, including Haitian voodoo, some American Pentecostalism, or the Taiwanese Religion of Compassion (Cihui Tang), whose possessions may have resembled the God Worshipers. I witnessed a local sect of the Religion of Compassion celebrating the birthday of their chief goddess, the Golden Mother of the Jasper Pool (Yaochi Jinmu) in 1976.[39] This cult is the largest of a set of pietistic sects that are very popular in Taiwan; many of them center on mediumship through spirit writing (see Jordan and Overmyer, 1986). The Religion of Compassion stands out from the others, however, through its practice of "jumping" (*tiao*). Any member of the cult is liable to experience jumping, that is, direct possession by the cult gods.

Such uncontrolled possession occupied the gathered faithful as I arrived to watch their festival. Possessed believers filled a field in front of their temple, some shaking, some falling to the ground, and some brandishing swords in the style of Chinese martial arts. They sometimes wandered into the surrounding crowd, occasionally infecting others with their trance. Especially in contrast to most ordinary Taiwanese religion, where trance is largely limited to professional mediums, the excitement and sense of altered context pervaded the crowd. The power of the occasion further increased a little later, as possessed cult members began to cure other members on the temple veranda. Still quivering with trance, they would tap on their patients' chests, speak spells, and draw smoke charms with sticks of incense. The experience clearly thrilled and compelled the patients. Many went into trance themselves, further enhancing the thrill of the event. The immediate power and excitement of such an occasion (even to a non-believing anthropologist), and the visible ability of the gods to transform human personality made the cult strongly appealing. The aesthetic and religious thrills of possession trance are part of the powerful ability of possession cults to attract followers.

All of this suggests that the God Worshipers might also have gained in both the unity of the group and the number of followers through the power of God's direct presence in their midst, along with many other spirits. Certainly the local traditions of possession on which these God Worshiping mediums drew were as colorful and dramatic as any. The spate of trance episodes during this period, accompanied by their effective cures and rival claims of religious authority, could easily have created an atmosphere of excitement that greatly increased popular interest in God Worship, just as occurred in possession trance movements in other parts of the world.

The surviving records unfortunately show far more concern with what God and Jesus said than with the quality of the performance itself. Yet while direct evidence is brief, we know that numerous individuals were possessed – we have at least surnames for five mediums in the material I have already mentioned, and many others are implied. We also know that many trance performances took place in front of large gatherings of followers, and that at least some of them were dramatically powerful. In the early moments of the rebellion itself, for example, Jesus spoke to the combined troops:

> Suddenly he called out to the Southern King [Feng Yunshan]: "Bring Snow in the Clouds [the sword God had given to Hong]." The Southern King presented Snow in the Clouds, and the Heavenly Elder Brother began a great battle against devils. The Heavenly Elder Brother said: "If they come on the left I stop them on the left! If they come on the right I stop them on the right! They can come where they like, I will stop them as I like!" He also said: "No matter where you devils run, you cannot escape my net on Heaven or earth" (*Tianxiong Shengzhi* in Wang, 1985:210).

This performance strongly recalled Daoist exorcism, but must also have been commandingly charismatic. It could easily have helped to cement a group of followers already familiar with such performance. At the very least, evidence on the God Worshipers is plausibly consistent with what we know about how comparable cults worked.

## Transcending Boundaries

Spirit possession, because it allows free and innovative new revelations beyond the power of the usual institutions, can provide a powerful validation for breaking accepted social boundaries. Possession movements thus often spread beyond conventional groups by appealing to both genders, to dissatisfied intellectuals, and to diverse social groups. Crossing the boundary between human and spirit makes more secular boundaries easier to cross as well. Interpretive communities, and conventions of all kinds, cannot stand against the multiple voices of mass possession.

Possession cults often cross ethnic boundaries and form new kinds of coalitions, facilitating recruitment and leading to the possible development of a large-scale movement. The New Guinea Taro Cult, for example, united several groups around a prophet who had been "struck down" by the Spirit of Taro (Worsley, 1968:59–67). In 1914 the cult began to spread through several villages as the Spirit possessed new people. In trembling trances, followers received messages about the planting of taro and other crops. They also cured and performed magic to ensure a good crop. One of their most important tenets was "good fellowship" toward each other. This, added to the infectious character of their trances and a tendency to proselytize, allowed the cult to spread very rapidly among neighboring groups, crossing both ethnic and linguistic boundaries. In fact, the reliance on trance made it very easy for the cult to spread, and to adapt itself to new areas and new leaders. Many other cults offered similar innovations.

In much the same way, the God Worshipers appealed across ethnic boundaries, in spite of a recent history of massive conflict between ethnic groups in the area. While the ethnic composition of the early God Worshipers is not fully clear, the Hakka undoubtedly found the movement especially attractive, and joined in large numbers. The main founders of the sect, Hong Xiuquan and Feng Yunshan, were Hakkas and originally settled with Hakka families. The arrival of perhaps 3,000 Hakkas fleeing a losing ethnic feud with natives in Gui County gave the God Worshipers a crucial edge in the local balance of power. The God Worshipers offered them a way of uniting in the face of their enemies. Kuhn (1977) and especially Kojima (1983) have argued that the God Worshipers' religious ideology peculiarly suited the needs of Hakkas newly arrived in a peripheral area, offering a religious unity to people with no geographical unity or local tradition of their own. In the absence of their own religious structures, the movement offered them both a unifying ideology and social organization.

Yet the God Worshipers by no means simply expressed Hakka ethnicity. They had included Zhuangs and some Yaos from the beginning, and their egalitarian ideology promised to erase standard ethnic divisions (Guangxisheng . . ., 1956:75–77). The movement's leaders consistently wrote of the brotherhood of all people: "Since our Heavenly Father gave us birth and nourishment, we are of one form though of separate bodies, and we breathe the same air though in different places. This is why we say all are brothers within the four seas . . . When there is clothing, let all wear it; when there is food, let all eat of it" (*Tianqing Daoli Shu* in Michael, 1966–1971:388).[40] Denying equality meant denying humanity itself, and the term "imps" thus came to mean the ruling Manchus in addition to its earlier use to condemn gods like King Gan. The God Worshipers' egalitarianism had strong Christian roots for Hong. Locally, however, evidence from possession movements elsewhere suggests that God's and Jesus's (and perhaps other mediums') presence on earth may have been one of the factors that promoted the movement's openness to various ethnic groups, even in the face of deep-seated conflicts. God and Jesus regularly spoke to the group about the need for harmony and cooperation, even if they did not address ethnicity directly (e.g., *Tianming Zhaozhishu* in Michael, 1966–1971:99, 100).

Among the top leadership, the newly powerful locals used cross-ethnic ties, like the religious interpenetration I have already discussed, to bridge the gaps among the groups. Shi Dakai, for example, apparently had a Zhuang mother and Hakka father, and Wei Changhui may possibly have been Yao. In any case, both were bilingual and could thus help appeal across standard ethnic lines (Guangxisheng . . ., 1956:74). In addition, Xiao Chaogui showed great familiarity with Yao spirit possession, often using the more Yao form of leading people up to Heaven.[41] The opening up of set social structures through the immediate presence of spirits on earth surely gave a power to Hong's egalitarian message that he could never have achieved on his own. The process further deteriorated conventional community boundaries in the area, weak as they already were in the 1840s. At the same time, it added still more complexities to the brew of ideas available to the movement.

## New Roles and New Rituals

Possession cults appeal so widely as the basis of social movements because the direct presence of a god can facilitate political and cultural innovation, breaking both cultural convention and social boundaries in an outburst of charismatic enthusiasm. In the Taro Cult this first took the form of new gardening ritual, which featured songs filled with "foreign" words (Worsley, 1968:60–61). They also introduced new large feasts that differed from traditional feasts by including curing ceremonies, singing new songs, and introducing new ways of cutting and cooking taro. New greetings and cries appeared, and many new vocabulary words began to replace old words. The converted took these symbols of new life to their extreme by adopting new names (Worsley, 1968:63). Their doctrine of amity among all the tribes was a critical cultural innovation that helped the movement spread; a fad of shaking hands accompanied the new doctrine.

Several years later, the people of Palau (in the Western Carolines) similarly used possession cults to create an innovative religious movement (Leonard, 1973:159–163). A precursor of the movement had begun in 1905, when a low-ranking man named Rdiall broke with Palauan tradition by building a non-traditional house, erecting a flagpole, and, most shocking of all, doing women's work – tilling the soil. The cult built around the trances of this prophet had died out by the time the Japanese arrived to occupy the islands in 1914, but a similar group called Modekngei ("Get Together" ) soon arose, apparently inspired by Japanese repression of traditional religion. The leader was first possessed in 1916, and like Rdiall, began breaking taboos. In his case, he ate bananas without suffering any evil consequences. This proof of his power established his reputation. Later leaders represented Modekngei as the only true Palauan way – they forbade foreign songs and foods, and took a number of Christian beliefs for their own. In both cases, innovations that challenged local tradition proved critical in gaining a following.

Possession cults often further transcend normal social lines by allowing a relatively powerless person to rise to authority as a possessed leader, or by allowing women a more active role than other organizations. Possession can dissolve conventional political boundaries by allowing people who are normally cut off from political power to occupy places of significant respect and authority. Lewis, for example, writes that women's possession cults become especially important "in traditional societies and cultures where women lack more obvious and direct means of forwarding their aims" (1971:31). Women also play important roles in possession cults in Taiwan, including the Religion of Compassion. They may comprise a major proportion of the membership, and often occupy major positions within these cults.

Like these possession cults elsewhere, the early God Worshipers gave opportunities to people who might not have had them otherwise, including dissatisfied intellectuals like Hong Xiuquan and Feng Yunshan, a river pirate like Luo Dagang, a poor mountain farmer like Xiao Chaogui, and a charcoal burner like Yang Xiuqing. Xiao and Yang in particular used possession to build their places within the movement, but some women apparently used similar techniques. Xiao Chaogui's wife, for example, told in 1847 of her spirit journey to Heaven a decade earlier:

> during a very severe sickness, when she lay as dead upon her bed, her soul ascended to heaven, and she heard an old man say to her, "After ten years a man will come from the east and teach thee to worship God; obey him willingly." She was eminent among the female God-worshippers, who used to say as a proverb, "Men ought to study Fung-Yun-san [Feng Yunshan], and women the conduct of Yang-Yun-kiao [Xiao's wife]" (Hamberg, 1854:34).

At least by the time the movement had organized as a rebellion, it allowed women a powerful role, including women's military units with their own officers and independent women's production units. The specific role of possession in this is not clear, but the similarity with the innovative appeal of the Religion of Compassion and other possession cults to women is striking. A few cases of God Worshiper possession, at least, suggest an active role for women. For example, one conversation between Hong and Jesus in 1848 implied that Guanyin, one of the most important goddesses in China, had been possessing people, probably women:

> The Heavenly King [Hong Xiuquan] asked, "Is Guanyin a good person?" The Heavenly Elder Brother [Xiao as Jesus] replied "She is a good person. She now enjoys good fortune in the highest

heavens, but is also not allowed to descend to earth." The Heavenly King asked, "While Guanyin enjoys the highest heavens, how do you address her?" The Heavenly Elder Brother said, "I call her younger sister." The Heavenly King asked, "How should I address her?" The Heavenly Elder Brother answered, "You also call her younger sister" (in Mao, 1989:36).

"Descent to earth" was the standard Taiping reference to spirit possession, and the passage appears to indicate that further possessions by Guanyin are inappropriate. Quite clearly, Hong and Xiao put themselves in a higher position by making her their younger sister. Just as important, here was another case of a local medium accepting a popular deity into the hierarchy, and of Hong accepting the polytheism.

Finally, just as in other possession cults around the world, the early period of God Worshiper possessions saw innovation and creative movement-building, as the innovations announced by a medium had immediate divine sanction. As usual, we have very few concrete details, but the period of widespread possession saw the beginnings of congregational worship at flag-raising ceremonies and an increase in followers due to the trance cures performed by Yang Xiuqing.[42]

Hong had entered Guangxi with a fairly tidy ideology, but by 1849 his ideas had been thoroughly dissolved and transformed in the cauldron of local traditions. Neither the local religion nor the God Worshipers would emerge the same. The dynamics of spirit possession elsewhere suggest that mediumship often empowers these movements, attracting followers through the aesthetic excitement of trance performances, creating new political opportunities while transcending old ethnic boundaries, and innovating cultural and political ideals through direct divine inspiration. The available evidence about the God Worshipers remains too scanty to assert confidently that all the same processes also took place there, but the evidence at least never contradicts such an inference. At the very least, early God Worshiper possession helped break old social boundaries and expand the potential base of support.

The thick mixture of 1849 teemed with possible interpretations, many of them incompatible but coexisting. Their connotations ramified through territory as diverse as local ethnicity, strongmen, gender, bandits, curing, and state power. While the situation was chaotic, it was also tremendously powerful and creative, quickly attracting an enormous and diverse following. Spirit mediums added to both the chaos and the power, further dissolving the movement in a new local brew.

At the same time, these developments further disassembled Guangxi's already very weak interpretive communities. Uncontrolled spirit possession, more easily than other forms of religious communication, undercuts authority of all kinds. No mere mortal can impose an authoritative interpretation when the gods themselves speak directly and through many mouths. The situation in Guangxi at the time, with its weak lines of authority and relatively uncontrolled and open-ended religious interpretation, encouraged the kind of Carnivalesque overflow of meaning I have been discussing.

By 1849, the God Worshipers had pushed local saturation to its limits. They had moved far away from any kind of Weberian rationalization, undercutting both the authority of the new movement leaders and the power of earlier structures of control. Especially with the long absences of their original leaders, and with the immediate power vested in any possessed medium, neither the God Worshipers nor the communities they sank their roots in could maintain established mechanisms of authority. Two very closely interrelated processes thus occurred during these years: the further complication and thickening of religious meaning and the further breakdown of interpretive communities.

Truly powerful symbols, from the cross to the flag, tend to be rich with meaningful possibilities. The evidence from Guangxi may never be conclusive, but it certainly suggests that the dissolution and enrichment of Hong's ideas had given the God Worshipers enormous power and appeal in Xunzhou. Much of their recruiting success stemmed from the dismemberment of Hong's ideas into the local mix, and then the potent addition of charismatic possession. Possession provided a maximum of saturation. Just as the Tristan chord constantly hinted at a resolution into a key but instead slipped into something different, so the God Worshipers also constantly suggested new interpretations but settled on none as a new medium would be possessed. Even as the movement gained in popularity, however, its very organization threatened to collapse. The process of multiplying interpretation that lent it strength also sapped the leaders' ability to control interpretation. The excitement and free reign of all those divine voices plausibly helped rouse the masses, but also threatened cacophonous chaos. The next chapter examines how the God Worshipers orchestrated those voices by establishing powerful interpretive communities as they built the institutions of their new state, and again concentrated and enforced a thinner ideology under their control.

# 6

# Precipitation and Institution: The Taiping Rises Up

The late 1840s utterly transformed the God Worshipers' movement, from the arrival of its two founders with their odd religious ideas in 1844, to the proofs of God's power in temple destruction and curing a few years later, and finally to the charismatic chaos at the end of the decade. In 1850 the movement suddenly crystallized into a rebellion waiting to rebel, with both new social patterns and a new self-identification as rebels settling out from the multiple possibilities that had flooded them the year before. Calling their scattered following together in the town of Jintian, the group encamped in the gender-segregated units that would characterize them for the next several years; they realized their communal economy through the creation of a Celestial Treasury; they created a full range of military and political titles; they developed official dress and ceremonies, including a yellow imperial robe for Hong Xiuquan; and by no means least important, they put a forceful end to uncontrolled possessions and recaptured control over interpretation. Only at this point did they dub themselves the Taiping Heavenly Kingdom (Taiping Tianguo), a political entity for the first time. Within a year they were occupying their first city, publishing texts and perfecting their new state apparatus.

The transition from uncontrolled spirit possession, with all its creativity and all its fragmentation, required constructing new interpretive communities – an enterprise that is just as much institutional as ideological. Pulling a single dominant interpretation from such a powerfully complex and mixed set of possibilities challenged the movement leaders with the extraordinary task of quickly building the social means to control meaning. They succeeded by drastically limiting spirit possession, creating clearer institutions of political and military authority, and by agreeing on a single master interpretation of the movement as a rebellion. They forged their cannons and their canons at the same time. While Taiping records on the early competing voices I discussed in Chapter 5 are hazy, much clearer evidence shows how the eventual leaders took control of the movement. As usual for the victors, they documented their own accomplishments better than they remembered their rivals'. Before I turn to that evidence, however, I want to return again to a comparative analysis of similar movements elsewhere in the world. The God Worshipers resembled many other possession movements, both in the problems that too many divine voices created and in the possible solutions. A general understanding of the dynamics of such movements suggests useful ways of looking at the Taiping transformation. At the same time, the Taiping case adds an important instance to the general theory, as one of the few where the movement retained and controlled spirit possession over the long term. The complex and indeterminate nature of such movements everywhere typically spawns very similar crises, and allows for only a few potential resolutions.

## POTENTIAL PRECIPITATIONS

The qualities that give uncontrolled possession trance cults such a powerful potential to become social movements – the aesthetic appeal, the transcendence of conventional social boundaries, and the creation of new cultural and political ideas through direct divine inspiration – gravely endanger the consolidation and organization of the movements. In fact the great majority of possession cults never attempt any wide political organization.

A few manage to continue as apolitical, unofficial cults often centered around curing; they are what Lewis (1971) calls amoral marginal cults. Horton (1969) gives a clear example of such a group among the Kalabari of Nigeria, who had a female-centered curing cult based on worship of amoral water spirits. This sect existed alongside, and sometimes challenged, a generally male and politically central cult based on ancestral and community heroes. The early Greek Dionysian cult may have been a similar institution. It was a popular movement that even slaves could join, in contrast to the state-controlled Apollonian cult (including the Delphic oracle) (Dodds, 1951:76–77).

From the very beginning, however, the God Worshipers demanded a greater role than these cults played. Amoral marginal cults
cede the political and religious center to others. The God Worshipers
ceded nothing, but instead put their God directly up against the
most powerful popular gods, and thus up against the definition of
community itself. Their mediums spoke with the voices of the most
powerful beings, and their statements thus carried more serious
consequences.

## Collapse and Repression

Possession cults that do develop into social movements usually
collapse in fairly short order; long-lived movements like the Taiping
rebellion arise only rarely. The frequent collapses stem from the
impossibility of maintaining political discipline when anyone can
speak with the authority of the gods. Attempts to create central
political organization out of mass possession thus frequently shatter
into a number of small sects. Even when the natural divisiveness of
these movements does not cause their direct internal collapse, it
makes them easy prey to outside repression.

Just a small twitch of colonial military muscle, for example,
crushed the millenial Watchtower movement in Northern Rhodesia
(now Zambia) after World War I before it could develop any very
large political organization (Fields 1982). Based on the American
Watchtower movement (now Jehovah's Witnesses), the sect taught
that when the End came, only those baptized in the movement
would survive, and whites (including the deceitful, not-Watch-
tower missionaries) would be enslaved or driven away. Until the
great cataclysm, however, adherents were to offer only passive
resistance – they had no immediate political agenda.

The movement shared many of the features I have been discussing. Converts held nightly prayer meetings with a powerful
aesthetic appeal: preachers proselytized loud and long, while
drumming, hymn-singing and speaking in tongues lasted well into
the night. The real political threat, at least as the local chiefs and
colonial authorities saw it, lay partly in the movement's passive
resistance; they refused, for example, to take part in wage labor. Yet
the danger also lay equally in possession by the Holy Ghost;
possession had been a tool of traditional political authority (just as
it had been for the community hero cult among the Kalabari), and
the Watchtower followers had usurped this critical symbol of the

chiefs' authority. Their mediums thus resembled the God Worshipers in speaking directly in the voice of the highest authorities. The movement peaked in 1919 with the forcible suppression by fully armed police of a New Jerusalem built on a hill.

In suffering an early demise, the Zambian Watchtower movement typified many possession cults whose cultural innovation and crossing of conventional boundaries themselves created enough of a threat that the extant powers took steps to repress them. At the same time, the constant creation of new leaders through possession discouraged Watchtower organization on a scale large enough to stand up against any kind of organized repression. Marginal cults survive only because their political and social innovations are limited, and they stick to an established, marginal position in their societies. The Zambian Watchtower overstepped these lines in the turmoil after World War I, but could not overcome the weakness of its organizational base in mass possession.

Internal collapse is as common as successful repression among possession groups attempting their own new social organization. Another group of Christian millenialists, this time the Apostolics of the Yucatan, provide a clear example. The Apostolics had grown dramatically under the charismatic leadership of their village preacher in 1970 (Goodman, 1973). A wave of speaking in tongues overtook the group, and they saw clear signs of the Second Coming in the immediate future – the Devil had appeared to a local prisoner, the Holy Spirit had given a vision of dirty churches that had to be cleaned before Christ arrived, and so on. Many people fell into trances, often not recovering for several days.

The movement included the charismatic power and aesthetic appeal of mass possessions, cultural creativity as possessed followers prescribed new forms of dress and ritual, and social innovation as many followers moved into the church. Yet the Apostolics fell into a total shambles when different individuals began to give apparently equally holy, but contradictory ritual commands – exactly the pressure point that also threatened the God Worshipers with disintegration. Followers of the movement began to accuse each other's trances of being Satanic. They finally collapsed into chaos, claiming in retrospect that the entire event had been a test from Satan. Here, the inherently indeterminate and multivocalic nature of mass possession prevented the movement from developing very far, quickly undercut the leadership position of the preacher, and blocked the development of any effective organization. Like

most such movements, they never reached the necessary activation
energy to create new social institutions of interpretation that would
have allowed the movement to consolidate the gains from its period
of mass possession.[43]

The chaos that overtook the God Worshipers by 1849 thus closely
resembled similar movements. I will discuss later the numerous
attempts to silence competing voices within the movement. The
situation grew so bad that the followers asked Hong to differentiate
true and false possessions, and to judge "the spirits according to the
truth of the doctrine" (Hamberg, 1854:46). Only he could see
through the conflicting claims to divine truth. The really remarkable thing was their ability to overcome the dissension without
falling completely apart. Possession cults that attain any long-term
political organization must always eliminate the dangers of too
many voices. They desaturate mass possession by creating and
controlling new interpretive communities. Yet while overcoming
the disadvantages of free possession, they often also lose the
advantages.

### Gaining Control

One possibility is to ban possession entirely, controlling interpretation instead through a priesthood or other institution that can keep
religion under the control of the movement leadership. For example,
the Palau Modekngei leaders – a case I have already cited for the
success of their mass possession – stopped acting as spirit mediums
after the initial organizational period (Leonard, 1973). Instead they
interpreted whistling sounds made by their dead founder. With a
monopoly on access to the sounds, the leaders could freely interpret
these whistles however they preferred. The new form of communication with the founder immediately gave the leadership an
effective means to control interpretation, even if it lost the excitement of spirit possession.

The Catholic Church of the fifth century apparently went through
a similar process. By this time, the Church was the prosperous and
official religion of the Holy Roman Empire. Its theologians reinter-
preted their chiliastic texts as spiritual allegory, saw the Millennium
already realized in the Church itself, and discouraged any further
direct divine inspiration (Cohn, 1957:13–14).

The Taborite heresy experienced a comparable transformation in
the early fifteenth century. Inspired by possession, prophets

preached the imminence of the millennium, leading to the usual cultural innovations and transcended social boundaries. Their followers abandoned their home communities for a new life where traditional norms and laws would no longer govern their behavior, and all goods were held in common. Yet as soon as this new society began to take concrete form at Tabor, inspired prophecy began to give way to institutionalized control over religious interpretation:

> The ideology of the movement – chiliasm – could not become the ideology of a society, and when Tabor began to come to terms with the facts of ordinary life in the world, she began to move away from the chiliast inspiration. Thus, almost as soon as the Taborites returned to South Bohemia, after the defense of Prague in the summer of 1420, we find evidence of what may be called a party of order, which promoted ideas and institutions of stability against the chiliast insistence on tension, enthusiasm, and total dynamism (Kaminsky, 1962:171).

Like the Palauans, the Taborites settled the divisive problems of multiple voices by ending spirit possession. And like the Taiping, they accomplished it hand in hand with a radical transformation of their social organization.

Each of these movements gave up the powerful appeal of possession as a means to recruit and retain the enthusiasm of followers. They substituted conventional means of political control over a civil population for the inspired enthusiasm of a prophet-led following. Other movements have instead restrained and controlled possession rather than eliminating it entirely. They hoped to channel its powerful appeal, while not falling victim to its dangers of collapsing under the weight of too many alternate prophets.

Many African and Pacific societies have controlled possession cults with direct political influence, where the mediums' power ties directly to the chief's.[44] Some ancient states also helped maintain legitimacy with the help of possessed mediums. The best known case is the Delphic oracle. Here, the masters of the cult controlled interpretation by keeping people from direct access to the medium. People communicated with the oracle and received interpreted responses only through the intercession of the Prophetes and Hosioi (Dodds, 1951:72–73). Limited and controlled as it was, the Delphic oracle could not have held the broad appeal of cults featuring mass festivals of possession and prophecy, but it must have retained some of the charisma of possession for those privileged to address it.

The ancient Chinese state also relied on apparently possessed mediums. Direct access to heaven was an important proof of legitimacy, and the Shang Dynasty king was the chief medium (Chang, 1983:45). Shang oracles existed primarily at the court, and relied on the use of bronze ritual objects. Bronze was a crucial form of wealth monopolized by the court, and the king thus held tight control over mediumistic contact with spirits (Chang, 1983:97). The Guoyu, a fourth-century BC text, has a possible reference to the concentration of the right to communicate with the spirits in the hands of the kings, at a time (supposedly the twenty-sixth century BC) when "virtue was in disorder":

> Men and spirits became intermingled, with each household indiscriminately performing for itself the religious observances which had hitherto been conducted by the shamans. As a consequence, men lost their reverence for the spirits, the spirits violated the rules of men, and natural calamities arose. Hence the successor of [the current emperor] charged Ch'ung, Governor of the South, to handle the affairs of heaven in order to determine the proper place of the spirits, and Li, Governor of Fire, to handle the affairs of Earth in order to determine the proper places of men. And such is what is meant by cutting the communication between heaven and earth (Bodde, 1961, quoted in Chang, 1983:44–45).

From this point on, only the imperial court controlled access to heaven. Here again, central political control required limiting the independent power of mediums, sacrificing the enthusiastic support that possession cults can create for the stability that state control required. Much like the Taiping several millennia later, the social transformations of state formation accompanied a new kind of control over possession – thinning and defanging the dangers of too many possessed voices.

The American Shakers offer one of the few cases where we can see in action the political consolidation of the right to interpret by blunting the dangers of spirit possession. While still in England, Ann Lee rose to the leadership of a small millenial sect called Shakers because of their frequent trances. Her claim to authority rested on powerful visions she had received while in prison for "profaning the Sabbath;" she had realized that only souls who had freed themselves from "the works of natural generation" and the "gratifications of lust" could follow Christ in the world to come (Desroche, 1971:29). Another vision in 1774 (and probably conflicts within the movement over her new direction) led to Mother Ann's emigration to the colonies with eight followers, where they created a radically new social life.

The trances of Mother Ann and her followers helped form the distinctive social and cultural patterns of this celibate and communal sect. Not surprisingly, each period of Shaker revival saw an increase in possession trance alongside an increase in followers. Yet the Shaker leadership already frowned on trance by the end of the eighteenth century. They replaced their thickly saturated and charismatic trance dancing with far thinner dancing in formal patterns. This occurred just over a decade after the sect had gathered into its communal form, again showing the close ties between interpretive control and social transformation (Desroche, 1971:117). By 1794, the Shakers felt that the period of inspiration had ended, and that they had entered a new phase (Desroche, 1971:115).

One reason for the reaction against possession trance must have been the competing divinely sanctioned claims to inherit Shaker leadership (Desroche, 1971:218); the new leadership moved to prevent this problem of too many authoritative voices from recurring. Some possession did continue through this time, however, and threatened the central leadership again in the Great Revival of 1837–1847. Revelations supported various sides in internal disputes, including an especially bitter one over vegetarianism. Yet the central leadership already had enough control that they held the potential threat within bounds. Conveniently enough, the leaders took control by validating "a revelation from Mother Ann in which the founder declared that she would have no 'gift' for any of her children except those who lived in perfect union with the ministry and the elders. The clever trick was, of course, to draw out of prophecy itself a means of neutralizing its own effect on the believers" (Desroche, 1971:106). Finally, "gifts" of revelations ceased entirely in the group.

Possession cults thus have an internal dynamic that leads them into new forms, which in turn have new dynamics. The very qualities that give them a powerful potential to become social movements make the consolidation and organization of these movements truly precarious. As they move to resolve their problems by institutionalizing or prohibiting possession, they create new kinds of limits on their organizational prospects and political structures. In every case, social transformation, political consolidation and religious interpretation are inseparable. Each case also makes clear just how difficult the transition to new interpretive communities always is. The few movements that did not simply collapse underwent drastic changes in organization as they sacrificed the excitement of mass possession. Hammering a dominant interpretation out of multivocalic enthusiasm poses a major political, social, and cultural challenge. Let me return now to the God Worshipers, who had to face these problems squarely by the end of 1849. The God Worshipers were unusual both because they succeeded in building a strong political movement out of such a shifting base, and because they continued to use spirit possession, but in an entirely new way.

## BUILDING A STATE AND PRECIPITATING AN INTERPRETATION

The God Worshipers' spirit possessions, for all their thick appeal, threatened to tear the movement apart in 1849 through the "disorder and dissension" that Hamberg described (1854:45). Hong's return to the area in 1849 and the local request to cull the true from the false gods, at last began to resolve the internal dissension. At this point Hong made one of the most crucial steps in the movement's development – he limited all future possessions only to Yang Xiuqing as God and Xiao Chaogui as Jesus. Only their possessions had been genuinely divine; all the others were false or inspired by imps and devils. From this time on, the leadership assumed increasing political control over possession, continuing to affirm Yang as the only true vehicle for possessions from God, and Xiao as the only one for Jesus.

In some ways, Hong Xiuquan's (and presumably Feng Yunshan's) affirmation of possession seems surprising. Spirit possession, after all, had no part in Hong's initial ideology. When he returned in 1849, he had recently spent several months with Issachar Roberts in Canton. While Roberts himself, with his revivalist background, surely accepted possession by the Holy Ghost, such performances apparently had no part in his Canton mission (Wagner, 1982:11–17). Furthermore, Hong was embracing a very local form of possession that must have been rather foreign to someone with his background, and embracing as well two local leaders with little education from poor families – men very different from hopeful scholars like Hong, Feng and the other original converts. Most important of all, he was acceding to the particular reading of the God Worshipers that Yang and Xiao had promoted, a reading that explicitly pushed the movement toward rebellion. Out of the saturated mess that the local people had made of his original Christianity, Hong now accepted a new line of precipitation that redirected the movement from his initial concern with religion alone to political change and the overthrow of the dynasty. Why did Hong choose this course that cast the die of revolt?

For several years the concrete events involving the God Worshipers had made their self-interpretation as rebellion increasingly reasonable, even though rebellion had not yet become the dominant interpretation. In part, the early successes of nearby rebels must have emphasized the weakness of the state and made revolt look plausible to the followers. Beginning in 1847, just after Feng's arrest and the first mass possessions, major uprisings shook several parts of east–central Guangxi. Chen Agui took control over the area between the Xun and Qian rivers, and Zhang Jiaxiang had united numerous Triad groups in a major uprising in Hengzhou (Li, 1981:139).

At the same time, the God Worshipers increasingly discovered that purely religious acts nevertheless brought political consequences. Their destruction of popular temples in 1846–1847 had angered a number of people, including some members of the local elite, particularly a local degree-holder named Wang Zuoxin. After the God Worshipers foiled his attempt to arrest Feng with the local militia in 1847, Wang petitioned the district officials early the next year, asking them to charge Feng with planning a rebellion. There is no evidence for actual plans to rebel at this stage; instead Wang used a standard technique for bringing the state in on his side – he accused his enemies of political heterodoxy. The magistrate refused to act at the time, but Feng was finally imprisoned for a while later that year with the help of Wang's militia. Wang Zuoxin continued to harass the God Worshipers from that point on. Thus even from 1847, outside forces had begun to define the God Worshipers as a political movement. This external definition of the group as an opposition helped shape them into one, especially as they found one of their top leaders in jail. In spite of themselves, they had little option but to respond politically by opposing the local militia and its elite leadership.

At some point in 1848, the idea of Hong assuming the imperial throne began to float in the movement, receiving a kind of support from the possessions of Yang and Xiao. Late in 1848 three followers petitioned Jesus (possessing Xiao) for permission for Hong to assume the Golden Dragon Throne. The idea apparently took Jesus by surprise, because he stalled and told the three to return later and ask God (Yang). Unfortunately, we have no record of God's response, but in numerous possessions afterwards, Jesus clearly said that Hong could not yet assume imperial trappings (Wang, 1985:202–203). Jesus certainly promoted the idea that Hong would be an emperor; the timing of the claim was the only question. At roughly the same time, Jesus began to talk about who the generals would be when the Taiping era began (Wang, 1985:193). These were among Xiao's earliest possessions, and Jesus thus interpreted the movement as a nascent rebellion right from the beginning. At the time, however, his voice remained only one among many in the jumble of possessed interpretations.

This particular line of interpretation must have appealed to Hong in several ways, in spite of the departures from his original expectations for the movement. First, the move to politics could still be consistent with Hong's original Christianity. Both the millenial streak in Christianity and Hong's vision could support the idea that a new Kingdom of God on earth would have to accompany the religious transformation of China. The re-reading of imps and devils from false icons and false gods to the Manchu government required only a small step. Imps and devils, whether human or supernatural, stood in the way of a Christian China. Second, Hong apparently enjoyed the idea of being a real king. In 1849 he often asked Jesus if the time had yet come when he could wear the dragon robe (Wang, 1985:203). Finally, both Yang and Xiao had created sizable personal followings within the movement by using their local ties and their charismatic possessions. As Hong moved to end the chaos threatening the movement by the end of 1849, he could not afford to alienate such large factions.

The most important key to Hong's settling on a single interpretation was the dissension and chaos that threaten all such possession movements. By the end of 1849, Hong either had to force a precipitation or accept the collapse of the movement. Faced with such a decision, Hong bowed to the many influences that combined to make rebellion the most plausible potential line of interpretation, and asserted a radically new kind of control over meaning. As uncontrolled possession lost its mandate, and as Yang and Xiao gained their monopoly on divine interpretation, the entire movement underwent a complete metamorphosis as it created a new interpretive community.

### Consolidating Interpretive Control

Merely announcing new lines of interpretation did not automatically create control: that would also require a new social organization. The reorganization of the God Worshipers into the Taiping Heavenly Kingdom required working through a newly forged ideology, creating new social structures, and silencing alternative interpretations by force. Spirit possession records from late 1849 and 1850 show a sudden surge in attacks on alternative mediums. The leaders forced the first alternate medium out of the congregation shortly after Hong granted interpretive control to Yang and Xiao (Hamberg, 1854:46).[45] They could act on such a condemnation only after Hong had sorted the divine possessions from the impish ones.

Jesus, speaking through Xiao, exposed many cases of evil possessions. Late in 1849, Jesus descended to earth because "the following did not share a single heart." Hong said to him, "Various celestial spirits are descending, and always aid the imps with their false hearts. Those who aid imps are themselves imps. Heavenly Elder Brother, the Heavenly Father sent you as the Savior Lord of all nations, and you are also my own blood brother. Please forward this petition to my Heavenly Father: do not let the celestial spirits speak." The same day, Wei Changhui (another top leader) again asked Jesus to intercede to stop celestial imps in one of the local villages. Jesus agreed to both requests (Wang, 1985:201). A similar case from the same period involved a woman named Huang Ermei, who came into Xiao's presence followed by a demon whom Xiao vanquished in a fight (Wang, 1985:200–201).

In 1850, Jesus also acted several times to control "lies" (*luanyen*) spread by some of the followers. The "lies" could well have been alternative possessed voices like the celestial spirits, but were in any case competing interpretations of the movement. In some cases the perpetrators suffered beatings of a thousand strokes and other fatal punishments (Wang, 1985:218). In other cases a threat sufficed, as when Jesus promised the death sentence to a medium if the "demon" who possessed him ever returned (Wang, 1985:201). Interpretive control meant silencing other voices by any means necessary.

Yang and Xiao consolidated their personal positions at the same time as they solidified control over interpretation. A number of their early possessions seemed quite transparently self-serving. For example, when Xiao demanded that Hong Xiuquan recognize him as Jesus during one of his earliest possessions, he was already creating the grounds for Hong's final valorization of Xiao and Yang a year later (Wang, 1985:192). In addition, when Xiao/Jesus first spoke of rebellion in late 1848, he named only himself, Yang, and Feng Yunshan as top generals, clearly serving his own possession faction at the expense of other leaders like Wei Changhui or Shi Dakai (Wang, 1985:193).[46]

God acted much like Jesus in this, although we have many fewer records of Yang's earliest possessions. In early 1851, for example, God again demanded recognition of his genuine presence through Yang's body, and reaffirmed the new Taiping authority structure:

> The Heavenly Father instructed the multitude, saying, "Do you all truly recognize your Heavenly Father and your Heavenly Elder Brother?" The multitude replied, "We truly recognize the Heavenly Father and the Heavenly Elder Brother." The Heavenly Father again said, "Do you all truly recognize your Sovereign [Hong Xiuquan]?" The multitude replied, "We truly recognize our Sovereign." The Heavenly Father said, "I have sent your Sovereign down into the world to become the T'ien Wang [Heavenly King], and every word he utters is a heavenly command. You must be obedient" (*Tianming Zhaozhishu*, in Michael, 1966–1971:99).

Yang and Xiao did not hesitate to consolidate their own positions, and simultaneously the new institutions of interpretation, by criticizing even other recognized leaders. In 1850, Jesus had prevented Feng Yunshan and Wei Changhui from carrying out one of their plans, scolding them for making Him bother with things no more important than fingernails (Wang 1985:195).

The ability to expose criminals and traitors further reinforced the divine authority of the two mediums and strengthened the new interpretive institutions. These miraculous exposures also began around 1850, just as the movement transformed itself. I have already mentioned God's exposure of the Triad bandit and faithless ally Big-head Goat (*Tianqing Daoli Shu*, in Michael, 1966–1971:375). The best documented case occurred in late 1851, when God suddenly exposed a follower named Zhou Xineng as a traitorous demon (*Tianfu Xiafan Zhaoshu*, in Michael, 1966–1971:87–97). The Taiping leaders were on the verge of promoting Zhou to office when God dramatically appeared to order his arrest. Zhou had brought a group of 190 followers to join the main Taiping camp, but had to enroll all but three in the enemy camp as a subterfuge. God exposed him instead as a turncoat and spy, first suggesting that the loss of the followers to the enemy was surrender not subterfuge, and then revealing details of spying that only an omniscient being could know. God knew all, from secret meetings to reconnaissance of Taiping defenses and assassination plans. The Taiping executed Zhou, his wife and son, and his demon accomplices.

Jesus had performed a similar coup a few months earlier, exposing a friend of Luo Dagang who had stolen some jewelry from Luo's wife after she died. He also received a death sentence, although Jesus allowed him to appeal the sentence to God (Wang, 1985:218–219). The dynastic camp reported another case from late in 1851, when the Taiping occupied its first city, Yongan, and was besieged by the Qing armies. Yao Ying, who was Judicial Commissioner of Guangxi (but would be demoted to hardship duty in Taiwan for failing to stop the Taiping), wrote in a letter that

Commander Wu sent the bandit leaders a letter that concealed an explosive charge. The bandits realized that the letter was rather heavy, saw through the plot, and threw the letter far off, where it exploded. The bandits cunningly claimed that the Heavenly Father had descended, warning of the explosive. Otherwise how could they have known? The followers believe this deeply, taking it as truth (Yao, 1867, juan 1:23–24).

These powerful reaffirmations of God's and Jesus's power continued on occasion as long as the two mediums lived (e.g., *Tianqing Daoli Shu*, in Michael, 1966–1971:385).

In concert with the new Taiping transformation of the social world after 1849, God and Jesus also interceded directly in family life. In late 1849, Jesus had sentenced an adulterous couple to 140 strokes for the man and 100 strokes for the "lascivious wife" (Wang, 1985:219). Jesus also gave frequent lectures to various people on proper family behavior. In 1850 He grilled someone named Li Dali about why he did not look after his wife better. When Hong's family arrived from Guangdong later that year, Jesus individually instructed all the women on proper and obedient behavior (Wang, 1985:220–221).

Within a very short period of time the Taiping had consolidated powerful control over religious interpretation, precipitating new social relations of interpretation along with new dogma. The transformation had created order from chaos. Yet the change also went far beyond the personal positions of Yang and Xiao. While the dangers of uncontrolled possession provided a key catalyst, once the new interpretive control began it cascaded into all aspects of the movement, creating a newly detailed ideology and drawing clear lines of social power that would strive to keep the new ideas in control while it pursued a rebellion.

### State-Building and Institutional Control

Once the Taiping created itself as a rebellion, some earlier acts lost their complex ambiguity, just as spirit possession had lost its multiple possibilities. For example, the Taiping resumed destroying temples in 1850, after a hiatus of over two years. The earlier attacks had concentrated on morally questionable temples, at least from Hong's point of view, and had been satisfied when the defeated god recognized God's greater power. Now, however, the group attacked the core community temples – the Three Generations temples – that they had carefully avoided in the past, and then began utterly destroying every temple they found (Guangxi Shifan Xueyuan . . ., 1981:273). The destruction of major Three Generations temples in Xinxu and Caicun in 1850 made unambiguously political claims. The earlier attacks had allowed multiple interpretations: Christian iconoclasm for some, a test of God's might for others, an attack on immorality for still others, and a political act for only a few. Yet now they attacked a clearly moral god in the most important community temple, which housed the local militia; this was a religious rebellion. From then on, local witnesses would lament the Taiping's apparently blind destruction of all temples they encountered.

At the same time, the Taiping solidified its newly unified interpretations with a massive publishing program. They controlled the dissemination of knowledge by publishing only carefully selected and edited texts, just as they controlled divine inspiration by commandeering possession for the top leaders. Although handwritten copies of Hong's writings apparently circulated in Xunzhou (Jian, 1958:1744), the first printing of Taiping texts occurred only with the capture of Yongan in 1851 and the official organization of a Taiping state. Yang and Xiao, often speaking with their divine voices, played a crucial role in editing even the most key texts, including Hong's own description and interpretation of his original dream vision. Indeed, Taiping descriptions of this seminal event seem to have changed several times. Wang Qingcheng (1985:213–214) describes several sessions in 1848 where the possessed Xiao supplied details of the dream that Hong had supposedly forgotten.

The new publishing program began to chisel Taiping religious ideas in stone (or at least to carve them in woodblocks). In 1852, for example, they published a set of fill-in-the-blank official prayer forms. Communication with Heaven had thus thinned by this time from the uncontrolled enthusiasms of mass possession to formalized repetition of standardized prayer. By publishing everything from educational texts to travel passes to the Bible (complete with Hong's annotations) in the next few years, the Taiping attempted to exercise full control over information and interpretation, ending the interpretive free-for-all of the late 1840s.

This rationalizing ordering of the movement covered all areas. In 1850, as part of the ongoing transformation, the leaders announced and began to use an elaborate structure of official titles, flags, robes and offices (Jian, 1973:45; Mao et al., 1980:43–44). Hong Xiuquan already had a yellow imperial robe in 1850, although Jesus would still not let him wear it in public (Mao, 1989:33–34). His robe was just the tip of a vast bureaucratic iceberg, however. The elaborate military system that suddenly crystallized in 1850 spelled out every detail. For example: "A corps general commands five colonels; altogether he commands 13,125 men. His flag is four and one-half feet in length and width" (*Taiping Junmu*, in Michael, 1966–1971:133). The system got its final polish during the long occupation of Yongan in 1851–1852, when the major leaders (including Yang and Xiao) received their official ranks as kings. The elaborate system of titles published in 1852 included details like:

From colonel to sergeant, all are commanders of troops; therefore their sons shall be addressed as Sons of the Commanders; they are also clean and undefiled; therefore their daughters shall be addressed as Snow, for snow is clean, white in color, and lovely to look upon.

Chancelloresses, women senior secretaries, women commanders, and women generals shall be addressed as Chaste Person, because chastity in a woman is most honorable . . .

When one royal father-in-law addresses another royal father-in-law, they shall address each other according to their precedence of birth, and call each other Royally Related Elder Brother, or Royally Related Younger Brother (*Taiping Lizhi*, slightly revised from Michael, 1966–1971:126–127).

The detail goes on and on, as pompous bureaucracy replaced uncontrolled possession. All of this systematizing formed part of a total social reorganization in 1850. The Taiping actually began to use these ranks and titles at the same time as they resettled their followers in sex-segregated camps in the town of Jintian.

This chapter began with the God Worshipers facing an interpretive problem – the great multiplicity of competing voices formed an irresolvable mass of indeterminate meanings, and threatened to tear the movement apart. The answer could not lie simply in coming up with the right interpretation, or in convincing through the power of logical reasoning. The very nature of such overloaded situations undercuts such answers. Instead, the Taiping had to erect an entirely new social system, creating institutions of interpretation, from controlled spirit possession to military hierarchy, that could allow them to impose a single dominant interpretation. Unlike many comparable movements, the Taiping actually succeeded. The result was a transformation in 1850 every bit as radical as the real chemical change from saturation to precipitation. Spirit possession had made the new social organization possible, and the new social organization in turn utterly transformed spirit possession.

The change happened quickly, but not easily. It required an enormous range of action, from creating a monopoly over critical knowledge (by publishing texts and controlling communication with Heaven), to a complete social redefinition (in the creation of new ranks and titles, and in physical resettlement on the ground), to a full range of punishment of dissenting voices (where God and Jesus met alternative interpretations with humiliation, beatings, or executions). In the middle of 1849, the Taiping had been a wild hodge-podge of possessed voices. Just over a year later, they were a powerful rebellion with clear leaders, a new religious orthodoxy, and a sharply defined social and military organization. This new unification could only occur with the social transformations that created new interpretive communities and institutions.

## NEW POWERS AND NEW PROBLEMS

Part of the power of the new system lay in its local roots. In contrast to the ideas Hong had brought to Guangxi in 1844, the new Taiping of 1850 had become sensible in local terms. God now spoke to local issues of power, ethnicity, curing and spirit possession. Even more importantly, the new control over interpretation itself brought major benefits to the Taiping movement. Above all, the change removed the immediate danger of internal collapse, even as it added the eventual dangers of rebellion. In doing so, the movement developed a structure of authority that would allow it to make decisions and undertake actions effectively.

Yang's ability to speak for God, and to determine correct interpretations of those speeches, helped the Taiping to make strategic decisions quickly and confidently. The possessed Yang, for example, exhorted the troops to break out of the siege of Yongan, and led to the stunningly successful drive through central China to Nanjing (*Tianming Zhaozhi Shu*, in Michael, 1966–1971:109). God, speaking through Yang, often issued direct military orders, providing an unquestionable line of authority that did not exist before Yang and Xiao monopolized possession. Just as the early mass possession episodes had helped build a popular following for the God Worshipers in Guangxi, centralized control over possession gave the Taiping stronger possibilities for coordinated action and ended the dissension that typifies movements based on broader opportunities for possession.

Yet even though they had created the essential prerequisites for political action, the transformed movement also experienced a new dynamic, whose problems would prove just as serious as the earlier chaos. The continued use of spirit possession itself posed one of the greatest difficulties, even though the early possessions had given the God Worshipers enormous advantages in recruiting, and the new monopoly on possession had created a strong structure of authority. As the movement expanded out of its backwater base in Guangxi, its heavy reliance on very local possession traditions became a fetter.

Spirit possession itself probably found a more skeptical audience in the sophisticated population of the lower Yangzi valley core around Nanjing. Strongly local traditions like leading other souls up to Heaven would have had even less appeal. In so far as people outside the leadership had contact with Taiping possession in the later years (and they did not have much), the practice could have provided very little legitimacy for the movement. The loss of possession as a popular organizing tool, and the inability of the movement to adopt and adapt local traditions the way it had in Guangxi, help explain the general lack of a true mass base after the Taiping left Guangxi. The Taiping borrowing of aboriginal techniques of possession, and its plausibility in an area used to very odd deities, doomed its potential religious appeal outside Guangxi.

As the movement developed over the next decade, dominating central areas of China under Yang's de facto leadership, the nature of possession continued to change. Xiao had died in battle in 1852, silencing Jesus's voice forever. Yang, however, continued to speak for God up until his murder by other Taiping leaders in 1856. With his monopoly on the voice of God, Yang's possessions gradually lost many of the radical ideals of the early God Worshipers while their Confucian content increased. Even though the earlier Taiping had banned Confucian texts, God in 1854 affirmed that the classics had many positive points, expounding on "the True Way of filial piety toward relatives and loyalty toward rulers" (Wang, 1985:215–216). The more Yang institutionalized his power, the more the Taiping began to resemble just another dynasty.

Yang also began to communicate with God in ways that totally sacrificed the charisma of possession, but that left interpretation even more firmly in his own hands. In particular, he began to have dream visions in Nanjing, which he could interpret at his leisure and according to his own whims. Yang thus came to dominate communication with Heaven through techniques that no longer involved large numbers of followers or any of the enthusiasm of possession, but that allowed him to claim final authority on any issue (Xing, 1981; Wang, 1985:222–223).

At the same time, Yang's possessed pronouncements grew more and more obviously self-serving. In an infamous case in 1853, after the Taiping capital had already been established at Nanjing, God publicly berated Hong for mistreating women officials and being too lenient with his son. He sentenced Hong to forty blows, although Hong was so contrite that God agreed not to carry out the punishment (*Tianfu Xiafan Zhaoshu*, in Michael, 1966–1971:198–220).

Yang's final act of possessed hubris came in 1856, when God announced that Yang should be addressed as *wansui* (Ten Thousand Years), a term that had been reserved for Hong and that traditionally had honored the Emperor alone. When asked how Hong should now be addressed, God lightly suggested a ludicrous neologism, One Hundred Million Years (Jian, 1973:290). The subordinate Taiping kings, quite possibly in consultation with Hong, saw this as the beginning of a coup. They killed Yang, his household and his bodyguard, leaving thousands of corpses and a badly torn movement. Although the Taiping hung on in Nanjing for eight more years after this slaughter, it never really recovered from the internal decimation. Just as the early movement could not tolerate too many voices of God, the later movement found that it could not tolerate the structural split in its leadership – between Hong, who was himself God's son, and Yang, who spoke with God's voice and authority. While Yang as man remained subordinate to Hong, Yang as God stood supreme.

By centralizing and controlling communication with Heaven, the Taiping sacrificed popular participation in the ecstatic charisma of the large trance episodes that had characterized the early years of the movement. The immediate reality of the spirits for followers, and the convincing legitimacy offered by actually witnessing such ceremonies, had been lost to the movement, even as possession became a powerful (and eventually self-destructive) political tool for Yang Xiuqing. By the time the Taiping settled in Nanjing, spirit possession had become Yang's personal tool for consolidating power among the leadership. His increasing reliance on dreams and his monopoly on possession opened him to the accusation that tends to accompany professional mediums anywhere – faking. His murder resulted in part from the loss of legitimacy of his spirit possessions, which had become a problem from the moment the Taiping centralized control over possession. The very act of institutionalizing control over possessed interpretation created the possibility that the possessions were mere artifice. While even believers agree that some possessions can be faked, the public possession of many people carries a kind of convincing charisma that Yang Xiuqing's monopoly sacrificed. Accusing Yang of faking undermined the entire movement, while accusing a single medium among many makes little difference.

The routinization of other aspects of the early movement similarly diluted their power. The concentration of all the early miraculous cures onto Yang as the Redeemer of Sickness, for instance, simply removed such cures from the daily repertoire of the movement. While the title appeared over and over again after the movement left Guangxi, no evidence points to any actual curing. A direct proof of God's power had devolved into a mere formalism.

The other major early proof of God's power – temple destruction – continued unabated throughout the movement, but it also lost its original potency. What once appeared as God's challenge to the local gods simply became an act of military destruction. Attacks on temples no longer formed part of an effort to make a positive claim for Christianity; they were just attacks on temples. The new religion itself saw very little propagation on the ground after the Guangxi period (Li and Liu, 1989:1–36). The failure of the Taiping as a religious movement outside of Guangxi also helps to explain why no trace of the religion remained after the military destruction of the rebellion, in great contrast to the White Lotus ideology that no military victory ever managed to stamp out.


CONCLUSION

In some ways, the Taiping pursued a Weberian path of rationalizing authority, at least from a situation with very little established authority to a clear case of charismatic authority. Any form of authority had largely broken down during the period of the uncontrolled spirit possessions. By the 1850s, however, they had imposed a new order. Like Weber's ideal type, the Taiping had charismatic leadership with supernatural properties, followers who lived in a communal order under the leader, and an economy based on gifts and booty more than pursuit of a regular income (Weber, 1978:242–245). They had the succession problems that Weber would have expected in the struggle with Yang Xiuqing. While a few areas grew more routinized, especially military and official ranks, the system remained primarily charismatic. Weber did not directly discuss this kind of transformation from no authority to charismatic authority, but it seems broadly consistent with his general push from less to more "rational" authority.

Yet for all Weber's insights, a focus only on an evolution toward more rational authority bypasses some of the most critical dynamics of the early God Worshipers. In fact, one of the movement's most crucial prerequisites was the initial move away from rational authority as the people of Xunzhou made Hong's ideas their own, changing them fundamentally in the process. Running Weber in reverse, they took over Hong's original religion, overwhelming it with new interpretive directions based on their own lives. By its nature, such overloading also undercut existing authority by leaving meaning up for grabs. The possessions of 1849 reached the zenith of anti-rationalization, where each new voice suggested a new ultimate meaning, but the multitude of competing voices thwarted any single unification by undercutting all authoritative institutions of interpretation.

While reading Weber quite properly suggests the organizational disadvantages of such a situation, it also leads us to underplay the advantages of saturation, which had been at the core of the God Worshipers' success. That initial hijacking of Hong's Christianity built the movement through legitimizing and emotionally powerful trance performances, by transcending conventional social and cultural boundaries in direct speech from the gods, and in the ability to make God sensible locally through curing and competition with other gods. The surfeit of meaning and inevitable breakdown of authority that accompanied it made the Taiping rebellion possible; the effervescent energy of overflowing meanings pulled followers to the movement. At the same time, of course, the situation planted the seeds of its own destruction in divisiveness and resistance to any new structures of authority.

More than just a push toward greater rationalization, a constant tension between overloading meaning and rationalizing simplification drove the system. As meaning became more heavily loaded and social relations of interpretation weakened throughout the 1840s, the threat to the survival of the movement created a powerful incentive for imposing a single dominant view, even as new followers flocked in. The Taiping surmounted this first level of difficulty by channeling interpretation through the mouths of two top leaders. Yet this thinned-out resolution soon showed its own new limitations, shackling the movement to a religious ideology with little appeal outside of its base area, and finally contributing to insoluble dissension among the Taiping leaders.

Perhaps most important of all, the Taiping experience suggests that the very process of centralizing interpretive authority creates new free space for alternative interpretations.[47] As interpretation united around a single voice, systematically impoverishing the rich and noisy mixture of possible interpretations in order to establish control, it also threw away the power and conviction of the earlier situation. Personal experience made the possessions and cures of the early God Worshipers convincingly legitimate. As soon as those wild early scenes paled into Yang's distant interpretations of his own dreams and formal enfeoffment as Redeemer of Sickness, official Taiping interpretation became open to doubt.

Centralization of meaning inevitably accompanied centralization of authority as it created new social relations of interpretation. Yet that process itself created twin problems: thin and formalized interpretations lost their inherent power to convince, and the clear ties between political institution and official interpretation opened the possibility that leaders simply acted for their own benefit. These two problems killed Yang Xiuqing, as his speaking for God no longer convinced anyone, even among the original leaders, and his motives thus appeared cavalierly self-serving. New followers continued to join in great numbers after the movement was formalized, but we no longer see any evidence of religious enthusiasm, or even much basic understanding of Taiping religious principle among these newcomers. The complete disappearance of Taiping beliefs after their military defeat confirmed their inability to make imposed interpretations into the powerful recruiting tool that saturation had been.

The Taiping movement thus suggests that the chaotic meaning and the move away from rational authority in the 1840s had important benefits as well as causing organizational problems, and that the later unification caused new problems even as it rationalized authority. The Taiping did not progress simply to better forms of organization. Instead it pushed and pulled against competing pressures to complicate and simplify interpretation. Each new phase created the conditions for the next transformation, and each transformation brought its own history that differentiated it from any earlier phase. Hong's original ideology of 1844 differed dramatically from the new one in 1850, in ways that tied in detail to the very local experience of the movement. Yet each saturation contained the seeds of a new precipitation and each precipitation opened new free spaces for saturation.

The Taiping also suggests that overloading and simplifying meaning may occur through different processes. The multiplication of meanings can occur through a slow dissolution, much as Hong's original Christianity gradually merged with local ideas in several steps over a number of years. The inevitable free space, where interpretive communities are weak, allows the continuous addition of new lines of interpretation and the possibility of leaving things uninterpreted. Unification around a single dominant interpretation, however, requires a massive investment of energy and may take place as a sudden transformation. Taiping metamorphosis into an elaborate ideology clearly articulated as rebellion was no simple cultural reinterpretation. Reinterpretation by enforcing a single reading required thorough social transformation as the new leadership forcefully silenced opposition and forged new social relations of interpretive (and social) control.

The Taiping rebellion fits anyone's definition of resistance. Yet this conclusion, which is so obvious in the clear vision of hindsight, should not mislead us into reading resistance into its earliest roots. The early God Worshipers in fact bring us directly back to the arguments about accommodation and resistance, to the complex realities of interpretation and institution, with which I began. From Hong's original vision through most of the 1840s, the God Worshipers may have exemplified cultural difference, but resistance was only one of many potential readings. The Xunzhou region of Guangxi offered an extraordinarily free space for alternative interpretations in the 1840s, with a weak state, plentiful bandits, ethnic strife, a strong tradition of spirit possession, and generally weak religious interpretive communities. Such massively free space created interpretive opportunities of all kinds, deluging the local world with a flood of possibilities by no means limited to active resistance. Even though Taiping claims about God and the brotherhood of all questioned social boundaries, and therefore made a political interpretation plausible, it still remained only one possibility.

That single reading as resistance became louder as Yang and Xiao expanded their influence in the late 1840s, but it could not dominate the movement until the multiple voices of spirit possession were silenced. The key transformations occurred very quickly in late 1849 and 1850 with a massive mobilization of interpretive authority and social reorganization under the influence of looming internal chaos and external pressure. With the new interpretive authority, real resistance could begin.

The early God Worshiper movement did not simply presage massive rural unrest. Its beginnings quite fundamentally resembled other centers of complexly indeterminate meaning around the world, whose so-called cultural resistance never erupted into a movement of any kind. The Taiping movement's differences from other such cases lay less in the content of that early mixture than in its ability to resolve the competing voices into a single chorus by forging new social relations of interpretation.

As I now turn from the Taiping to a contemporary Taiwanese ghost temple, I will again begin with free space, multiple meanings, and centers of possible alternative interpretations. The apparently enormous differences between the two cases – one a shattering rebellion and the other a politically quiescent religious oddity – should not disguise the fundamental similarity of the processes in both cases. For Taiwan, however, hindsight provides no benefits. In spite of many attempts to force a unified interpretation there, the solution still remains saturated, and any potential political resistance remains unrealized. If the similarities help to reveal the nature of indeterminate meanings, the contrasts clarify the great difficulties of achieving interpretive control.

# Part III

## TAIWANESE GHOSTS

# 7

# Hot and Noisy Religion

Overloaded cultural space that weathers any push toward total control inevitably seems less important than a conflagration like the Taiping rebellion. Yet the lack of official decrees and bloodied spears should not disguise the importance of mundane life. The religious developments I will be discussing from Taiwan have issued no grand pronouncements, raised no political hopes, and forged no cannons. Resisting nothing, however, need not imply accepting everything. The early Taiping, after all, also resisted nothing. These chapters will concentrate on some apparently minor corners of Taiwanese culture, which nevertheless have much broader implications for resistance, acquiescence, and the nature of indeterminate meaning.

I leave aside the many daily acts of petty opposition that are not overloaded with meaning yet clearly resist. Feigned incompetence or stupidity is open to multiple interpretations if well performed, but stealing toilet paper or driving through a red light is not. Such mischief is important, but tends to be either idiosyncratic or routinized into minor acts over tangential issues, avoiding real confrontation. I concentrate instead on situations where interpretation and lines of opposition are far less clear, but the potential for large-scale organization may be much greater, as the Taiping rebellion showed.

The origins of the Taiping movement showed the great importance of free religious and social space in Guangxi in the 1840s, along with the inherent weakness of attempts at cultural domination under such circumstances. Taiwan's early history in some ways strongly resembles east–central Guangxi on the eve of the Taiping. Both were wild frontiers of China, with large aboriginal populations, endemic feuding among various Chinese ethnic groups and between Chinese and aborigines, local strongmen, and only a tenuous political hold by the central authorities. They even shared some economic features, like the production of charcoal, indigo and other mountain forest products.

113

Like peripheral Guangxi, Taiwan also fostered more than its share of revolt, and much of the violence was organized through religious channels. Taiwan averaged one rebellion every other year in the first half of the nineteenth century, nearly always organized through religious sworn brotherhoods (Hsu, 1980:84). In 1786–1788, Lin Shuangwen led thousands of rebels in the first known revolt led by the Triad Society (Tiandi Hui). They gained control over most of the settled part of the island within a few months, and the Qing had to send more than 100,000 troops to quell the rebellion (Cai, 1987:66–122). Dai Wansheng led another rebellion, almost as large, in 1862–1863, just as the Taiping rebellion was in its final throes. This one also had secret society and Triad leadership.

As the nineteenth century wore on, however, Taiwan began to lose a little of its frontier turbulence. The island finally achieved provincial status in 1885, and the new governor attempted a host of modernizing reforms in administration, finance, transport and the military (Speidel, 1976). The really overpowering change, however, happened in 1895 when Japan forced China to cede the island. Local Taiwanese fought the Japanese up and down the island, often organizing through major community temples. Yet the resistance was patchy and disorganized. The Japanese crushed it, and often took retribution by burning temples. The occupying troops left no doubt that the era of rebellion and communal feuding, of organized violence in any hands but the government's, had now ended forever. Open resistance under the fifty years of Japanese occupation nearly always remained spontaneous, unorganized and small-scale (Wang, 1980:60–138).

China's Guomindang (Nationalist Party) government reclaimed Taiwan after World War II. In 1947 they powerfully reiterated the old Japanese message from 1895 – the government would leave no room for local political ambition, and would tolerate no resistance. Popular unrest in 1947, which had its strongest origins in the domineering but incompetent new state, claimed perhaps 10,000–20,000 Taiwanese lives. As in 1895, the government showed its intention to muzzle dissent with much authority and little mercy.

The Communist military victories in 1949 caused the flight of the top state officials, the best of the Nationalist armed forces, and a good portion of the mainland economic elite to Taiwan. This marked the beginning of Taiwan's new economic path, but brought no change at all to the political straitjacket. Explicit resistance, as under the Japanese, remained a piecemeal and very dangerous affair for decades. Only in the last few years has Taiwan again allowed space for significant political action from below, as President Jiang Jingguo [Chiang Ching-kuo] initiated a remarkable period of democratic reform shortly before his death.

Under such circumstances, the relative political quiescence in Taiwan (until recently) need not necessarily imply happy acceptance of shared hegemonic politics and culture. The literature on cultural resistance implies that apparent cultural hegemonies are challenged everywhere, and the lack of open political space in twentieth-century Taiwan further suggests that such passive cultural resistance may be especially vivid and resourceful. The more powerful the pressure, such views suggest, the more creative the response.

Just as much of Taiwan's unrest took religious forms in the eighteenth and nineteenth centuries, religion in the twentieth century offers one of the most promising areas to look for such expressions of cultural difference. The remarkable resurgence of Taiwanese popular religion in the last few decades has many explanations, including especially the nature of recent economic changes. Yet cultural resistance theorists might also easily take it as evidence for their views. The inherently decentralized structure of Chinese religion, combined with its complex multivocality, created a resilient free space. Political control over religion grew even more difficult with the secular states and constitutional guarantees of religious freedom in modern times. As the explicitly political arena closed down in Taiwan, religion potentially offered a space for cultural alternatives and safe expressions of resistance.

Taiwan, like much of the world now, challenges the early modernization theorists' expectation that economic development would necessarily walk hand in hand with the replacement of traditional customs by new civil ideologies. Statistically the watershed for Taiwanese popular religion occurred in the early 1970s, after which the steady increase is unmistakable. This time also marked the beginning of Taiwan's stunning period of independent economic development, when the base developed over the past two decades began to support rapid increases in standard of living.

Government figures on numbers of popular temples are very unreliable – many temples do not register legally, and many others, especially small shrines to neighborhood Earth Gods or unworshiped ghosts, are too small to be picked up consistently by even a more determined census. Nevertheless, the statistical bias should be roughly consistent from one year to the next, and government figures show trends over time that should be reliable. After having decreased slowly over the years since the end of the Japanese occupation in 1945, both the absolute number of temples and the number of temples per capita increased significantly after about 1970. The numbers of registered temples went from 2,930 in 1956 to 6,251 by 1980, an increase of 113 percent. Temples per capita increased 18 percent over the same period, with a steep rise beginning around 1972 (Qu and Yao, 1986:657).[48] The growth in popular temples easily outpaced even Taiwan's high population growth rate.

A walk down the street (nearly any street) quickly confirms the statistical impression. Major temples are booming, and old Earth God shrines have been rebuilt in high style everywhere. In the large cities, every few blocks seem to offer a sign advertising a new shrine, usually in someone's apartment. The owners often do not register legally, and the government has found these shrines very difficult to control, in spite of increasingly loud complaints from neighbors kept awake by the divine racket. In the countryside, empty hilltops also often sport new temple construction. Consumer demand drives much of this temple boom, as worshipers contribute enough in return for spiritual favors to turn a profit for the owners.

Hill Gates [Rohsenow] was one of the first Western scholars to note the increase in religious activity in Taiwan, and to see it as a kind of resistance (Rohsenow, 1973:84-87). She argued that participation in popular rituals "serves to mark off the majority of traditionally-minded Taiwanese from Mainlanders," and that government attempts to control worship further strengthened religion's role as an ethnic and social marker (Rohsenow, 1973:18). Emily Martin [Ahern] developed similar ideas in her much more detailed symbolic analysis of the large pig offerings that I discussed briefly at the beginning of this book (Ahern, 1981b). Comparable arguments have also been made for gender, for instance in the religious societies in parts of Guangdong, which provided havens for marriage resistance (Topley, 1975). Similarly, Emily Martin wrote about Taiwanese funeral ritual that "women as a subordinated gender frequently use contradictions in the total ideological field against the system and for themselves" (Martin, 1988:176).[49]

Yet as with all cases of routinized cultural "resistance," no clear line separates resistance from accommodation. This creates the possibility of drawing quite different kinds of conclusions from similar data. Steven Sangren, for example, argues that broader structures of meaning transcend the apparent resistance of heterodoxies, just as *yang* (the principle of light, male gender, etc.) opposes but also encompasses *yin* (the principle of darkness, female gender, etc.).

> Heterodoxy and orthodoxy are not sociologically polarized. Depending on context, nearly all Chinese have access to both. It is always useful to have an idiom capable of questioning particular hierarchical orderings, but few can convert this idiom into a sustainable and encompassing worldview. Thus the "minor" heterodoxies . . . are best viewed as being encompassed within the orthodox orderings that define them as heterodox (Sangren, 1987:185–186).

The power and efficacy of gods (*ling*) for Sangren lies in their ability to incorporate chaos, heterodoxy and *yin* into order, orthodoxy and *yang*. Such an analysis sees far less scope for real cultural opposition in religion than cultural resistance theories.

Any argument between these views disappears, however, if we see political interpretations as potentials rather than givens in ritual scripts. As I have already discussed, many Chinese simply leave religion relatively uninterpreted, and rituals themselves are structurally open to multiple interpretations. Analysis as resistance or accommodation often offers insightful and accurate readings of potentials, but also tends to lose sight of the surface play of kaleidoscopic possibilities that characterizes Chinese religion just as much as any simple underlying order. That messy exuberance itself, which separates successful rituals from mere bores, guarantees a diversity of possible interpretations. In this chapter I will thus focus more on the luxuriant overgrowth of much Taiwanese ritual, in order to reveal the various potentials for interpretation as they are grounded in concrete social contexts. After all, people do not simply choose their favorite interpretation as if they were blank slates; they interpret (or not) only within sets of social relations.

Such social relations of interpretation are changing rapidly with Taiwan's recent economic and political transformation. Chapters 8–10 will concern innovations in ghost worship, a relatively minor area of Chinese religion that has suddenly boomed in Taiwan. The ghost cults remain very thick with possible meanings, and no one has been able to impose a single dominant interpretation, although many have tried. Yet in spite of the lack of explicit interpretation, the cults clearly provide a lively and robust arena for people. They included some of the most popular temples in Taiwan in the 1980s, and launched successful movies and television soap operas.

Chapters 8–10 explore this new fad in Taiwanese worship in some detail, again looking for the interplay of saturation, precipitation and resistance. I will begin with a look at indeterminate interpretation in Taiwanese religion in general, and at one of these ghost temples in particular. Chapter 8 takes up the potential interpretations of the ghosts as they relate to social and cultural change in Taiwan, and concentrates especially on the plausibility of seeing the cults as resistance. Finally, in Chapters 9–10, I will look at the many efforts to precipitate an agreed-upon interpretation out of these cults. The greatest difference from the Taiping movement lies in the failure of all these attempted precipitations of ghosts, in great contrast to the successful transformation of the God Worshipers into the Taiping Heavenly Kingdom.

## SATURATED RITUAL IN TAIWAN

Beginning with several seminal essays on Chinese religion in Taiwan (Jordan, 1972; Wolf, 1974), anthropologists have been unraveling the broad structures of Chinese religious practice, where gods form a rough parallel for secular hierarchy, ancestors define the family, and ghosts fill in the marginal space. While this line of analysis has been very revealing, and indeed forms the base for any study of Chinese religion, it also tends to abstract away from the irresolvable complexity of actual ritual experience. In this section I will instead concentrate on the ambiguous and multiple interpretations inherent in all major Taiwanese rituals.

This analysis builds on my earlier discussion of how free religious space encourages variable interpretations of gods (Chapter 4). Bearing in mind how a single deity like Tian Hou/Mazu can receive markedly varied interpretations (Watson, 1985), I turn here more directly to temples and their rituals. In a broad sense, this is an analysis of the aesthetics of "heat and noise" (*lauziat*, Mandarin: *renau*). Any successful large event in Taiwan, from a market to a ritual, provides plenty of heat and noise – it should be packed with people, chaotically boisterous, loud with different voices, and clashingly colorful. The word for "heat" also occurs in the medical hot/cold distinction that most people use to think about food. Hot foods are more *yang*, the active, moving principle. Chocolate, coffee, and meat are hot. Hot foods give you diarrhea, while cold foods constipate. The word for "noise" can also mean to make mischief, and the combination strongly recalls Bakhtin's description of ludic medieval marketplaces. Temples, both as social spaces and architectural creations, provide a good example of the dynamics of *lauziat* and its various interpretive possibilities.

## Architecture

Temple plazas, even when no ritual animates them, are among the hotter and noisier parts of a town. They are usually crowded with conversing people, and with hawkers selling souvenirs, incense and snacks. In Sanxia, the town I know best, the shops surrounding the plaza also include several tea houses, known as haunts for the less respectable side of town life, where young ladies will join you for a price. On weekends, when religious tourism surges, the plaza brims over with cars, people, and buses bearing tourist-pilgrims. The heat and noise peak during major rituals, when the plaza simply over-flows until traffic throughout the town reaches gridlock. Major temples everywhere attract a kind of hustle and bustle that enhances their aesthetic appeal, even if it has little to do with more apparently "religious" feelings. Temples with no heat and noise are on their way to disappearing.

Temple architecture gradually controls the mild chaos on its outskirts through its broad structure. Yet at the same time, temple decoration reproduces the heat and noise. Taiwanese temple construction directly recalls the yamens of imperial times – the combined offices and residences of magistrates. Both consist of concentric courtyards, leading by stages to the magistrate or god himself. The ultimate in such architecture was the Forbidden City in Beijing, where visitors gradually approached the Emperor through a series of small buildings leading further in toward the center. No visitor ever reached the center, however, which the Emperor ruled alone. The architecture, like the ideology, made the Emperor the moral exemplar for a world that extended down in concentric circles from his palace, even as it pulled people centripetally toward a center they could never reach.

Major temples in Taiwan make the same statement, though on a far more modest scale. Visitors enter past the doors and their door gods, into a front hall where most of the worship takes place. After an open courtyard just ahead lies the central hall, which houses the primary god. Side and rear halls may also house images of various secondary deities. Temples may sport more or fewer concentric rings of courtyards and halls, but the main deity always holds the center. The broad strokes of temple architecture thus reinforce Sangren's (1987) image of ever more inclusive hierarchy.

Yet many of the details of worship and of construction blur the hierarchy and confuse the center. Except on rare occasions, for example, people worship as individual representatives of their families, and never as congregations. Most worship thus occurs with no explicit social organization, as a constant and uncoordinated flow of people suit their own needs. The resulting clamor is one of the important ingredients that make a hot and noisy temple.

Even space does not divide into as neat a hierarchy as the architecture suggests. While most people do not approach the central hall very closely, there is no reason not to. In fact, the inner courtyard is often full of running children, and anyone can walk up to the central altar.[50] Similarly, temporary altars set up for ritual purposes tend not to be treated as sacred spaces. People can and do walk all around such altars, carrying on their own conversations quite freely. I have even seen unruly crowds reach directly onto altar tables in front of priests.

Multiple temples to the same deity, which occur in the case of every major god, further blur the center. Such temples usually have a historical hierarchy, based on when they branched from the original temple on the mainland or from another branch temple in Taiwan. In practice, though, many temples will claim to be the top of the hierarchy in Taiwan. At least four Taiwanese Co Su Kong temples make that claim, and all of Taiwan knows the hot and noisy rivalry among Ma Co (Mazu) temples jostling for recognition as the true center of their cult. Central altars often also recall this confusion in hierarchy by seating multiple images of their primary god. Temples keep multiple images so that villages or families can borrow them, but each image also forms the seed that could plant a new and competing temple. The idea of an ultimate and overarching hierarchy remains strong – after all, everyone agrees that some temple must be the ultimate one. Yet the potential challenge is always there.

Temple decoration fosters still more disordered heat and noise. All major temples swarm with decoration – every spot has dragons writhing, phoenixes flying, lions sitting, or people fighting. Sanxia's temple to Co Su Kong epitomizes rather than typifies this style. It has been undergoing a total reconstruction for over forty years, and the end is still not in sight. Li Meishu, a well known artist in Taiwan who was also politically active in Sanxia, designed and supervised the new construction. He hoped to create a masterwork of Taiwanese temple architecture, faithful to both traditional style and technique.

Huge, hand-carved stone pillars support the central hall, some entwined with dragons and others with dozens of birds fluttering among plum branches, and all carved in such high relief that the animals seem almost separate from the stone itself. Near the ceilings, even more detailed gilt wood carving covers every surface. Each piece is small, with individual characters only a few inches high. Each shows a separate scene, usually from a famous popular novel like the *Romance of the Three Kingdoms*.

As I have watched the reconstruction at intervals over the last fifteen years, the carving grows both more extensive and more intensive. There is a kind of centripetal involution of detail, as the eye moves from the facade of the temple as a whole, with its complex pattern of multiple roofs and doors, to the intertwined carvings of the pillars, and finally to the detailed intricacies of the wood. The wood carving has even deeper involutions, with moving chains cut from single pieces of wood and balls that rattle inside lions' mouths, all high up under the eaves.

Just as the halls and courtyards pull toward a center they never reach, the decoration draws viewers into ever greater detail, beyond their capacity to see. Most of the wood carving, in fact, is too high to identify clearly, and details like a ball carved free inside a lion's mouth are simply invisible from the ground. In addition, the decoration does not particularly draw the eye toward the central altar. Any spot in the temple offers the same possibilities for involution, as any fragment of a hologram retains the entire image. At the same time, every spot also offers new stories with no particular relation to each other or to the temple as a whole. The heat and noise are everywhere.

Temples thus have two faces. One offers a sort of official orthodoxy – an image of successively encompassing hierarchy. The other complicates that hierarchy at each level, from the surfeit of teeming decoration to the multiple claims over hierarchical ranking. Everyone believes that a center exists, but no one can quite find it for sure. Unlike the Forbidden City, where a sufficiently august visitor would finally meet the Emperor at some point on his journey to the center, in temples the center recedes forever. An old adage in Chinese holds that behind every heaven lies another (*tianwai you tian*), and the same is true for temples and their gods: it is heavens all the way down, leaving people without an ultimately authoritative interpretation, but with an involuted surface of saturated possibilities.

### Ritual and Impenetrable Experts

Temples hire priests to perform their major rituals, and the rituals again provide laymen with a multitude of rich images, most of which people find quite impossible to interpret. While they are confident that all the detail means something to some expert, they happily accept the confusing complexity, the heat and noise, without much concern for proper interpretation. Daoist ritual dress, for example, sparkles with arcane signs like trigrams and star patterns, embroidered in gold thread. Priests may also move in mysterious ways, from Daoist ritual dance patterns to esoteric Buddhist hand mudras. Even their speech usually evades interpretation, as it involves peculiar pronunciations of difficult texts. Ritual music furthers the effect by drowning out most speech and song, and through the polyrhythmic complexities of the drums.

Major rituals also offer music in the form of outdoor opera in the temple plaza. An especially large and successful ritual might have three operas taking place at once, all amplified and all in the same temple plaza. Typically, the extra heat and noise more than compensate for the loss of comprehension. On such an occasion, hundreds or even thousands of people may be milling about, watching one opera or another, offering incense, watching the priests, checking out the offerings, or just talking to their friends. The general chaos of the scene marks its success, with the cacophonous surplus of sound, movement, color and symbol themselves creating one of the main goals of the ritual.

Even minor rituals and priestly services offer a profusion uninterpreted symbols. Daoists performing simple curing rituals in their homes may use forms of paper spirit money not known to most people, and often speak quite mysterious spells. The minimum ritual service usually consists of writing a small paper charm (*hu-a*) whose checks, curlicues, zig-zags and totally illegible characters render them completely enigmatic to the people who will use them. In fact, much of the message may be very simple, something like "let the evil spirits depart," but the priest will carefully write one character on top of the other to guarantee the proper mystery.[51] When I once asked a Daoist why he did that, he gave the same answer I heard when I had asked about that other uninterpretable, the cleaver in the pig's head: it just looks better that way. The opacity of such ritual to interpretation provides a major part of its appeal, with the proviso that some expert somewhere can really explain it. There is a final truth, but no one ever gets to it: the center recedes forever.

The priests themselves have a far greater fund of interpretation. Unlike their clients, the ability to interpret is important to priests professionally, and often personally as well. Yet even for them, a fuller interpretation always seems one step away. Daoist priests in Taiwan, especially if they are serious, search out various masters in an attempt to increase their knowledge. Daoist gossip often turns to who stole what secret knowledge and how they did it, as people strive to come closer to full knowledge. This idea that truer and better knowledge always lies just out of reach recurs in many areas in China, especially where master/disciple ties form the primary means of organization. From martial arts to religion, folklore has it that masters always withhold some vital piece of knowledge, dying before they can pass it along to their favorite child or student. The classic example in martial arts is the ability to destroy the balance of a victim's vital forces with a mere touch, or even with just a point of the finger, causing inevitable death (*dian xue*). I have often heard that this most powerful of techniques was lost, only to have someone else suggest that his friend had a friend who knew a mountain recluse who could do it. Even for experts, the true center is always just out of reach.

## Interpretation

The general lack of popular interest in interpretation ties closely to the existence of experts. It is enough to feel confident that an explanation exists somewhere, even if expert knowledge follows the same kind of infinite recession into unresolved detail as temple decoration. Such confidence allows people to revel in the relative chaos of hot and noisy religion, without having to worry much about orthodox interpretation. The social organization of religion

furthers the effect, with experts who make a living off their knowledge and thus prefer to keep it secret. The result is very different
from Christian churches, which strain toward explicit interpretation
through Sunday schools and sermons, catechisms and confessions.
With no formal congregations and no ministers, Taiwanese popular
temples could not pursue such a path even if they wanted to.

For most people, interpretation is far secondary to ritual practice,
which should ideally be complex, busy and entertaining.[52] By
turning the infinitely receding center over to the experts, people
are free to celebrate the aesthetics of heat and noise as they pursue
the more mundane goals of worship – peace, profit and happiness.
Temples and their rituals provide an extraordinary wealth of
saturated material. In spite of people's belief that a correct interpretation of everything exists in principle, in practice the possibilities leave them with enormous (but usually unrealized) interpretive
potential.

One of the most crucial questions about resistance centers on how
a movement can make the transformation from so many indeterminate possibilities to an explicit interpretation as resistance. When, in
other words, do people begin to realize interpretive potentials and
to rationalize religion or other forms of "cultural resistance"? Spirit
possession catalyzed this transformation in Guangxi. No such
transformation has occurred in Taiwan, and that difference offers
a telling point of comparison.

This emphasis on the saturation of hot and noisy religion does not
make all worship an unrestrained celebration of chaos, a cultural
challenge to authority and hierarchy. Such an analysis would
overinterpret much of what really goes on, while also ignoring the
reiteration of hierarchy and confidence in expertise that parallels the
heat and noise. Yet the pleasure of saturated ritual in China
nevertheless creates a plethora of interpretive potentials, which
cannot be drained into a simple reproduction of structural hierarchy. Overinterpretation as either resistance or accommodation saps
the life from vivid and vivacious ritual.

## THE EIGHTEEN LORDS

Let me turn now to the temple that will form the core for most of the
material that follows. The Eighteen Lords temple at the northern tip
of Taiwan often astonishes people familiar with Chinese popular

religion, as it amazes and sometimes scandalizes Taiwanese themselves. Two decades ago the temple was a simple roadside shrine for unidentified bones – the sort that sits unattended and almost unnoticed all over the countryside, quite appropriate to marginal beings like the dog and seventeen anonymous corpses buried there. Ghosts like these deserve no better and should not be treated like gods, who are known spirits of generosity and morality. People build shrines to ghosts more out of pity for their unworshiped spirits than out of devotion. Yet Taiwan in the 1980s experienced a sudden burst of ghost worship, and the Eighteen Lords became one of the hottest and noisiest temples anywhere, along with a few similar shrines.

The Eighteen Lords temple backed up traffic on the northern coastal highway for several kilometers at its peak in the late 1980s, and still attracts thousands of worshipers each week. While clearly within the traditions of popular worship, the temple turns much standard ritual procedure on its head. Worshipers normally do not touch images of deities, but here they caress two large bronze dogs. Most typical worship takes place during the day, but here peaks in the small hours of the morning. Nearly all deities are honored with sticks of incense, but the Eighteen Lords prefer burning cigarettes instead. Other temples stand above the ground, but the heart of this one is in a basement. The scale of its popularity alone is odd; such temples to unworshiped ghosts never grow to a large size.

I first heard about the temple in 1986, when a Taiwanese friend who knew I was interested in religion told me I had to visit this bizarre new twist in Chinese ghosts. In fact, many people shared his opinion that the temple offered something both new and weird, and I frequently heard it mentioned along with current fads in social deviance like gambling or "motorcycle gales" (*biao che*), the occasionally suicidal races down Taiwan's expressway that erupted into a brief craze in the mid-1980s. In spite of its unconventional features, though, this is clearly not a new religion. It is instead a new proportioning of everyday religion, a kind of spirited play that has magnified previously lowly and unworshiped ghosts to rival the gods themselves.

The shrine's origins will always be murky, but everyone agrees on certain basic features of its story. The temple sits at the northernmost tip of Taiwan, a coastal fishing area. At some point, probably about a century ago (but in the seventeenth century according to one version), a fishing boat washed ashore. The boat itself was badly

battered, suggesting storm and disaster in the Taiwan Strait. It held
the dead bodies of seventeen men, along with a dog who had
somehow remained alive. The local fishermen who found the boat
had no way of identifying the bodies; the wreck may have blown
over from the mainland. The fishermen proceeded as one normally
proceeds in such cases in Taiwan – they buried the bodies in a
common grave on a cliff overlooking the shore, thus creating a new
and quite typical ghost temple. Only the dog makes this story a little
different from most others. This was a dog of outstanding steadfast-
ness and loyalty to its masters. According to some versions, it
insisted on jumping into the grave with the bodies, until the people
finally buried it alive. According to others, it starved itself to death
in front of the new grave, and was finally buried along with the
men. The dog is thus the eighteenth of the Eighteen Lords.

Informants in the area remember the shrine from the 1950s and
1960s as a simple gravestone and incense pot; the grave itself was so
old and unkempt that it had lost its characteristic rounded form and
was just a bit of flattened earth. Soldiers on coast guard duty
occasionally worshipped there, and an old woman (now rumored
to have made a fortune off the temple) swept up once in a while.
Even by the low standards of a ghost shrine, the Eighteen Lords
temple was not very important or active.

The transformation of the temple began in the early 1970s, when
Taiwan broke ground for the construction of a nuclear power plant
just a stone's throw away from the grave. Construction of the plant
required shoring up the cliff overlooking the sea, and in the process
the Eighteen Lords shrine was to be buried. Construction sites in
Taiwan are known to suffer from problems caused by ghosts – they
frequently turn up old bones – and construction workers regularly
make offerings to appease them. This construction site was no
exception. According to informants now, there were an unusually
high number of "accidental" injuries and even a few deaths. The
most alarming event in current versions of the story happened when
the crane suddenly stopped dead as it was poised just over the
shrine, on the verge of destroying it. No one could explain this crane
suddenly frozen, looming over the shrine. The large number of
accidents and the crane problem finally brought construction to a
halt.[53] Both workers and local inhabitants wanted the temple saved;
the government wanted its power plant finished quickly.

In the end the government and project managers decided to
"respect local customs" by rebuilding the temple. They fixed up

and preserved the original grave in a small underground chamber, and built a large temple overhead, on the new higher ground level. The rebuilt temple contains an exact replica of the underground grave, directly above it, plus a further wing with wooden images of the Eighteen Lords. Rebuilding the temple marked the transformation of the Eighteen Lords – both a physical transformation into an inordinately large ghost temple, and a spiritual transformation into a group of beings with unusual efficacy. They had, after all, brought the government itself to do their bidding. Just as important, they accomplished this in front of thousands of workers who came from all over the island, and thus set the stage for an unprecedented expansion in popularity for such a temple.

The result is an extraordinary lode of saturated ritual in a temple that carries heat and noise to a Carnivalesque extreme. A night-time trip to the temple, after a long fight with the traffic jam that the temple itself creates, begins in the parking lot that stretches along the side of the cliff, just below the level of the road and the temple. The boldest hawkers swoop down immediately, usually old ladies trying to sell packets of incense, paper spirit money, and amulets with dogs on them. The long approach to the temple forces visitors through a shanty town of rickety shacks that house completely secular Carnival attractions – rings to toss over posts, balls to throw at bottles, and appropriately seedy hawkers to take the money. This is also the point where visitors start nervously checking their wallets and purses: the temple is famous for its pickpockets.

After running the Carnival gauntlet, visitors go up a few steps to the road and the chaos of the temple itself. The crowds can be huge and intimidating, especially late at night when most people come. Distinctly earthly elbows help worshipers get their burning sticks of incense to the crowded incense pots, and the sheer quantity of burning incense often causes the pots to burst into roaring flames. The largest mass squeezes toward the right side of the temple, where the artificial grave stands flanked by two life-size dogs.[54] Here people offer incense and burning cigarettes at the grave and then fervently rub their hands (or one of the amulets the hawkers sell) over one of the dogs, reciting a bit of doggerel about the good luck that will flow from different parts of the dog's body.

People come because the Eighteen Lords really grant wishes. Even better, these spirits will grant any wishes at all, as long as they are properly repaid. As ghosts, they have none of the moral prudishness of proper gods. Their laissez-faire attitude gives the temple a reputation as a haunt for gamblers, prostitutes, and gangsters. For the hundreds or thousands of relatively honest citizens who also came every night during the temple's peak of popularity, that reputation added a sense of titillating danger to the real efficacy of the spirits and to the consummate pleasure of all the heat and noise. Like the nuclear power plant that sparked its fame and now glows quietly in the dark behind the temple, the Eighteen Lords combine power and danger. Vaguely immoral without being illegal, frequented by dangerous people but not really dangerous, and powerful in areas that respectable gods spurned, Taiwan found the Eighteen Lords temple irresistible.

The temple grew out of popular religious practice, and resonates with much traditional religion. Yet the new magnification of ghosts in Taiwan, and the consequent reproportioning of religion, also speaks to much that has changed in the last two decades. Typically for Chinese religion, there is no worked out interpretation of the phenomenon; people go for the heat and noise and to get favors granted, not for the quality of the theology. In Chinese popular religion, with its already weak social relations of interpretation and resulting surplus in possible interpretations, this temple offers the very acme of overloaded religious indeterminacy. In Chapter 8, I will explore worship at this temple in more detail, spelling out some of the rich detail and its potential lines of interpretation, and finally offering an interpretation of my own.

# 8

# Saturated Ghosts and Social Change in Taiwan

The Eighteen Lords (Shiba Wanggong) temple innovates, but only as bricolage – a creative recombination of elements already at hand. A trip to the temple offers a disorienting reformulation of old ideas, but no new worlds. Even though every ritual offering and every architectural detail can conjure up a wealth of old associations for people, the combination is fresh and complexly evocative, a view of the world through a kaleidoscope. I begin by tracing out some of the lines of evocation to suggest plausible potentials for explicit interpretation, while illustrating the rich surplus of meaning at the temple. The chapter concludes with an examination of the intimate ties between these cultural changes and Taiwan's economic growth. The Eighteen Lords delineate a world of individualistic, utilitarian and amoral competition, easily adapting to changing social relations of interpretation. The rich evocations of the temple stir up a host of possible interpretations, but as we shall see, none has come to dominate thinking about the temple. Certainly the implied critique of Taiwen's economy and polity, comparable to what other authors have seen in some ritual elsewhere in the world, has never been brought to the surface.

## INTERPRETIVE POTENTIALS

While Taiwanese recognize that the Eighteen Lords resemble gods in some ways (the eighteen wooden images and the sheer scale of the temple imply gods), and are just strange in others (the cigarette offerings, the underground chamber), everyone also knows that above all, they are just a gang of ghosts. Ghosts are marginal beings, the unincorporated dead who have no proper place as either gods or ancestors. As we have seen, gods protect community interests, from neighborhood Earth Gods to the patron gods of whole districts, and the community takes responsibility for their

129

temples and major rituals. Ancestors define the world of family and lineage. That leaves ghosts – the residual category, with no legitimate political, geographical or family position.

Ghosts most broadly are simply dead souls (as are gods and ancestors), but the term refers especially to the dead who are left lonely and starving because no one worships them. This happens particularly to people who die before marriage, by suicide or other violence, or unknown to their relatives. Ghosts can sometimes become gods (through promotion) or ancestors (through spirit marriage with the living), but generally remain a good Mary Douglas (1978) sort of liminal category – ill-defined and dangerous (see Weller, 1987c:65-66; Yu, 1990). In the Durkheimian terms that characterize most of the anthropological literature, gods are bureaucrats, ancestors are kinsmen, and ghosts are beggars, bandits and strangers, who fall into no proper social category: they are asocial and individual.

Ghosts receive offerings in several contexts. Unidentified, individual ghosts sometimes command worship because they make someone ill. Occasionally, people even see ghosts. More usually, though, people worship ghosts as a generic and anonymous group in rituals conducted by large temples during the seventh lunar month (see Weller, 1987c). In these rituals, the temple hires priests to provide spiritual alms on behalf of the community for these pitiful beings; it is a form of ghost welfare. Offerings on these occasions further individualize ghosts. People thrust individual sticks of incense into their food offerings; ghosts do not get the communal incense pots that honor gods and ancestors[55]. Finally, ghosts often have tiny temples of their own, at which they receive offerings during the annual ghost ritual or when supplicants have specific requests to make. Such temples typically begin when people build a small shrine to house unidentified bones or bodies, discovered during road construction or on a battlefield, for example. Except for the seventh-month festival, people worship ghosts as individuals, for their own personal benefit. Ghosts have none of the community ties of gods.

As a rule these shrines are comparatively tiny; the largest might hold half a dozen adults, and many more are too small to enter. In general, no committee or individual takes responsibility for them (unlike the elaborate arrangements that run god temples), although communities or individuals may repair a deteriorated ghost temple on an ad hoc basis. The temples contain no images of ghosts, but usually just a gravestone and an incense pot. Many often also invoke the Earth God (Tho Te Kong), whose responsibilities include protecting the living from the dead. They never have the decorated roofs and nested buildings of god temples, nor do they rate door gods, or even doors, or even front walls for that matter. People often call them "three-wall temples."

Ghosts are much weaker beings than gods, and most people thus prefer to make important requests at temples to gods. Yet gods generally behave as upright and moral beings, in spite of the spirit money offerings they require. They refuse to consider entire categories of requests. For example, most gods will not help gamblers or people with illegitimate business requests like prostitutes and gangsters. Ghosts, on the other hand, are desperate. They will grant any request at all, and their temples typically sport banners reading *"iu kiu pit ieng"* (all requests shall be answered). People usually call them Iu Ieng Kong temples, a shortened form of the slogan, meaning Lord Who Grants All Requests. While many people might in fact occasionally worship at these temples, they are considered the special arena of the lower strata of society, whom the ghosts are especially willing to help, and whose lives the ghosts also reflect most closely. Taiwan probably has thousands of such temples, although their small size and lack of organization makes a census impossible. They rarely develop beyond the level at which they begin – small roadside shrines that see only an occasional supplicant.

In spite of its incongruously large scale and huge popularity, the Eighteen Lords temple leaves no question about its origin as just such a minor shrine. All informants describe it before the nuclear power plant was built exactly as a Lord Who Grants All Requests temple, and a rather minor one even by those lowly standards. More importantly, the new temple makes no attempt at all to disguise its ghostly nature. Not only did they preserve the original grave underground, but they built a new one on top. The temple does not sport the curved eaves of a god temple, nor does it have a front wall. Even the number eighteen can spark images of ghosts. Dead souls pass through eighteen hells, and Taiwan has at least three other temples to eighteen unknown ghosts (Qiu, 1979:588–589).[56]

The alleged constituency of the temple again reflects its fundamentally ghostly nature. People describing the Eighteen Lords invariably point out how popular they are with gangsters, prostitutes, gamblers, and similar people – the standard patrons of lowly spirits who will do anything for a reward. These are the sorts of people whose requests proper gods would ignore. The pickpockets who frequent the temple are thus not just taking advantage of the big crowds; they are there to worship as well.

While this popular image fits the general atmosphere of the temple, it cannot be true in practice. Far too many people worship at the temple for the constituency to be limited to these underworld types. In addition, images and amulets from the temple adorn the altars and cars of a great many people in Taipei. Taxi drivers and other small businessmen with perfectly legal sources of income clearly frequent the temple. When I asked the temple management about this, they also insisted that people who come to ask questions of the gods are a fair cross-section of the entire population. The temple is thus less a haunt of gangsters and gamblers, than a lure for ordinary people who find some thrill in the sort of temple appropriate to the underworld. They like the idea of a temple not too punctilious about issues of morality, and clearly have needs that the Eighteen Lords can fill better than any proper god.

Yet for all its obvious roots in little ghost shrines, the temple also harbors a wealth of anomalous features and an unorganized bounty of evocative connotations, even more than most other temples. Many of these features stem from the peculiarities of the temple's reconstruction and the worshipers' creative promotion of the weird. Together, they make up the temple's richly indeterminate interpretive complex, and weave a tangled web of potential interpretations.

## Oppositions and Inversions

The architect who designed the rebuilt temple must have been a folk post-modernist: it contains bits and pieces from various different traditions, with nothing quite in its right place. The most discordant aspect is the awkward juxtaposition of a ghost temple and a god temple. The reconstructed temple has expropriated one of the most important elements of god worship – the use of wooden images of the spirits on a raised altar. The stage-left (and higher ranking) side of the temple strongly resembles a god temple. The god images sit against the far wall, fronted with an altar table and two incense pots. The only reminder of their ghostly nature in this section of the temple is an extra god. The sharp-eyed (but probably no one else) notice that one extra image accompanies the expected images of seventeen men and one dog. This is Tho Te Kong, the Earth God, who sits there to keep the ghosts in line. The broader temple architecture itself, with no front wall and no curved eaves, also clashes with the implication that these are gods.

The god imagery emphasizes that these are extraordinarily powerful spirits, but the temple stresses its ghostly origins just as much as its godly claims. In addition to the ghostly temple construction, the grave itself (actually the artificial grave built over the original site) dominates the stage-right side of the temple, which functions more like an overgrown Lord Who Grants All Requests temple. Everyone worships at both sides of the temple, but judging from their enthusiasm, this artificial grave is even more important a center of worship than the god altar. The incongruous architecture clashes most strongly in the direct center of the temple. The center should always house the main locus of power in a temple, usually a gravestone for ghosts and statues for gods. Here, however, the center offers only the amorphous no-man's-land between the ghost half and the god half, containing nothing but the crowded chaos of visitors trying to shove their way from one side to the other.

The oddly overlapping structure of the temple contains a further opposition on the ghost side, which inverts space itself. Real enthusiasts of the temple will explain that the most powerful bit is neither the god altar nor the reconstructed grave, but the original grave, now hidden in a basement room. The original grave lies directly below the fake grave, and looks just like its copy; both were rebuilt with the same mosaic-covered mound. Supplicants enter the room by a dark staircase at the back of the right side of the building. Although most people seem to know about it, there is a happy fiction that the underground chamber remains something of a secret, and that only the real insiders know this esoteric place of power. In the eyes of its patrons, the chamber is in fact a bizarre and unique feature of this temple – a case where the necessities of reconstruction have reinforced the liminal weirdness of ghosts. In other god or ghost temples, power concentrates in the center; here it lies underground and off to the right. This reverses all the usual hierarchy, where higher is superior to lower and left is superior to right.

What passes for an incense pot sits in what was once the normal position just in front of the gravestone. Yet because of the peculiar construction of this temple – the gravestone was originally at the edge of the cliff, and thus now closely abuts a wall – the incense pot is crammed between wall and grave. Worshipers can only approach it by squatting or crawling in the dirt and leaning over the grave. This is by no means a respectful posture, the way pilgrims may sometimes approach a god temple on their knees. The contrast with typical offerings – even to ghosts – is striking; ghosts normally receive offerings above ground from standing supplicants. The inversion of space, which moves power into the lowest possible position, thus extends to the reversed orientation of the grave, reducing the normally respectful approach with incense to a kind of awkward clowning.

Not content with space, the temple also inverts time. The Eighteen Lords are especially efficacious at night, and worship peaks in the small hours of the morning. Like worshiping on one's knees underground, this is also an inversion of normal practice that particularly emphasizes the contrast between the ghostly nature of the Eighteen Lords and the gods. Night is the period when ghosts are strongest, and their perceived amorality fits with the general image of night-time activities – sex, crime, gambling, and illicit endeavors of various sorts. Most ghost worship elsewhere, however, takes place during the day. This is partly for convenience and partly for safety; people usually prefer to avoid strong ghosts, who can be capriciously violent. Yet the danger is part of the appeal of this temple, as is the inversion where power peaks in the usually inferior period. The more mundane danger of pickpockets and purse snatchers also characterizes the place at night and reinforces the entire image of the temple. In classic Carnivalesque style, the Eighteen Lords reverse everything, emptying the usual seat of power in the temple's center, and moving it to the lowest possible position in space and time. The receding center of most temples has been overturned.

## Righteous Dogs and Sex

With its architectural oddities, its inversions of space and time, and its celebration of power at the bottom of the hierarchy, the Eighteen Lords temple both parodies and partakes of more standard religious traditions. This is the sort of "resistance" by inversion that analysts of Carnival favor. Yet even the clashing overlap of gods and ghosts and the removal of the center only begin to suggest the many thick possibilities available here. The suicidally faithful dog who became the eighteenth Lord offers one of the temple's most striking features, and opens up a new range of associations.

Although the dog is just one of many images on the altar, and the two life-sized bronze dogs that flank the fake grave do not have their own incense pots, dogs nevertheless command much of the ritual attention. The table in front of the altar brims over with images that people place there (as in other temples), but they are almost invariably little ceramic or metal dogs, not images of the human ghosts. The office at the side of the temple, which sells paraphernalia of all sorts – charms, banners, books, even an Eighteen Lords movie sound track tape – specializes in dogs, from little cast replicas of the dogs in the temple to fluffy poodles. Many of the banners for sale also feature dogs. Most conspicuous, even shocking by the standards of most Chinese worship, is the treatment of the two bronze dogs by the grave, where avid worshipers rub various parts of the dogs' bodies to bring good fortune. Late at night, during the temple's peak hours, the dogs seem covered in a swarm of fondling hands as bodies crowd to get at the images.

People occasionally worship animal images in Taiwan, and at least two other small temples also enshrine a dog along with unidentified ghosts, much like the Eighteen Lords before their reconstruction (Qiu, 1979:323; Shahar, 1991:69). They are usually called Righteous Dog (Yiquan) temples, and arise when dead dogs appear with unidentified bodies, usually on battlefields. Yet the very physical, almost sexual stroking of the dogs at the Eighteen Lords temple is unusual. While this particular dog claims to be a simple allegory for loyalty, dogs generally in Taiwan are associated with unclean sexuality as much as with higher virtues. Seaman describes a story of a woman using a black dog fetus to poison a man, the use of "black dog blood" as a euphemism for menstrual blood (also an ingredient in magic charms), reference to ladies' men as black dogs, and destruction of a supposedly evil Black Dog Demon cult (Seaman, 1981:392–394). People also sometimes eat dog meat in Taiwan. They only eat it in winter, though, because dog meat is very hot in the medical sense – proper for sexual action and for a hot and noisy temple. The highlighted dogs thus add a peculiar combination of loyalty, sex and danger to the overloaded mix of the temple.

## Offerings

The act of worship itself closely follows standard ghost worship, with incense sticks offered first on the god side and then on the ghost side, followed by burning paper spirit money appropriate to ghosts. Two additional offerings, however, make this temple stand out from all others, and again increase the range of potential associations – sesame oil chicken (*mayou ji*) and cigarettes. Unlike the incense and spirit money, these offerings are optional, but still very frequent. People usually bring the sesame oil chicken when they choose to offer food, because they know the Eighteen Lords relish it above other dishes.

Sesame oil chicken has one major connotation in Taiwan: it restores strength to women who have just given birth. All new mothers must eat this soup made of chicken, wine, and sesame oil. In Chinese folk medical terms, sesame oil chicken is restorative (*bu*) and hot (the hot of "hot and noisy"). The pollution and general blood loss of labor leaves women weak and cold. They must therefore scrupulously avoid cold foods (again referring to medical properties, not temperature), eating only restorative foods like chicken, and warming ones like sesame oil and wine (Gould-Martin, 1976:128).

I asked several people what sense it made to offer such a dish to seventeen dead men and a dog. The answers invariably drew parallels between these ghosts and new mothers. Most people explained that, as drowning victims, the Eighteen Lords were cold and weak, with a great need for restorative and warming foods. Like new mothers, ghosts are also polluted beings (Ahern, 1975). Childbirth and menstrual blood pollute women so badly that the eighteen hells reserve a special Bloody Pond of bodily fluids to punish them. Funeral experts hang scrolls showing the hells at funerals, illustrating how the women suffer up to their necks in blood and birth fluids, and of course also encouraging their sons to pay for special funeral services to save them.[57] Menstruation alone prevents women from worshiping gods.

The cold and pollution of new mothers and the Eighteen Lords is one side of their great power – the mothers' power to reproduce and the ghosts' power to grant wishes. Like ghosts, female sexuality provides a combined power and threat. No family continues without it, yet sex is also a major danger. Chinese express this in social terms when they accuse sisters-in-law of forcing families to divide by breaking the brothers apart. They express it in folklore with stories about ghosts and fox fairies who appear as beautiful women to seduce men to death by draining all their semen. In some ways, the offering of sesame oil chicken thus reinforces the celebration of *yin* in the Eighteen Lords temple by drawing a comparison between the ghosts and the most *yin* of humans, new mothers. Yet the message also contradicts the reversals that put the Eighteen Lords in the most *yin* positions in space and time – the bottom right in the middle of the night. Sesame oil chicken, after all, makes the ghosts more *yang*. Like any good chicken soup, it cures a "cold" – the pun works in Taiwanese as it does in English. Even as the offering marks the *yin* nature of these ghosts, it attempts to ameliorate their condition instead of just celebrating its power. The food offerings thus do not mesh neatly with the architecture, and further muddle the possible meanings. If the architectural inversions seemed to promote an interpretation as resistance, the sesame oil chicken instead suggests accommodation.

Cigarettes, the other unusual offering, open up quite a different range of associations. Below ground in the temple, as supplicants crawl around to reach the awkwardly placed "incense" pot, they do not place sticks of incense, but instead erect burning cigarettes by thrusting them into holes drilled in the concrete pot. Most people offer only incense at the above-ground grave, but some also impale cigarettes on a small bed of nails just in front of the incense pot. This is a very unusual use of cigarettes in Taiwan, which I had never seen before. People sometimes offer whole packs of cigarettes at the annual ghost festival, but not as a substitute for incense. Cigarette smoking is widespread, especially among men in Taiwan. Yet it is also viewed as it once was in the United States – just a little bit wrong, and not really appropriate for women, children, or religious people. It would be very disrespectful to offer a cigarette to a god.[58] The contrast between cigarette and incense highlights the underworld associations of ghosts and of this temple in particular.

People at the temple could not explain where the custom of using cigarettes came from, but it seems to be spreading. A similarly overblown ghost temple, this one to a Japanese period robber named Liao Tianding, also gets offerings of single, lit cigarettes.[59] Several people told me how burning cigarettes stood on end can bring ghostly spirits down to *die xian* ("bowl spirit"), a sort of Ouiji Board in which three players hold a bowl that moves across a sheet of paper printed with characters and spells out messages. Ghosts typically motivate the bowl, and behave generally like weak versions of ghost temples, granting requests for information about anything at all. Single cigarettes also show up in the New Territories as offerings on the graves of village toughs, the enforcers who guaranteed the power of lineage strongmen.[60] All three of these cases fit the slightly unsavory character of cigarettes in Taiwan.

Each case also recalls the social functions of cigarettes, especially in male gatherings. Nearly any friendly encounter begins with someone offering cigarettes around; others will reciprocate as time goes by. While whole packs or cartons of cigarettes may often serve as minor gifts to superiors in the hope of encouraging a favor, the offering of single cigarettes to smoke instead immediately marks ties between equals. Such an offering thus goes beyond just reinforcing the lowly status of ghosts compared to gods. It differs fundamentally from offerings to gods (or even to ghosts at the annual ghost festival), which reinforce the hierarchy of supplicant to superior. Instead, it emphasizes an exchange among equals, a relationship based on contractual ties rather than fixed political and social hierarchy.

Each transaction with the Eighteen Lords indeed resembles a contract far more than a petition to a superior like offerings to gods. If the Eighteen Lords grant a request, the worshiper must repay them or face sickness and misfortune, perhaps even death. Just like contracts with mobsters, broken deals with the Eighteen Lords need not await the slow turning of the wheel of law; justice is swift and merciless. Gods also appreciate repayments, but do not require them so cold-bloodedly. In a sense, gods expect a thanks of tribute, but the Eighteen Lords must be paid in full by giving gold medallions, sponsoring an opera or puppet show for their entertainment, or contributing money to the temple. This strict calculation of contractual repayment is one of the most discussed features of the Eighteen Lords.

One further use of cigarettes offers still further interpretive possibilities. In the summer of 1988, at a small restaurant in northern Taiwan, I glanced up at the small altar near the cash register. This altar resembled the altars in many small businesses, and held a statue of the Cloth-bag Monk (Budai Heshang) as one of its images. The Cloth-bag Monk is a fat, jolly character with a big bag draped over his shoulder; he is a minor figure on many family and small business altars. The cloth bag is stuffed with presents and cash that, like Santa Claus, he hands out to little children. He strongly resembles popular images of Maitreya, the Buddha of the next age, and many people say he is an incarnation of Maitreya. He is not normally an important object of worship in his own right, but he is the sort of symbol of easy wealth falling into your lap that small businesses in Taiwan like. Such symbolism is usually fairly crude. Many people simply glue the character *fu* (wealth) to their cash register at every lunar new year, and stylized images of old coins are also very popular.

This particular image, however, with its chubby cheeks and big grin, had a burning cigarette hanging out of its mouth. Somehow the cigarette transformed the smiling, fat monk into a typically stereo-typed sneering, overweight hoodlum. I have also heard of people who bring dog statues back from the Eighteen Lords temple, and who worship them by placing burning cigarettes in their mouths. The tie between eighteen dead bodies and the Buddha of the future is the idea of easy money and the amorality of earning it. The temple itself strengthens the association: the most popular items the temple sells after little dogs are statues of the chubby monk. Both the Eighteen Lords and the Cloth-bag Monk act as sources of unearned wealth, and the cigarettes are a reminder first that unearned wealth tends not to be very moral wealth, and second that wealth comes from a kind of tit-for-tat reciprocity rather than the hierarchy that gods personify. The Cloth-bag Monk suggest resistance again, but this time through the subversive irony of the cigarette, rather than the inversions of the architecture.

## Goals of Worship

The Eighteen Lords and similar temples owe much of their rise to fame to their ability to meet the needs of their worshipers. Like all ghost temples, they have a particular comparative advantage over gods when people have needs irrelevant to the orthodox morality of the gods. In the last two decades, when such places suddenly got so hot and noisy, many people looked to them for help dealing with capricious, dangerous, and not especially moral financial situations. Most important of these was an illegal lottery that swept Taiwan in the 1980s, followed closely by the stock market craze and the general uncertainty of small business.

The lottery came in various versions, but people refer to it generically as "Everybody's Happy" (*dajia le*). Everybody's Happy depended originally on Taiwan's national lottery, which chose three numbers to share the seventh (and last) prize. The odds of winning any of the prizes in the national lottery, as usual for such lotteries, were astronomical. In the original form of Everybody's Happy, people bet on the last two digits of the seventh-place prizes, and the odds of winning on a single bet could thus be as high as three in one hundred. Anyone could organize a betting pool by photocopying sheets of paper with boxes numbered 00 to 99, and taking one bet on each number. The amount of the bet varied with the pool, and could range from a few dollars to very large sums. When enough bets were down (usually when at least fifty of the numbers had been taken) the pool was closed. If not enough people made bets or if none of the numbers won, the organizer would return all the money; if one or more people bet on winners, the organizer would take a 10 percent cut and divide the rest among the winners.[61] Bettors could join any number of pools and bet on more than one number within a pool. Organizers (*zutou*) could organize any number of pools. This led to the development of some betting specialists – the largest caught was said to have over 17 million NT dollars on hand (over half a million US dollars).

The ease of organization of a pool, and the lack of any centralized organization running it made Everybody's Happy almost impossible for the government to control. They tried altering the national lottery and finally canceled it, but people always found new ways to play. Many games became tied to the Hong Kong lottery, but even tour buses played off the last two digits of the license plate of a passing car. A 1987 police report (Jiang, 1987:1) estimated that 3 million people were betting on the lottery.

Bets were often very high, and one of the reasons for the interest was the excess of capital in Taiwan in the last few years with very few routes for productive investment. As labor costs have gone up, many people have been afraid to invest in new labor-intensive enterprises, yet have not had the resources for capital-intensive industry nor the opportunity and knowledge to invest abroad. Combined with the great success of Taiwan's export economy, the result by the mid-1980s was unproductive uses of capital – passive investments in land or stock for people who saw no plausible alternatives. The illegal lottery provided a similar form of investment, riskier but with a much greater profit for winners, and far more fun than other investments.

Like any good investors, many players of Everybody's Happy tried to reduce their risk, in this case by getting an idea of the winning numbers in advance. Religion provided one of the most popular means for learning numbers. Numbers came from two types of sources: deities could give indirect hints about numbers (through patterns in incense smoke, for example), or they could communicate the numbers directly, often through spirit possession. As a rule, however, temples to more respectable deities would have nothing to do with such activities. Instead, people would ask ghosts or marginal deities who do not really fit the standard bureaucratic model, like the lowly Earth God, Taizi Ye (a small child turned god), Sun Wukong (popularized in the West as the mischievous Monkey), or Ji Gong (the inebriated Buddhist monk) (Hu, 1986).

Small and large ghost shrines were even more involved in this, and there were close ties with ghostly death. People would spend the night in graveyards hoping to be inspired with dreams. According to widespread rumor, people would also come to traffic accidents to see what number the bodies resembled, or to get the numbers of the license plates. High community gods, on the other hand, would refuse to give such information, or would give false numbers to punish people who asked. Only gods known for bucking the system, and especially ghosts, would cooperate with these requests for help in an illegal activity.

One result of this has been a further increase in privately run possession cults, and a real economic boom for larger ghost temples. In her important study of such cults in the Taichung area, Hu T'ai-li (1986) cites evidence that the numbers of temples seeking to enter the Daoist Association almost tripled in 1986 compared to the annual rate for the previous six years, and that the number of spirit medium altars applying for such registration quadrupled at the same time. Similarly, the number of officially registered Ji Gong temples increased from 12 to 120 between 1981 and 1986. She also gives many examples of ghost shrines that have become extremely popular, sometimes seeing up to 10,000 worshipers at a time. One such shrine commemorates convicts put to death during the Japanese occupation. Reminiscent of the Eighteen Lords temple, they are worshiped with dog meat, cigarettes and betel nut – all "hot" and all considered less than fully respectable vices.

Temples suggesting numbers would usually be ambiguous, offering up three or four digits that could be combined into five-ten two-digit numbers. With each number having three chances to win, and more numbers generated by people watching incense smoke or candle drips, the odds of a temple coming up with a winning number were very high. A temple that helped the winner would see more and more business come its way. In addition, the iron-clad rule that all ghostly favors must be repaid in full meant that winners had to present the temple with donations of cash or gold medals, or arrange for outdoor opera performances, puppet shows, striptease shows or movie showings in front of the temple. Some ghost temples had a ten- to twenty-day waiting list for puppet show performances (Hu, 1986). Unsuccessful temples, on the other hand, suffered serious consequences. For instance, newspaper reports described smashed Earth God images that washed ashore at a river bend – apparently the result of angry revenge from disappointed worshipers (Hu, 1986). As in the capitalist marketplace, there is the possibility for great gain or loss for both parties, and successful performance counts for more than traditional values or social ties.

## Summary

The Eighteen Lords offer a cornucopia of inconsistent interpretive possibilities: the celebration of unorthodox power in the reversals of space and time, the combined loyalty and sexual overflow of the dogs, the healing warmth of chicken soup for new mothers, the seamy reciprocity of the cigarettes, the contracts enforced by threat of violence, and the amoral caprices of making money. As a set, these possibilities offer no obvious and consistent message, nor are they meant to. Reducing this simply to resistance or accommodation would badly oversimplify; the two possibilties are hopelessly interwined along with many others. The healing power of sesame oil chicken, for example, contradicts the celebration of *yin* power elsewhere, and has no connection to unearned wealth. The saturation results from the accretion of history and creative play with ghosts. At the risk of losing some of the exuberance of possible connotations, however, we can pull out a few major themes that run through most of this discussion and help to explain the greatest anomaly about the Eighteen Lords temple: how it could have achieved its huge scale, and why the temple blossomed exactly when it did. Ordinary ghost temples never even have regular traffic – days or weeks may go by with no offerings. No other ghost temple has achieved such a scale, where hundreds or thousands of supplicant/tourists come day after day. Only a handful of Taiwan's most popular god temples operate at a comparable level.

The first general theme is that the cult serves only the needs of individuals. The very definition of ghosts rests on their existence apart from any normal social ties. Requests to this cult are thus uniformly individualistic: for profit in the lottery, stock market or gambling tables, or for success in (not necessarily legal) business enterprises. Second, the Eighteen Lords work on a contract basis, creating the sort of marketplace ties that exchange cash for services and leave no lasting personal ties. Both the use of cigarettes and the threats about repayment reinforce this image. Third, the temple has no concern at all about orthodox morality. The physical association of the Eighteen Lords temple with pickpockets, the rumored appeal of its ritual netherworld to the secular underworld, the dogs and their associations with black magic and sexuality, and even a fat Buddha with a cigarette hanging out of his mouth continually reemphasize the disreputable implications of the cult. The Eighteen Lords offer none of the appropriation of official state morality which provides the mainstay of ordinary community god temples. They contrast even with other unorthodox spirits like Guangxi's King Gan or the Taiping God, both of whom served communities, even as they challenged other kinds of values. Nevertheless, arguing for the cultural difference of the Eighteen Lords is not the same as claiming they are resistance.

## WHY NOW?

Dealings with ghosts need not be immoral in Chinese terms; one can make the same requests to ghosts as to gods. The difference is that the ghosts grant requests just for the economic reward, while the gods require accepted morality and are less mercenary about payment. By the same token, one visits ghosts in the hopes of individual profit, and not on behalf of a community. If gods reinforce the idea of hierarchy, ghosts scoff at it. Spirits like the Eighteen Lords are by no means unique in China, or even in complex societies anywhere. For example, ghosts among the Edo of the West African Benin Kingdom could have come from a description of China: "While relations between the living and the incorporated dead have a strong, positive, moral component, ghosts are dealt with almost entirely in terms of expediency ... The incorporated dead are the recipients not only of expiatory offerings but also of acts of thanksgiving and commemoration. Ghosts can only be bought off" (Bradbury, 1966:131).

Our own unincorporated dead work much the same way in the West, coming out on Halloween and demanding payment while threatening tricks. In Thailand, to cite just one more independent case, the unincorporated dead consist especially of young men who died violently and women who died in childbirth, "precisely the persons whom the elders have been unable to initiate and install into the ordered sequence of community statuses" (Tambiah, 1970:315). Expert mediums can exploit these spirits to achieve either good or bad, and cults to them tend to be peripheral, ecstatic, and dangerous (Tambiah, 1970:316). The idea of amoral spirits with no community ties thus frequently fills the cracks in an otherwise hierarchical system.

These systems for imagining the unincorporated dead, with their emphasis on payment and individuals, also seem well adapted to commodity economies, especially where they exist in tension with more politically incorporated economies under the control of the state. Just such an adaptation occurred in Colombia, where the Devil became a trope for the relations of capitalist wage labor (Taussig, 1980:13–38). Late imperial Chinese ghosts were similarly marginal, but in a way that matched the commoditized side of the economy. Their individualizing function contrasted with the community base of gods, and their faceless anonymity and insistence on keeping the terms of a bargain recalled the market in ways that political petitions and tribute payments to gods did not.

There is thus nothing startlingly new for China in the profit-oriented and self-serving motives that appear in the Eighteen Lords temple. A commodity- and individual-oriented undercurrent, relatively unconcerned with problems of morality, has always flowed below the surface. While ghosts typically did not reach the glories of the Eighteen Lords, they clearly formed part of this undercurrent – asocial beings willing to enter into any bargain to improve their own position. The annual ghost festival repeated the same message when the priests threw coins out to the greedy ghosts, and to the spectators struggling for them below. The same thing recurred at the annual grave-cleaning festival when parents scattered coins over the graveyard for their covetous children to gather up. The single sticks of incense in ghost offerings also emphasized their individuality and lack of community ties, recalling those single cigarettes for the Eighteen Lords, and contrasting strongly with the massive piles of incense and combined clouds of smoke in more standard shared incense pots for gods or ancestors.

In addition, Chinese funerals include a reimbursement of the celestial treasury to repay the loan of life with interest by burning piles of spirit money. As Gates argues, this simulates the circulation of profit-making capital, treating life itself as a commodity (Gates, 1987:266–274). Maurice Freedman provides a different kind of example: in the specialist system of geomancy, which includes siting graves for the benefit of the offspring, one brother may manipulate the burial for his own benefit, even to the detriment of his other brothers. In this kind of geomancy "the accent is put upon the paramountcy of selfish interest, the subordination of forebears, and private action," while in ancestor worship it rests "on the supremacy of the common good, the dominance of ancestors, and collective behavior" (Freedman, 1966:143).

The very existence of an avowedly amoral, individualistic and grasping cult like the Eighteen Lords emphasizes a commercial and competitive side to Chinese religion, which is paired against the more bureaucratic and Confucian model that occurs in many other contexts. Although this seamy side of late imperial religion has seen much less scholarly attention, it should come as no surprise in a place where the commodity economy was developed as strongly as China's by the eighteenth and nineteenth centuries. The Ming and Qing dynasties saw a rapid increase in petty commodity production (especially in silk and cotton), and an enormous volume of market trade, especially in grain and cloth (Huang, 1990:90–91). This trade did not particularly fit into the political hierarchy, and spirits like ghosts represented its new tensions better than the bureaucratic gods. Late imperial China's uncomfortable connections between bureaucracy and commerce existed just as strongly in religion.

In some ways, then, the Eighteen Lords seem aberrant only because we have paid too much attention to precipitated versions of religious hierarchy, and too little to the full range of religious practice. The new proportioning of religion today is less a structural break than a repositioning of values that had always been implied by some aspects of Chinese religious practice, even as they were being denied by others. Yet this sudden magnification in the 1980s itself has great significance. The Eighteen Lords do not shock Taiwanese because they are greedy ghosts, but because spirits who should be marginal have suddenly become the center of a huge cult. Ghosts who should typically be kept at a great distance, unseen and unheard, suddenly occupied one of the hottest and noisiest temples in Taiwan.

## Religious Change in the 1980s

The Eighteen Lords temple is only one part of a general reproportioning of popular religion in Taiwan in the 1980s. The primary growth areas in all popular religion since about 1970 have been in its most individualistic aspects, rather than in those that most emphasize family or community. The ancestor cult and major community god temples are holding their own, even increasing, but the striking growth has been in worship through private spirit mediums or involving ghosts. Both these areas have especially weak institutions of interpretation compared to ancestors or gods in community temples. Their interpretive looseness let them adapt easily to changing social relations of interpretation in Taiwan.

Even with China's relatively weak control over religious interpretation, marginal ghosts fell beyond the scope of most interpretive institutions. In addition, possessed mediums are fundamentally resistant to control, as I argued for the Taiping. China never had strong mechanisms to control the meaning even of ancestors and gods, but at least those spirits had written genealogies, experts and their texts, and expensive temples. All these things attempted to freeze interpretation in ways simply not possible for ghosts or mediums. By remaining more thickly indeterminate, these aspects of popular religion responded most easily to rapid social change.

Spirit mediums (*tang-ki*) who provide advice and perform cures while possessed by various gods have long been popular in Taiwan. Some major community temples have spirit mediums attached to them, but most mediums work out of private, unregistered altars, usually in their homes. Most of their work is very utilitarian – they cure the sick, find lost objects, pronounce on the probable success of a business venture, and so on. Most have no ties to the communal interests of major temples dedicated to gods and they serve individual clients rather than communities. The potential for lucrative rewards from the great popular demand for spirit possession has led a number of mediums to leave community temples in order to open up their own altars, as well as creating the great increase in the number of the privately owned cults (Li, 1988:7–8).

At the same time, more and more different gods are appearing on these private altars. Community temples usually feature one primary deity, often captured in many images. Other gods may appear on secondary altars, or in minor positions on the main altar. The horde of different gods on private spirit medium altars – as many as forty or fifty different images – reinforces the utilitarian functions of such cults. With each deity having its own specialty, these temples can meet the needs of a wider variety of clients, just like a shop that expands its selection of wares (Li, 1988:11–13). While the possessing spirits are not ghosts, much of the message is the same, concentrating on utilitarian functions for individuals rather than communities. Not coincidentally, spirit medium shrines themselves are profit-oriented petty capitalist enterprises.

Ghosts (*kui*) in general represent the other major growth sector, and they relate even more clearly to utilitarian and individualistic needs (Li, 1988). The Eighteen Lords temple itself is just the most fashionable of a series of similar cults. At least three similar ghost temples rose to unprecedented popularity during the last twenty years. The others tended not to share the systematic inversions of the Eighteen Lords temple, but they all centered around the graves of ghosts and their willingness to grant disreputable requests.

One temple honors a general named Li Yong who was killed fighting aborigines during the nineteenth century. He is perhaps the least ghostly of the group, but still his violent death far from home marks a basic similarity to other ghosts. The second temple commemorates a sort of Robin Hood figure named Liao Tianding. Liao was a thief during the Japanese occupation who was very generous with the poor. The authorities could never find him, but he was finally murdered in his sleep by a brother-in-law who wanted the reward. His shrine sits in the middle of a graveyard, and he also receives offerings of cigarettes. The third temple houses the remains of a mainland soldier who robbed banks with great success, and supposedly used the profits to support a friend's child. He was shot by firing squad. All of these temples share two important features: they honor figures who are beyond official control, and they are willing to help people at the bottom of society. As ghosts, they are far more flexible about honoring requests than proper gods.

The growth and transformation of ghost shrines is not new in the last decade or so. A number of temples that now appear as ordinary god temples began as ghost shrines, whose transformation stemmed from their reputations for great efficacy (Harrell, 1974). Even an eminent goddess like Mazu began life as a ghostly spirit, a girl who died violently and without descendants. As such temples succeed, their ghostly origins recede. The new development in ghost temples in recent years, however, differs in retaining, and even celebrating strong ties to the world of ghosts. The graves stand out conspicuously in all cases, offerings are appropriate to ghosts, temple structure resembles overgrown ghost shrines (no curving eaves, no door gods), and the beings worshiped happily honor the sorts of requests that gods would refuse to recognize. The critical change is thus that these temples insistently retain their ghostly appeal, not acceding to orthodox morality the way they must to become god temples.

Taiwan has thus fostered the increasing prominence of a set of ideas and ritual acts that encompass ghosts, dogs, cigarettes, private spirit mediums, and an illegal lottery. Certain potential lines of interpretation come up repeatedly within this set: a general perception of amorality, at most a kind of utilitarianism, and a narrowing of focus from family and community down to the individual and his or her private needs and desires. While my pulling out these general features sacrifices some of the temple's thick evocation, it also points to a close relation with Taiwan's economic pyrotechnics of the same period. It suggests in particular a close look at the rapid development of small-scale entrepreneurial capitalism and of a kind of "gambling mentality" in Taiwan in the 1980s. The new proportioning of religion has both reflected and affected the questioning of identity that has accompanied Taiwan's dramatic transformations of the last decade. Ghosts and mediums – the most saturated aspects of Taiwanese religion – have responded most effectively to those changes in social relations.

## Profits and Religion

It should be no great surprise that this religious embodiment of individualism has grown most at exactly the same time as Taiwan's small enterprise-based capitalism has thrived. The relation of the individual to the marketplace in capitalism, along with the associated breakdown of many communal and particularistic ties, has been recognized since Marx on commodity fetishism and Durkheim on anomie. The new version of the ghost cult also implies that success in wealth is capricious and a little corrupt. Several informants described this as a new respect for *piancai*. *Piancai* literally means "biased wealth," and is originally a term from divination. It refers especially to unearned wealth, and sums up the attitudes in gambling, playing the illegal lottery or the stock market, or offering cigarettes to the Cloth-bag Buddha (whom one informant described as the God of Biased Wealth). Its special popularity in recent years stems in part from real economic experience of the market.

Any market is to an extent capricious and unpredictable, especially for the small entrepreneurs and investors who have created much of Taiwan's growth. The situation was especially bad, however, in the late 1980s, when many people felt that small, labor-intensive enterprise would no longer be profitable in Taiwan, yet saw no plausible alternatives. The result was a huge increase in relatively unproductive investment – an exploding stock market, skyrocketing land prices, the thriving illegal lottery. One of the most powerful symptoms was a booming underground futures market that held perhaps 6 billion US dollars in deposits and offered returns of over 50 percent annually (Friedland and Kaye, 1990:54). Essentially pyramid schemes built on quicksand, these companies collapsed in early 1990. Unregulated margin loans led to an equally wild stock market frenzy, moving the market index from 1,000 to over 12,000 between 1986 and 1990 (Winn, 1991:10). The craze extended to all levels of society, as housewives lined up to buy shares and the news began broadcasting prices of the entire market. As the *Financial Times* put it, "casino-style gambling on the stock market had replaced the work ethic" (Elliott, 1990). The inevitable crash occurred in early 1990, when the market lost 75 percent of its value.

Profit appeared less as a product of hard work and smart decisions, and more as a result of luck, greed and insider connections. At the same time, the crisis of economic confidence accentuated the tooth-and-claw image of the economy always implied as one side of petty entrepreneurial competition. While the stock market and gambling dens raged on, high labor costs were tightening the reins on small business. Success appeared increasingly as the result of self-serving utilitarianism rather than community morality, that is, more ghostly and less godly.

The capitalist market presents itself as an amoral phenomenon where commodities are qualitatively equated through money, and have no ties to systems of social relations. Polanyi (1944:163) described this as the subjection of labor to the laws of the market, which was "to annihilate all organic forms of existence and to replace them by a different type of organization, an atomistic and individualistic one." More recently, Taussig (1980:26) has described similar changes in Colombia, where "communality and mutuality give way to personal self-interest, and commodities, not persons, dominate social being." These critics of capitalism emphasize only one aspect of the capitalist transformation, and to an extent idealize the communal harmonies of pre-capitalist social life. Nevertheless, they grasp an important aspect of the growth of capitalism, which Taiwan's religious development has emphasized.

Cultural developments based on a perceived loss of morality have turned up frequently in the history of capitalism. The Romantics sought to fight it with values beyond an impoverished capitalist rationality, and conservatives from Matthew Arnold on resisted it with Culture itself. Much of the world-wide religious resurgence, especially in Islam and Protestantism, also attempts to re-introduce lost values. Taiwan has had similar reactions. They range from some intellectuals' reworking of the relationship between Confucianism and capitalism, to an esoteric Buddhism fad mostly among college students, to a Taiwan culture movement. The most startling growth has been in new religions whose spirit possession sessions offer to reclaim an earlier set of Confucian or Buddhist values (see Jordan and Overmyer, 1986). Yet while all these reactions attempt to combat a perceived loss of morals, the Eighteen Lords celebrate and utilize the loss, even as they imply a criticism of the market's lack of morals.

The Eighteen Lords' catering to individual and utilitarian needs fits this view of the economy as a place where success has less to do with morality and good social relations than with self-interest and competition against other members of the community. One of the episodes in the movie, *The Eighteen Lords* (which I take up in more detail in Chapter 9), describes a gambling incident that illustrates this well. A young gambler needs to make a lot of cash to help his friend buy off the contract of a prostitute he likes. He and the friend ask the Eighteen Lords for help. The spirits respond by leading him to a book that describes how to use the umbilical cord of a newborn infant as a gambling talisman. It warns, however, that such a use of the umbilical cord will permanently damage the fate of the baby. The man's wife has conveniently just given birth to a daughter, whose umbilicus he yanks off to the protests of the mother and wails of the daughter. The tactic proves a great success (except, perhaps, for the baby, who is not followed further in the film). Even family morality is sacrificed for profit. The film clearly celebrates the wonderful power of the ghosts, but their action also shocks in just the same way as the temple itself.

The increasing commodification of religion itself, especially of these newly popular cults, further emphasizes profit over community or family morality. Commodification is nothing new in Chinese religion, in which temples have asked for donations, specialists have sold their services, and people burn paper "money" to spirits of all descriptions. These cults, however, have pushed the profit motive to new heights. Tremendous fortunes have been made from the Eighteen Lords temple over just a few years. While the main source of income is donations in thanks for requests granted, the temple also charges for parking, and even for the toilets – a level of petty greed that other temples have yet to match.

The modern media have also added a new dimension to temple profitability, as the extensive news, soap opera and film treatments of the temple have been as rewarding for the temple as for the media. The temple sells the movie soundtrack alongside its little ceramic dogs, for example. People consider the Eighteen Lords powerfully efficacious, but that need not imply that the temple management is motivated by anything other than profit. The spirit mediums who are growing just as fast in popularity are open to the same kinds of criticism. Even believers know that trance can be faked, and that spirit medium altars are businesses like any other. Again, their profit motivation is not new; the tremendous popularity of such activities is.

By tying the popularity of ghost temples to the specifics of the "gambling economy" of the late 1980s, I have also implied that such cults should decline with further economic change. The stock market crash of 1990 brought just such a change. While people still play the market, they are considerably chastened, and other forms of gambling like Everybody's Happy no longer constitute major sensations. At the same time, the Eighteen Lords temple has lost a great deal of its former popularity. The change reflects both a decline in the more ghostly side of capitalism, and the obvious decline in the efficacy of spirit-world stock tips – as you might expect, the Eighteen Lords picked winning investments much better in a booming market than in a collapsing one.

The economic experiences of the last two decades have bent traditional religious practice in new directions. At the same time, however, those practices have given Taiwanese a partial way of making sense of their new experiences. The development of the ghost cult has played up a theme of individualism and greed that had previously been just a religious undercurrent. Peter Berger (1988:8–9) has suggested that popular images of gods provided a model of loyalty and cooperation that was pre-adapted to modern capitalism. There is a great deal of sense to this, but it is equally true that Taiwan's small-scale capitalism has also promoted an image of all against all, without any shared moral community. This is the image that the rise in the ghost cult played up: the nineteenth-century image of the free market, red in tooth and claw. The increase in ghost worship has responded to the economic experience of the last two decades, but has also helped shape that experience, providing a model of individualistic and amoral competition that is part of living in a society of small capitalists.

I began this chapter by discussing the rich and inconsistent complexity of the Eighteen Lords, and have finished with a single interpretation that represents my own analysis. That single thread inevitably thins the temple's exuberant possibilities, following certain lines of potential interpretation over others. Such a reduction is unavoidable when translating ritual to prose, but is even more inseparable from any academic argument. Academic orthodoxies, like political ones, are precipitates, and change similarly when new ones challenge them. Explicit academic analysis thus relates closely to the more political processes I have been discussing. I will address intellectual versions of the Eighteen Lords (including my own) more fully in Chapter 9, as one of many kinds of precipitation of the temple, none of which have had much success in altering the original mass of potential meanings.

The temple and its followers certainly agree on no such unified interpretation. The loose commentary on capitalism I have been discussing represents only one clear potential to emerge, rendered plausible by the social relations of interpretation of the late 1980s. Even that commentary, however, offers no systematic message, nor does it exhaust the potentials. On the one hand, it condemns capitalism as a greedy challenge to proper morality and a reversal of proper order. Yet on the other hand, it exuberantly celebrates markets, profit and competition. Pulling out only the critique or the praise, the resistance or the accommodation, drains the cult of its energy and loses sight of the full range of potentials.

Just like Taiping religion, interpretation here lies as much in the society as in the religious practice itself. For all its quirks, after all, the Eighteen Lords clearly remain an overblown ghost temple not fundamentally different from temples that have existed for centuries. The critical change was in the broader social relations of the 1980s. The ease with which ghosts have readjusted themselves to changing times results in large part from their saturation: a clear interpretation with clerical or elite enforcement could not react nearly so flexibly to the changing economy.

# 9

# Failed Precipitations

I have argued that an exuberant and messy multivocality characterized the beginnings of both Taiping religion and the Eighteen
Lords temple. The early Taiping nearly collapsed from the overload
of meaning, as the melting of Hong's ideology into local practice
foreshadowed the cacophony and chaos that followed during the
period of mass possessions. Although its roots were very different,
the Eighteen Lords also offered a surfeit of possibilities rather than
any single message. Both celebrating and condemning utilitarian
greed, these spirits evoked a range of images from new mothers to
merciless gangsters. Despite their diverse origins, the two cases thus
shared an extreme saturation. Each case also included a potential
reading as resitance among its complex possibilities. The crux of the
comparison between the Taiping and the Eighteen Lords lies in how
the one managed to realize that potential, forging a unified
interpretation as resistance, while the other defeated all attempts,
remaining a thick brew of unrealized and inconsistent possibilities.
This chapter will look in detail at the various attempts to forge a
unified version of the Eighteen Lords, and at how the temple
managed to soak up each one, just stirring it into the mix instead
of being transformed by it.

Attempts to thin out the overgrown meanings of the Eighteen
Lords temple were quite consistent and thorough in some cases, and
more cursory in others. At the very least, however, every attempt
froze some aspect of the many possibilities that the temple contained, and thus sought to limit the interpretive range. The least
systematic efforts (including a competing temple to the same spirits
and the *Eighteen Lords* movie) retained some of the multivocal
enthusiasm of the temple, while only partially limiting the interpretive possibilities. More sweeping efforts (including a television soap
opera and a claim on the Eighteen Lords as lineage ancestors)
forcefully promoted a single version of the temple. While some of
these efforts were profitable, and some probably further increased
the temple's popularity, all fell flat as efforts to determine meaning.
Each attempt succeeded, at least to a certain extent, in thinning out

possible readings of the temple, but each failed to convince the broader public that it controlled the single true meaning. I take them up here, roughly from the most superficial attempts to unify a single meaning to the most thorough.

## THE OTHER EIGHTEEN LORDS

In 1986, I began to hear about a "fake" Eighteen Lords temple, located on the same highway as the original one, but a few kilometers closer to Tanshui, the nearest city. Several people told me that the new temple was a crude attempt to siphon off traffic from the real one, since the usual route took most travelers to the new one first. The story seemed confirmed one night when I was taking a taxi to the original temple. The driver stopped at the new one, claiming it was the genuine article. We had agreed on a fixed fare, and the driver was trying to shorten his trip. Motivated by illegitimate profit, he acted quite in the spirit of both temples, and indeed worshiped the Eighteen Lords when we got to the real temple.

Like many new temples, this one began essentially as a business venture, founded by ten partners from the local area. It sits on a roomier site than the original temple, and is a little larger. Other than that, the new temple is a close copy of the old one: it has no curved eaves or front wall, the same oversized and brightly lit "Eighteen Lords" sign on top, and a god altar on the left with a tiled grave on the right. The new temple even copied the underground chamber, although the builders arranged the basement room so access to the cigarette/incense pot would be easy. The only thing it lacked was a following.

When I interviewed the temple manager and two of the owners, they vociferously and repeatedly denounced the charge of fakery. That false accusation, they said, stemmed from the original temple, which bought ninety minutes of television time to run an extended commercial attacking their temple. Their justification for the new temple involved a small but crucial rereading of the Eighteen Lords, an explicit interpretation that gave them equal claims to authenticity. Their claim also began with seventeen unknown fisherman and a dog, perhaps in the nineteenth century. In this version, though, the bodies were never found and never buried. Instead, the local fishermen decided that the ghosts were ruining the fishing in the area, and hired a religious specialist (*hoat-su*) to perform a ritual called "collecting the souls" (*siu hun*). Collecting the souls, they told me, allowed the spirits to rest peacefully in a grave, instead of roaming around bothering the fishermen. Other than this one clear detail, the owners of the new temple constantly insisted on how little anyone knew of the history of the temple or its spirits. This claim attempted to undermine alternative versions of the temple.

In 1985, the Eighteen Lords allegedly inspired a dream, complaining that the original temple was crowded, unpleasant, and possibly radioactive. The new owners responded with a new temple, and so hired another religious specialist to collect the souls again at the new site. Their claim to authenticity thus lay in having performed the same ritual act as the original temple, and in the implication that the original temple grave housed no bones. The result, they argued, is just like having two Mazu temples – both are equally authentic. Indeed, they argue for a kind of moral superiority, not just with comparisons to an eminent goddess like Mazu, but by pointing out that they do not charge for the toilets or for parking. Truly a pot calling the kettle black, they said the original temple only wanted to make money. They tried to back their claims further by registering as an official temple with the Daoist Association, which the original temple had never done. The Daoist Association responded that they could not register, because the Eighteen Lords were not known gods. Not to be stopped so easily, the new temple built a small altar to the major deity Guan Gong on the second floor, and registered as a Guan Gong temple.

The new temple appropriated much of the overloaded symbolism of the original, including the reversals of time and space, the combined god and ghost altars, and the offerings of cigarettes and sesame oil chicken. It insisted on explicit and consistent interpretation only in the origin story, because only that story supports its claims to legitimacy. Yet even that one small interpretive claim has been a failure, along with the temple as a whole. I visited the new temple twice during the day and once at night, and found it nearly empty on every occasion. The obvious financial opportunism of the new temple certainly made people suspicious, but in itself need not undercut the temple. After all, everyone knows the original temple makes huge profits.

Instead, the problem lay in their explicit interpretation, which convinced no one. The story simply struck most people as implausible. The idea of graves without bones is very unusual, but even worse, the claim about collecting the souls appeared false to everyone I asked. Collecting the souls is one of the most common curing rituals in Taiwan, performed by specialists for babies who have lost their souls, which are still loosely attached at first. People found any other use implausible, and the claim about doing the ritual for the Eighteen Lords just accentuated suspicions that this was really a fake temple that could not accomplish anything. In addition, and most crucially, the temple had no social mechanism for promoting its version of things; they could not afford lengthy television commercials. Even a more plausible precipitation would fail without the construction of a social structure of interpretation.

THE MOVIE

While the fake temple captured the shape of the original without its heat and noise, the movie came closest to the real spirit of the Eighteen Lords (*Shiba Wanggong*, 1985). Like the temple architecture, the structure of the movie offered a kind of parody on post-modernism. The disjointed plot slapped together a set of unrelated anecdotes, and its moral implications ran a chaotic range from the importance of loyalty and respect to the pleasures of sex and money. Even the language ran riot, with an unpredictable mix of Japanese, Mandarin, Hokkien, and Hakka. The movie pushed at the moral limits of Taiwanese society, with partial nudity and profanity right at the border of censorship. The film came off as a cheap attempt to capitalize on the commercial success of the temple. As such, it made an excellent mirror for the greedy and amoral temple it celebrated. Yet even the movie inevitably froze the heat and noise of the temple into a limited set of anecdotes, and thus lost much of the richness of the original.

After a short prologue of sexual punning between a prostitute and a Japanese tourist at the temple, the first major plot began with another prostitute, on the verge of leaping from a cliff to her death. A large dog saw her, and indirectly saved her life by running a motorcycle off the road. The two men riding the motorcycle saw the woman, and talked her into worshipping the Eighteen Lords instead of killing herself. These two young men were the handsome hero, A-kai, and his faithful sidekick, Ban-ji. Both gambled compulsively. At the temple, the prostitute realized that the dog must be the incarnation of the one worshipped there. She also learned from the Eighteen Lords that she would soon meet a "gentleman." With its sexual beginning and the focus on prostitution and gambling, the film already placed itself squarely within the dominant theme of the temple.

Viewers soon learned the cause of the heroine's depression. In her country ignorance, she had been tricked into debt bondage to her pimp. She no longer wanted to work for him, and he had taken her to court over the debt. The plot was transparent: handsome A-kai was the gentleman of her fate, and he would win enough money gambling to buy her from the pimp. In the middle of the sexual intercourse that followed A-kai's announcement of his intentions, the heroine quietly crooned, "Thank you, Eighteen Lords." The film worked its way to its climax through a series of episodes that showed the power of the Eighteen Lords, but that also painted the spirits as a wildly inconsistent mix of loyalty and perfidy, respect and mischief. First came a run-in with an exorcist and healer (*hoat-su*) named A-cui. In the process of trying to divine who the "gentleman" was, A-cui insulted the Eighteen Lords and pawed the prostitute. The Eighteen Lords responded by humiliating him.

The next day, A-cui set up a large outdoor altar to take magical revenge on the Eighteen Lords. This time, the response came on a much larger scale, wreaking mischievous havoc on a number of bystanders. First, the eighteen ghosts attacked the possessed medium assisting A-cui; from the steady shaking of his trance, the medium suddenly began involuntarily break dancing and moon-walking until he finally passed out. A-cui found himself sitting in a burning incense pot, and then chased through town in mid-air. During the chase, the Eighteen Lords also caused a concussion, a motorcycle crash, the destruction of a vendor's cart, and the humiliation of a young woman who found herself inexplicably stripped to her skimpy underwear, to the pleasure of the bystanders, the movie audience, and presumably the Eighteen Lords. All the mischief had no result though – A-cui fled to the temple of a higher god (the Dragon King), and the Eighteen Lords respectfully stopped at the door.

From A-cui's humiliation, the film switched to examples of the amoral power of the temple. At one point, for example, the evil pimp bemoaned his poor business, and commanded his workers to worship at the dog temple. Even though this man was the worst enemy of the heroine, the Eighteen Lords cannot resist any request, and business boomed for the pimp right away. In another such episode, Ban-ji, the sidekick, wanted help with his bad gambling luck. The Eighteen Lords told him the only cure was "spirit money under the ass." Ban-ji tried this by stealing celestial treasury money from a funeral he passed. This is the money repaying the original debt of the deceased, and stealing it will presumably harm the soul. Neither Ban-ji nor the Eighteen Lords seemed to care, though. He sprinkled ashes from the money under the chairs of other gamblers, whose luck suddenly turned sour.

This scene reproduced the dynamics of the biggest gambling coup in the film, which I have already mentioned – Ban-ji tore the umbilical cord from his newborn daughter, destroying her fate, but winning enough money to allow A-kai to buy the prostitute. The happy heroes repaid the temple, as they had to, with a large gold medal. The entire story painted an insouciantly inconsistent picture of the temple. While the Eighteen Lords saved the prostitute and punished the disrespectful exorcist, they also helped the evil pimp, celebrated gambling and prostitution, cost the fate of both a baby and a dead soul and thoroughly upset a throng of innocent bystanders. The contradictory moral dynamics of the film thus stayed close to the spirit of the temple. The possible reading as resistance lies close to the surface here.

An unrelated interlude followed, where a doctor and a coffin-maker got kicked out of the temple. People feared that they would pray for good business, that is, sicknesses to cure or deaths to bury. The Eighteen Lords will do anything, after all. The rest of the movie bore no relation to the earlier plot, except that some of the characters reappeared in new roles. Most of the new developments centered on A-cui, who had now given up the exorcism business. The ghost of a beautiful young woman was haunting him and his family. In an effort to find out who she was, A-cui and two friends tried the Ouiji-like "bowl spirit" that I have already mentioned. Unfortunately for him, however, the bowl attracted the very ghost he was trying to avoid. Once again, A-cui found himself terrorized and humiliated, and ran off to his daughter's house.

Meanwhile, his son came home on leave from the army. He ran straight into the beautiful ghost, who began a deadly seduction in the classic style of Chinese spirit femmes fatales. Just as the clothes were about to come off, though, a shining ray of light blasted from the sun (a Nationalist symbol) on his army hat, hurling the ghost back against the wall. "Take off your hat," she moaned, and foolishly, he did. A-cui interrupted them a few minutes later, and she fled, half-naked and leaving the unconscious soldier behind. Her rout was quite temporary, though, and she returned to terrorize A-cui and his family still further.

The daughter finally asked the Eighteen Lords for help, but they refused. They even appeared in a dream to A-kai, the hero of the first part of the film who now worked as a volunteer in the temple. They told A-kai that they were helping the ghost, and that he should not intercede on behalf of her victims. Nevertheless, when A-cui and his entire family showed up in a wild panic the next day, everyone asked the Eighteen Lords to help him, and the spirits felt compelled to accede. Suddenly the seventeen Lords (the dog did not help) turned on the ghostly woman. As ghosts themselves, they were having a hard time defeating her, when Guanyin, the Goddess of Mercy, finally intervened. A truly eminent deity, she commanded the instant respect of all the combatant ghosts. At last, the audience learned from the divine arbitration that A-cui had killed the young woman in a hit-and-run accident. She agreed to stop her haunting if reparations were paid and A-cui was arrested. With peace restored, the movie ended. While this final part of the film dropped the pleasures of prostitution and gambling (though it still has plenty of sex and profanity), it again showed the Eighteen Lords blissfully switching sides, from their defense of the wronged spirit to their attack on behalf of her murderer. Hardly a powerful moral voice, the temple just serves its customers, an equal-opportunity vendor of fee-for-service miracles.

I had not seen a Taiwanese film since the late 1970s, and this one amazed me. It simply could not have been made a few years earlier. The sex and profanity would have been censored out, and the happy prostitutes and gamblers would have been excluded as immoral. Even the linguistic range showed the extent to which official control over film had been relaxed – only Mandarin had been permitted earlier. The new freedom in film allowed this movie to respond to market opportunities quickly, and to reflect fairly well the spirit of the temple itself. Like the temple, the movie had plenty of standard moral bits thrown in, including the powerful role of the upright goddess Guanyin, the ridicule of exorcists and spirit possession (which reflected educated and often official attitudes), the importance of being respectful, and even a nod toward patriotism in the magical powers of the soldier's hat. Here it suggests accommodation much more than resistance. Yet the mischievous trickery and general antics of the Eighteen Lords stood alongside those moralistic bits, as did their willingness to serve anyone who promised a reward: they helped an unhappy prostitute against her pimp, but also helped the pimp make more money; they helped the ghost against A-cui, but turned against her when A-cui himself asked for help.

One might argue that such gross inconsistencies reflect the speed and greed that marked the making of the film at the expense of any kind of integrity, but much the same process went on in the temple, too. Like the temple, the film remained relatively free of unifying interpretation because no one created a more explicit and integrated message for it – neither the film nor the temple really cared about such precipitation. Yet compared to the temple, the film still looks thin and silly. Frozen into a hundred minutes, the movie necessarily lost much of the thickness of the temple. For example, cigarettes, sesame oil chicken, and the underground chamber played essentially no role in the movie, even though they add much to the evocations of the temple. The film was popular, but failed to focus any integrated interpretation of the temple because it neither offered a convincing single version of things nor fully caught the rich range of possibilities in the temple. The film was less of a failure than the other cases I discuss here only because it had much lower ambitions to impose a unfied interpretation. To the extent that it inevitably thinned out the possibilities of the original temple, however, it had no effect on consiousness. Its influence (like most films) was ephemeral, lasting a few weeks and then gathering dust in video stores.

## TELEVISION: THE EIGHTEEN LORDS GO STRAIGHT

The changes of the 1980s brought a great deal of commercial and artistic freedom to the Taiwanese film industry, but had much less influence in television. Taiwan still has only three television stations, all of them very conservative and well-behaved toward the government, in contrast to the press or cinema.[62] Quite unlike both the original and copy-cat temples and the film, a clear plot and a clear interpretation permeated the television soap opera, *The Strange Tale of the Eighteen Lords* (*Shiba Wanggong Chuanqi*, 1985). Although the soap opera appeared within a few months of the movie, the two media illustrated enormously different views of the temple, from the chaotic antics of society's margins in the movie, to heroism, patriotism and loyalty on television. In fact, the soap opera fit a broad pattern of politically safe historical tales in Taiwan, where patriotic Chinese loyalists fight off foreign conquerors and their dangerous ideas. The favorite example is the mass of Ming loyalists who fled to Taiwan to fight the invading Manchus and their new Qing Dynasty. The parallels to the Guomindang flight to Taiwan in 1949 are obvious to everyone.

The writers at the Chinese Television System network (CTS) squeezed the Eighteen Lords into this mold by inventing a history for the inhabitants of the grave.[63] Sometime in the 1850s, our seventeen human heroes formed a secret religious brotherhood, swearing a blood oath of loyalty in a Guan Gong temple. Typical for such oaths and such societies in southern China at the time, they swore to oppose the Manchu Qing Dynasty and restore the Ming, and to die on the same day even though they were born on different ones. Unfortunately, the Qing troops heard about the ritual and surrounded the temple. Just in time, though, the dog Blackie (actually acted by a borrowed police dog named Lisa, dyed black for the occasion) showed up to warn the plotters. The eighteen fled to the coast, with the army in hot pursuit. The heroes then fought an "explosive life-and-death battle for nationalist loyalty and righteousness, alarming heaven and earth, moving even the ghosts and gods to tears" (Chen, 1985:30–31). The seventeen humans all died in the end, fighting on the boat they were using to flee. The Qing troops were so awed by the heroes that they failed to burn the bodies, and the boat floated miraculously to Taiwan, where the soap opera no longer followed the story. This was a story of patriotism and heroism, with no sex or profanity, no gamblers or prostitutes, no mischief or miracles beyond a very clever dog. The interpretive complexity of the temple had been reduced to a simple story.

In the summer of 1991, another soap opera wrought the same transformation on the Liao Tianding grave-temple, whose popularity had boomed along with the Eighteen Lords. Like *The Strange Tale of the Eighteen Lords*, the Liao Tianding story dropped any reference to efficacious ghosts or to the kinds of requests related to the temple. In fact, the two stories clearly fit a single genre: the Liao Tianding soap just substituted one robber for seventeen young fighters, and Japanese colonial oppressors for Manchu conqueror overlords. Both cases featured brave but hopeless struggles against foreign exploiters of the Chinese people. Liao, of course, was still a robber in the television version of his life, but all his crimes aimed at correcting colonial injustice. He plundered only Japanese rulers and rich collaborators. Both stories bowdlerized their heroes, excising the very features that made them such powerful and popular ghosts. Both also claimed the temples as memorials to loyal patriots, ignoring their actual function as marketplaces for miracles. The official CTS viewers' magazine even imitated the fake temple's comparison of the Eighteen Lords to Mazu, Taiwan's most popular goddess, claiming that their worthy achievements made them gods in the popular mind, spirits worthy of respect (Chen, 1985:31).

In spite of the relatively clear, politically approved and morally upright intent of these serials, the single message they pulled out of their sources was neither as pure nor as thin as may at first appear. The efficacy of the temple itself, for example, frequently came up in publicity for the soap opera, although it had been carefully removed from the story. The official viewers' magazine reported that the Eighteen Lords themselves chose the names for their characters, when the director went to the temple for a divination session. The magazine also told how one of the stars went to worship there while waiting to hear if he got the role. As usual, the Eighteen Lords did their best, and he got the part the next day (Cai and Xiao, 1985:35). The lyricist also claimed to be a fervent devotee of the temple, and alleged that the idea for the story came to him in a dream inspired by the ghosts (Zhang, 1985:16–20). Thus while the front-stage performance itself attempted a consistent message enforcing a single version of the temple, some of the Eighteen Lords' actual complexity snuck in the back door, especially in attempts to drum up public interest.

The Eighteen Lords soap opera had some influence as entertainment, and partially succeeded in wresting a unified interpretation out of the temple. Yet it failed as an attempt to propagate a new interpretation. No one I met ever told the soap opera version as the real story of the temple. The producers, of course, intended only to entertain, not propagandize. Yet the consistent pattern of their productions also indicated the pressure to toe a certain political and moral line. Whatever their intention, the result proclaimed a certain vision of the temple, and provided a potential seed to crystallize a new interpretation. The seed failed to grow less because the story lacked any real evidence, than because the soap opera refused to capture most of what made the temple so appealing – the amoral power of the ghosts.

Worse still, the television show had no social mechanism to promote its version. Rather than achieving a unified vision of the temple, the serial found itself irresistibly sucked into the general mix, just another element of overloaded significance. The effect occurred both in the back-stage reports of the actual role of temple miracles in making the soap opera, and in the way people would include the television version as just one of many possibilities for the temple's origins. Any other result would have required a social organization of interpretation on a scale comparable to what the Taiping did in 1850. Like film, television freezes a certain version of things, but is finally ephemeral, disappearing back into the general babble of interpretations. If the Eighteen Lords someday evolve into a more standard god temple and attempt to lose their ghostly trappings, the soap opera version might come back to life as a justification. For now, however, with no social mechanism to overcome the black hole effect of the temple, the soap opera will create no unified interpretation.

## A GHOSTLY LINEAGE

The final twist on the Eighteen Lords appeared in a little booklet available free in the temple. Written in response to the supposed misinformation in the movie and television series, the book gave the "true" origins of the spirits, most of whom turned out to be ancestors of the local Lian family (two of whom wrote the book, Lian and Lian, 1985). The book named each of the spirits, and provided quick biographies of each, even the dog (called Black Dragon in this version). The biographical sketches characterized each person by virtue: filial piety, bravery, repaying past kindness, providing education for the poor, and wisdom. Each showed a worthy person, not at all ghostly. Sometime during the Tongzhi reign (1862–1874), twelve Lians, five others and the dog set out from their home village in Fujian to join relatives who had already settled in northern Taiwan. They died in transit, but the boat somehow washed ashore at just the village they had hoped to reach. Not knowing who they were, the local Lians buried the bodies. Some decades later, one of the Taiwan branch visited family back in Fujian, heard the tale of the lost relatives, and realized that the bodies were lineage relatives.

The rest of the booklet detailed specific evidence for the efficacy of the temple. Most of the stories, but not all, concerned the Lian family. All of them, however, typified the kinds of tales commonly told about community gods. A flying dog, for example, chased off an Allied bomber during World War II. When the local Japanese colonial office extracted too much tax on grain, the dog allowed the office to be bombed, first warning a Lian relative to escape. They also brought fishing boats safely to shore, saved maidens in distress, and mended broken families. Nothing ghostly remained of these ghosts; they had become protectors of community and family, not marginal challenges. Only one of the nineteen stories in the booklet even touched on the sort of ghostly figure that made the temple famous. Strongly reminiscent of the film version, the story told of a suicidal prostitute, saved by the Eighteen Lords and told she would soon meet and marry her savior. All this came to pass, and she became an upright mother of three. Yet unlike the film, this little tale disliked the prostitution and had no gambling. It was a moral fable of a woman saved from disgrace, not a celebration of illicit pleasure and profit.

This story is no more implausible than the story of the soap opera or the "fake" temple, nor is it any more effective. By no coincidence, the chairman of the temple committee is a member of this Lian family. In making a kinship claim on the Eighteen Lords, the book also claimed the temple's finances. Thus like the fake temple, financial motives immediately undercut the appeal of this attempt at a unified interpretation. Even more important, the booklet had a very limited circulation. Even temple employees largely ignored it, and told the more standard version of the temple as anonymous ghosts. Like the other attempts at interpretive control, the temple simply swallowed up and digested this one. With no social control over interpretation, each attempt to impose a clear meaning on the Eighteen Lords failed.

## ACADEMIC VERSIONS

Academic readings of the temple necessarily differ from these other interpretations in their intellectual context, goals, style and means of transmission. Yet like all the others, academic versions also impose a single interpretation, molding a single order on a saturated original that remains overstocked with latent orders but reducible to none. While academic analyses of this specific temple are rare, it nevertheless provides a good example for theories about cultural resistance or acquiescence. By taking up both possibilities here, I want to show how either of these possible academic readings – as resistance or as accommodation – captures real potentials of the Eighteen Lords. Yet, like the other versions I have been discussing, they also lose sight of the great allure inherent in the temple's interpretive chaos, and fail to capture most people's real experience. In fundamental ways, then, academic theories (including this one) resemble folk precipitations of the temple.

Much about the Eighteen Lords resembles other cases where no organized or open resistance takes place, but the argument for cultural resistance looks strong. In some ways, the temple and associated ghost cults in Taiwan bear a striking resemblance to Devil worship by the miners and rural proletarians in Colombia and Bolivia that Michael Taussig discussed (1980). In both cases, rapidly changing social conditions promoted elements of traditional religious practice that resonated with the amoral and competitive aspects of capitalism. For example, Colombian claims about huge profits from bedeviled money that had been baptized instead of a baby have a striking affinity with the stolen umbilical cord as gambling talisman in the *Eighteen Lords* movie. Both empowered their masters to make easy, unearned profits, and both doomed babies as a result. Taussig saw this as a metaphor for (and a damnation of) interest-bearing money under capitalism, and analyzed his Latin American cases primarily as a protest against the capitalist exchange-value economy pushing out earlier values of reciprocity based on a use-value economy.

This explanation will not work in Taiwan; Taiwan before 1970 was in no sense a use-value economy.[64] Yet Taussig's analysis helps clarify one facet of capitalist economic experience in Taiwan, and brings out some of the strong potentials for resistance in the temple that the movie especially emphasized. The Latin American cases help focus on the competition, greed, and lack of community values inherent as one aspect of capitalism. This seamy side of development came to the fore in the 1980s in Taiwan, where ghosts provided the natural carrier for such meanings. The temple offers plenty of evidence for such a reading as a critique of economic change: the anomic and individualized nature of ghosts themselves, the emphasis on the social underworld, the ties to illegitimate wealth, and the reversals of space and time with their valorization of *yin*, darkness, and danger.

I have argued from the beginning, however, that when meaning remains overwhelmingly multivocal, the claim for cultural resistance nearly always has a plausible twin reading as accommodation. The Eighteen Lords are no exception. Parts of the cult pick up on values that shed a very different light on economy and society. The cigarettes, for example, underscore reciprocity, and the dogs emphasize loyalty. When the soap opera made the seventeen humans a religious brotherhood sworn to mutual support, it was picking up on a possibility already inherent in the temple. Even more importantly, the very features that suggest the resistance reading also seem to celebrate capitalism. Ghosts are not really the Devil: they are not evil embodied, and worshipping them is no sin. Ghosts are just the unincorporated dead, pitiful and desperate. Unlike the Devil stories, worshipping the Eighteen Lords need not harm anyone, and in fact offered mostly fun and profit. Rather than condemning capitalist profit, this temple reveled in it.

The same twin readings show up if we focus on politics instead of economics, just as they did for the pig offerings on the community god's birthday. If god worship affirms the political hierarchy and community structure, the recent fad for ghost worship can be seen as a challenge to that structure. On the other hand, as Eco argued about Carnival, one could read all those reversals just as reminders of the structure itself. Every one of these academic readings robs the temple of its thick and complex meanings, just like the non-academic versions of the temple. It should come as no surprise that, in the absence of any institutions of interpretive control, no precipitation comes to dominate the field of possibilities, as each is engulfed by the deluge of meanings in the temple itself. Each of the attempts to control interpretation that I have discussed had self-serving goals (profit, propaganda, promotion), but could only realize these goals by successfully imposing their reading on people. None has managed this.

The benefits of hindsight make it easy to classify the Taiping rebellion as resistance. The Eighteen Lords offer no such luxury. On the contrary, even asking whether such a loosely interpreted cult resists anything forces a problematic reduction of its full range of meaning. The God Worshipers themselves were just as saturated in the late 1840s, but underwent a critical transformation that has never occurred for the Eighteen Lords. The difference between the two cases thus does not lie in some fundamental meaning of their ideas as resistance in one case and acquiescence in the other; the difference lies instead primarily in their very different social organizations of interpretation. Both had potential readings as resistance. The comparison allows us to focus on the cultural and social conditions that allow one potential to be realized while others are lost. What allowed the Taiping to forge a unified interpretation, but not the Eighteen Lords? Given the many attempts to control the meaning of the Taiwanese ghosts, both academic and popular, why have none of them made much difference? The following chapter takes up various broader attempts to control interpretation in Chinese religion, nearly all of which fail. Indeterminate meaning creates a free space that places powerful limits on any form of cultural domination. I will argue in addition that the particular nature of this ghost cult and its social relations make a unified interpretation as resistance – to either Taiwan's economic or political order – unlikely.

# 10

# The Limits to Cultural Domination

Attempts to forge a single, shared meaning fail when no strong social relations of interpretation support them. Only the enormous and difficult social transformation of the Taiping movement bolstered and energized the creation of their new ideology. In the absence of any comparable organization for most of Chinese popular religion, the maintenance of its free space against the propagation of explicit, unified interpretations should be no surprise. The one social organization large and powerful enough to exert an effective influence was the state. While Guangxi in the 1840s had a feeble and faltering state, Taiwan since World War II has had a powerful and intrusive one, especially concerned with control over ideas. That state has often tried to influence religious interpretation, yet it never succeeded, even at its most authoritarian. The power of indeterminate free space like the Eighteen Lords temple allowed it to digest attempts at control, and placed strict limits on the possibility of cultural domination. The temple illuminates the weakness of even a strong state, which cannot construct tight organizations of interpretive control everywhere at once.

## HEAT, NOISE, AND CHAOS

Chinese governments, including the imperial bureaucracy, Taiwan and the People's Republic, have always struggled against "chaos" (*luan*). Chaos describes the breakdown of the natural order of things, from revolutions and natural disasters to premarital sex and messily arranged furniture. Chaos, in other words, describes the very values of overwhelming sight, sound, action, and meaning celebrated in the popular concept of heat and noise, where neat structures collapse and order is unclear. Overmyer (1989) documents how the state consistently deplored this side of popular religion, hoping to detoxify it through official ritual regulations. The *Collected*

169

*Important Documents of the Song Dynasty*, for example, described the destruction of over a thousand spirit medium shrines in the year 1111. The point was to protect the world from those who "do weird and immoral things and damage popular customs," and who "lead astray the sons and daughters of good families to transmit their teachings and weird rituals" (Overmyer, 1989:40). As I have argued, spirit mediums imply an inherent threat to order, whatever they actually say. By their nature, the divinely inspired statements of mediums were chaos, challenging the authority of the state by providing a new and unquestionable voice outside official control.

### Controlling Chaos

In an unenforced attempt to control all the chaos of popular religion, the *Collected Statutes of the Great Ming Dynasty* banned most worship: "The common people are to make offerings to uncared for ghosts of the village and district and to the spirits of their grandparents and parents. They may also sacrifice to the god of the stove. All other [sacrifices] are prohibited" (Overmyer, 1989:23). These attempts to control chaos existed mostly on paper, more as self-proclamations of ideals than actual policies. Yet there were also regular state attempts to have a real influence on popular religious practice.

As I have documented elsewhere for the annual ghost festival in Taiwan, these attempts had very little effect (Weller 1987b). That festival had become a large, raucous affair in nineteenth-century Taiwan, when tens of thousands might gather for the rowdy ritual. Yao Ying (whom we met earlier as an official trying to stop the early Taiping) also spent time in Taiwan, where he attempted to manipulate the festival by writing a special ritual text to be read, urging peace in the fractious populace (Yao, 1957:85–87). Taiwan's first governor took the stronger step of banning the ritual entirely in 1889 (*Taiwansheng Tongzhi*, 1980:18). Neither attempt left signs of any effect at all in the historical record.

The Nationalists brought a much stronger state to Taiwan with some very different foundations. Yet almost immediately, they took similar steps to control the festival. Newspapers reported in 1948 that police would disperse any performance of the ritual in certain parts of Taiwan, as part of the general policy of "suppressing chaos and being frugal" (*kanluan jieyue*) (*Xinsheng Bao*, 9 August 1948:6). While they lightened their touch considerably in the years that followed, they continued to discourage large ritual performances as wasteful extravagance. In 1960, for example, the government held meetings to discourage large meat offerings and feasts during the festival (*Xinsheng Bao*, 3 September 1960:3). They offered prizes to communities that saved the most. Data on the number of pigs slaughtered, however, again showed that the campaign had no success (Weller, 1985:58).

The more indirect effects of the government's efforts appeared when I was living in Sanxia in 1978. The major community temple held a planning meeting, where the influential leaders of the temple called together all the village heads to plan for the ghost festival. Constantly appealing to the government for approval of various aspects of their ongoing reconstruction, the leadership urged a token gesture toward government desires by asking people to bring only vegetarian offerings to the festival. The village heads opposed the idea immediately, and as usual, the attempt to manipulate the festival failed.

Like most large temples, Sanxia's also made other relatively inconsequential nods toward official preferences. The temple management wrote a formal introduction to the temple, which is translated into English and offered only to occasional tourists. It suggests a version of the deity that neatly fits the pattern from the Eighteen Lords and Liao Tianding soap operas. Co Su Kong, we learn, tried unsuccessfully "to rally patriots to preserve the Sung [Song] Dynasty from invasion by Genghis Khan, who, in 1206, founded the Yuan or Mongol Dynasty. Inspired by his example, [the god's] descendants helped greatly in the overthrow of the Yuan Dynasty and the establishment in 1368 of the [ethnically Chinese] Ming Dynasty" ("Brief Introduction...", 1990). Once again a Chinese hero fights the good fight against the invading hordes. The description neatly ignores other aspects of the legend that fit the official line less well, like the hero's retirement to the mountains as a Buddhist hermit, or the locally far more salient stories of the miraculous help he has given not to the nation, but only to residents of his own turf around Sanxia. Except for the temple management and a very occasional tourist who picks up the information sheet, this is another interpretation without an audience.

Another very similar instance of this pattern occurs in "Mountainstreet" village (Feuchtwang, 1992:182–183). They have many versions of their god, Ang Gong, including the usual very local miracle stories. An official school version, however, associated the deity with two Song Dynasty patriots. In fact, these men actually existed in the Tang, several centuries earlier, but the transformation to the Song makes a more officially welcome tale of fights against barbarian occupiers.

## Creating Alternatives

A secular state like Taiwan no longer has the option of trying to control popular religion by offering a wholesale alternative, as the imperial state had done in the official state cult. The current government does, however, retain a small echo of the old rituals in an annual celebration honoring Confucius on his birthday. The ritual takes place at Taipei's Confucian temple, and claims to reconstruct traditional practice. Confucius' birthday differs radically from popular ritual. It is literally a performance, acted in front of an invited audience of seated notables, and quite different in character from the chaotic comings and goings and broad participation in popular ritual. It is strictly lineal in organization, with the name of each stage droned out by a celebrant, unlike the complex and multiple action of everyday religion. Even the music is simple and straightforward, in contrast to the polyrhythmic drums and wailing reeds in popular ritual. The Confucian ritual comes off as a thin and frozen anachronism, completely lacking heat and noise. In the spirit of Confucius himself, they have rooted out all chaos from the ritual. The advantage of a thin performance in front of a select audience lies in the ability to control interpretation, just as it did when the state cult really existed. Quite unlike popular ritual, everything is neatly boxed up here.

Unknown to most of Sanxia's people, the Co Su Kong temple performs a very similar ritual at the lunar new year. When I saw it in 1978, it began at 11:30 on the last night of the old year. The ritual had been organized by Li Meishu, the head of the reconstruction and a powerful figure in the town. The participants included some of his personal followers and much of the elite of the older generation, especially those politically allied with Li – people like the son of Sanxia's last official *xiucai* degree holder. There were no spectators at all, except for a few people who wandered in by accident. Li explained that when the temple reconstruction was finished, they would do the ritual with the doors closed, keeping the masses out. Li had designed the ritual on the model of the ceremony in the Confucian temple. It began with an announcer who gravely intoned each stage: three sets of solemn single beats on a drum, a procession of the participants, a hand washing, and three presentations of offerings and incense, interspersed with bows and musical interludes. The music resembled the Confucian performance, although they substituted elite instruments like the *guqin* for the archaic instruments in the official ritual. In both cases, though, the music was simple, quiet, and very different from popular religious music. The celebrant described the offerings with archaic terms (like "burying the hair and blood" ), but in fact they resembled standard meat offerings, paper spirit money, plus some wine in an archaic vessel.

By keeping the public away, and by keeping the ritual simple, linear and tied to Confucian texts, Li managed to eliminate most of the surfeit of meaning in popular ritual. By the same token, he also eliminated all the excitement and interest for most people. A marked contrast occurred just a few minutes after the Confucian ritual ended, when hundreds of people gathered in front of the temple, all struggling to be the first to offer incense in the new year. The stroke of midnight brought a wild flailing of burning incense sticks and waving arms as people pushed to be the first at the incense pot. The occasion had apparently led to violence in the past, and the temple management now collected all the incense and put it in the pot together. Quite appropriately for all the heat and noise, the huge pile of incense immediately burst into a roaring bonfire. The juxtaposition of the two rituals marked the contrast powerfully – the cool and thin Confucian ritual preceding the hot and thick popular affray, verging on the edge of social chaos.

Similar thinning occurs wherever elites take firm control over ritual, trying to make sure that neither interpretation nor social action get out of hand. Watson describes how a powerful New Territories lineage elite, which legitimates some of its power through a local Tian Hou (Mazu) temple, runs temple festivals that are "remarkable for their utter lack of religious fervor," and whose religious content "is understated in the extreme" (Watson, 1985:318). Typically, their effort to promote their own interpretation of Tian Hou as a symbol of lineage territorial hegemony has little effect, as other groups maintain very different interpretations. Even the use of the elite-controlled self-defense force to guarantee religious orthodoxy by "encouraging" attendance at temple festivals failed to control interpretation itself (Watson, 1985:315). This tension between lively saturation and thin precipitation creates a dilemma for anyone hoping to dominate interpretation: successfully limiting the possibilities undercuts much of the popular appeal, while retaining thick ritual risks losing control over interpretation.

## Sects

I have been arguing that attempts to unify religious interpretation in China typically fail, unable to construct the social institutions of interpretation that might overcome the necessary watering down of vivid ritual. Pietistic sects in Taiwan, however, offer an interesting and important exception. Like the Taiping, they succeeded through new kinds of social organization, although they have absolutely no interest in violent resistance. These sects have grown rapidly over the last few years in Taiwan, and now have millions of followers. While they come in many variants, they typically create focussed congregations of believers centered on spirit writing sessions, where a possessed medium writes messages from the gods. The selection of gods may be very eclectic, sometimes including Jesus or Mohammed as deities in the pantheon. Unlike popular versions of spirit writing, where the illegible characters allow any number of possible readings and people come and go freely, these are tightly organized sessions with easily legible characters. Wealthier sects often publish the results of their sessions, and often have study groups that propagate unified interpretations. Many of them also evangelize actively.

One sect I visited in Kaohsiung in 1978 received patronage from several very wealthy businessmen and politicians. Like Weberian Protestants, they emphasized especially the importance of actual accomplishments in the secular world. The group itself met about every third day. One man, an employee of the largest patron, led each session.[65] Dressed in a white robe, he lectured about a dozen followers on the meaning of the most recent spirit writing session. These Sunday school equivalents have no parallel at all in popular religious practice, and neither does the magazine (*Raozhi*, 1978) the group published to disseminate its ideas. This tight congregational order allowed a kind of unity in interpretation that is impossible for most Chinese religion.

After the lecture, everyone put on robes to worship at their altar and begin the spirit writing. Men stood on the left and women on the right. We bowed as a group to the altar, and four representatives offered incense, fruit, and tea. This neatly organized regimen

contrasted sharply with popular practice, but resembled the officia-
lized Confucian rituals a little in feeling. The medium went easily
into trance, when the god immediately asked that foreigners not
take photographs. The leader later explained that, although this
particular sect was legal, they worried about government disappro-
val. The god then wrote the continuation of his ongoing commentary on the Daoist classic, the Daodejing. From the neatly organized
ritual, to the study sessions, to the magazine, this group had created
a social organization that could effectively disseminate and enforce
an interpretation based in spirit mediumship. The mechanism was
not as powerful as the Taiping, which could enforce its precipitated
version through legal and punitive means because it had arrogated
the full powers of the state. Instead, these sects tend to fission over
differences of interpretation, much like their Protestant equivalents.[66] For both the Taiping and the sects, however, novel forms
of social organization allowed successful control over interpretation.

The largest of these sects, the Way of Unity (Yiguan Dao) was
illegal for many years in Taiwan, and only came above ground with
the general loosening up in the late 1980s. Chinese governments had
always disliked spirit mediumship in all forms, because it tends to
foment "chaos." In other words, they understood that possessed
revelations are inherently difficult to control, regardless of what the
medium may actually say. The state reserved most of its wrath and
power, however, for just such sects as the Way of Unity, which
successfully managed to unify and control an alternative interpretation. When new sources of meaning became organized and united,
they moved from chaos to heterodoxy (*xie*), and the state's reaction
moved up an order of magnitude. While such sects did occasionally
rebel, the Taiwanese versions as a group were politically conservative and morally upright by official standards. The problem lay in
their sources of legitimacy rather than their messages, in their
implications rather than their actions. The government disliked
the chaos of indeterminate ritual, but mostly tolerated it. Organized
interpretive alternatives, however, had to be crushed if possible –
until recently even in a secular state like Taiwan.

There is safety in overloaded meaning exactly because the multiplicity of possibilities always includes a potential reading as
accommodation, as when the Eighteen Lords appear as nationalist
heroes on television. Leaving meaning saturated discourages political organization, but also makes repression difficult – no clear
target exposes itself for attack. Organized and explicitly worked out

systems outside the state, however, lose their multivocal defenses and invite repression. In China, just the act of creating such an explicit system could be seen as a political challenge, no matter how innocuous the actual content.

## THE STATE AND INTERPRETIVE COMMUNITIES

In twentieth-century Taiwan, many of the social institutions of religious interpretation had weakened even further than the usual low level in China. Daoists had been cut off from the sources of orthodoxy in mainland monasteries, and other means of religious transmission like itinerant storytellers gradually died out. Most important, though, has been the gradual retirement of the state from the business of religious interpretation. From the founding of the Republic of China, its Nationalist Party leaders had been dedicated modernizers, as much in the cultural as in the economic sense. Part of that effort meant a dedication to rationality and science instead of "superstition," even as their Western-style constitution guaranteed civil liberties like freedom of religion.

The result was an awkward compromise, where organized, textual traditions like Buddhism gained approval as religion, while the bulk of popular practice became unpalatable superstition (Duara, 1991). In a series of laws created between 1928 and 1930, the Nationalists "spoke of religious authority as being obsolete in the age of popular sovereignty, of 'superstition as an obstacle to progress,' and of the superstitious nation becoming 'the laughing stock of the scientific world'" (Duara, 1991:79). They retained only the institutionally controlled traditions, plus a thin version of certain inspirational deities like Confucius or Guan Gong. As Duara argues, this flattening of religion did more than just reflect their modernist values; it also attempted to expand the power of the state by removing alternate sources of ideas (Duara, 1991:80–81). Like the other attempts at cultural domination I have been discussing, however, this one transformed nothing at the popular level because it failed to remake local social relations of religious interpretation.

The official attitude favoring religious freedom but against "irrational" ideas helps to explain the halting and ineffectual attempts at religious control in Taiwan since the Japanese occupation ended. With the real increase in civil liberties in Taiwan in the 1980s, the dedication to religious freedom has further undercut attempts at control. This culminated most publicly in the legalization of all the pietistic sects, and the sudden appearance of the entire movement from underground. By renouncing a religious stand of its own, a modernizing state like Taiwan finds it very difficult even to attempt to influence religious interpretation.

Unlike education, the media, or politics, the government has very little direct institutional control over religion. There is no priestly hierarchy that can be forced into particular interpretations, nor is there any real platform for preaching revised interpretations. At the same time, the political costs of repressing popular ritual altogether are too great, especially because the current secular government does not really see religion as much of a threat. Unable to speak from within a religious context, the state must choose between ignoring religion or simply repressing it. Taiwan has mostly ignored it, spiked with irregular and ineffective episodes of mild repression. As long as religious practice always left open acquiescent interpretations and never organized into open resistance, it remained a safe and free space.

The weakness of state control over religion is ironic. After all, Taiwan has had a powerful, authoritarian state with only a single ruling party (which learned its political organizing at the hands of the Comintern), a powerfully ideological education system, strong control over all the media, and few qualms (until recently) about crushing dissent. A stern sedition law allowed the government to silence voices of opposition, and the state of military emergency stemming from the Communist insurrection ended only in 1987. The tightly controlled media censored itself before the government could step in. When I first went to Taiwan in 1976, the television stations interspersed commercials with quotes from Jiang Jieshi [Chiang Kai-shek], and walls conveyed patriotic slogans about retaking the mainland. Magazines that spoke too freely quickly found themselves shut down, and the foreign press showed up heavily censored or not at all until the relaxation of the 1980s. Patriotism was a constant theme; people were expected to stand when the flag appeared, even if only at the closing moments of the day's television broadcast. School children had to refer to Jiang Jieshi as Lord Jiang (Jiang Gong) after his death, and were punished for speaking the local dialect in school.

At the same time, the government attempted to inculcate a revived Confucianism that would both replace the Japanese influence in Taiwan and challenge the Communist ideas across the

Taiwan Strait. From the schools to the legislature, one heard attempts to enforce a value system of filial piety writ large, where the proper respect of children for parents and wives for husbands paralleled a filial respect of citizens for the state. Each had his or her proper place in society. They were attempting to create a shared ideology based on patriotism, loyalty, and a kind of Confucianism read through modern eyes, stressing the family as a root metaphor for broader benevolent political control and obedience.

People learned to speak this language in appropriate contexts, and its fit with some aspects of daily experience made it more convincing. Yet it remained only one fairly clear thread in a knotted skein, and never replaced the competing moralities lurking in corners of popular religion. The government too slipped on Taiwan's uncontrolled and open-ended religion, in spite of all their attempts at unifying morality. The Weberian religious revolution, where new national, civic values would replace religion (e.g., Geertz, 1973a, Bellah, 1965:202–203), never took place in Taiwan. While government power successfully prevented the formulation of strong alternatives to its values, even such a strong state could not fully penetrate saturated space to create its own singular cultural world. As evidence for this, a chorus of competing voices quickly replaced the old monotone with the remarkable relaxation of state control over mental life in the last few years.

Intellectuals have quickly discovered Marx (although not as quickly as East European intellectuals have abandoned him), whose works had been forbidden until recently. Businessmen have discovered cheap labor in the mainland, politicians have discovered an opposition party, and popular religion has discovered the Eighteen Lords. All speak to the alternative values that lay just below the surface until recently, drowned out by the more speakable political orthodoxy. Public revelations of corruption and abuse of power by the Jiang family and other leaders have increased the new political and cultural freedoms. Most notorious were political scandals like the alleged involvement of the government in the murder of Jiang Nan, a Chinese–American scholar working on a biography of Jiang Jingguo that politically powerful members of the Jiang family found threatening. Financial scandals have also hurt credibility and helped speed the stripping of the old veneer.

The Everybody's Happy lottery provides a minor example of this. In addition to getting winning numbers through popular ritual, rumor held that there was also a secular alternative for those who knew how to get it. Members of the Bamboo Gang, a kind of Taiwanese Mafia, had allegedly carried out the murder of Jiang Nan at government request. When publicity about the case blew up, according to the story, members of the government paid off the mob for its silence by publishing in the newspaper a coded indication of the last two digits of the winning lottery number, in advance of the drawing. Those who knew how to read the code could make a fortune. This "newspaper method" of getting lottery numbers rivaled religious methods in popularity. It indicated a total lack of confidence in the honesty of the government, especially because the lottery drawings were televised and clearly random (Qu, 1987:30–31).

No state can fully control values. Any set interpretation faces the possibility of reinterpretation, placing fundamental limitations on conscious mystification and cultural domination. Taiwan faces the paradox of a modern, powerful state which has seen the resurgence of religious values that it does not fully share. Max Weber suggested one possible explanation for this modern combination of a strong state with growing religious ideologies. His description of the modern, rational, bureaucratic type of authority relies least on any kind of shared values beyond an acquiescence to the rule of law (Weber, 1978:217–225). In contrast, legitimacy in traditional authority rests on a shared system of custom and traditional values, and in charismatic authority rests on belief in the sanctity or special character of the individual leader (Weber, 1978:215). Only bureaucratic authority gains its legitimacy from what claims to be an abstract system, created by human intention for pragmatic ends. Values certainly continue to exist, and to an extent underlie the system of law, but they occupy a far less central position in creating an ideology of bureaucratic legitimacy than for the other types of authority.

The new religious growth in Taiwan and other modern states reflects a need for meaning that these states cannot meet, in large part because their legitimacy no longer explicitly rests on a shared set of traditional values. Implicitly, many values continue to be shared, but these are less the product of the active interference of the state than of the entire social formation. The problem is especially serious for religion, because the secular government can make no case for legitimate interference, nor does the decentralized nature of the religious organization allow for much direct intervention. Religion, especially under the very loose political and clerical control it has typically had in China, is inherently open to multiple interpretations. This is even more true for Carnivalesque religion like the Eighteen Lords, where no one has clear authority to impose an interpretation and the ritual itself is filled with innovative and complex possibilities.

The Eighteen Lords in action affirmed the lack of fully shared values in Taiwan, certainly a lack of consistent Confucian values. If the lack stemmed from the rapid social transformations of the last few decades, and especially the last few years, it has not been remedied by the government, in spite of repeated attempts. While decades of firm control over information and education helped eliminate alternative political voices, they also helped rob the government itself of legitimacy. People may not have heard other versions of the world, but they knew that the one version they were receiving was bent to particular purposes. The political relaxation of the last few years, the opening to new voices, has thus created a babble of competing interpretation.

Contrary to some predictions, then, this evidence suggests that the advent of modernizing states has actually increased free space for religion by removing the state's right to create religious interpretations of its own. Even more unexpectedly, the Taiwan case suggests that even authoritarian states have only ineffective and partial control over culture, in spite of extensive campaigns. Crushing alternative explicit interpretations leaves the ironies and ambiguities of uncontrolled space untouched, and even encourages their spread. As long as no challenging, organized interpretations ever come openly to the front, areas like popular religion can remain a safe haven for all kinds of meaning, like a desert waiting to bloom at the first hint of rain. At the same time, the thin and ideological alternatives that the state offers in exchange have little inherent power to convince. I will take these issues up again in Chapters 11 and 12.

## SATURATION AND RESISTANCE

This look at nineteenth-century Guangxi and twentieth-century Taiwan suggests some broad patterns in the relationships between saturation and precipitation. Far from confirming the inevitability of rationalization, the evidence suggests that the teeming overgrowth of unclarified meaning remains an important aspect even of modern societies. Guangxi disintegrated Hong Xiuquan's more rationalized ideology, and the Taiping finally retook interpretive control only by a wrenching transformation of their entire social organization. Taiwan has fostered a thriving, expanding indeterminate world in popular religion, in the face of both a successfully modernizing economy and a disapproving authoritarian state.

One reason these Carnivalesque areas survived so robustly is their easy response to social change. With no dogma to defend and no sacred canon, with few technicians of the sacred and no powerful social institutions of interpretation, little stood in the way of new developments. The inconsistent multivocality of these heaps of meaning also provides them with a prior fund of new directions for adaptation to new circumstances, just as a genetically diverse species will adapt more easily to a changed environment than a species of clones. The Eighteen Lords sprouted from just such a process. Based on standard ghosts, they patched together elements that had been there all along, but that suddenly became prominent with the economic and political changes of the 1980s.

Much the same process explains how disorganized interpretation (or no interpretation at all) defuses attempts at cultural domination. In a world of multiple and inconsistent possibilities, suggestions of explicit and organized interpretations just get thrown into the pot along with the rest of the stew. They may complicate the mix a little, but generally induce no major changes. Nearly every attempt to control interpretation that I have discussed failed, from the modernizing frowns at popular religion to the television version of the Eighteen Lords. The only exceptions invented new social organizations: the Taiping took control over spirit possession as they took up arms, and the sects developed congregations centered on explicit interpretation.

This surfeit of possibilities makes overloaded interpretive space a home for irony and ambiguity, where meaning seems to shift, like the Tristan chord, with the first effort to pin it down. Attempts to impose an interpretation thus face the jeopardy of ironic readings. This has been the fate of the carefully documented genealogical claims of the Lian family about the Eighteen Lords, and of the equally carefully performed ritual justification for the fake Eighteen Lords temple. Both versions suffered rereadings as greedy claims on temple income. Authoritarian control promotes this kind of shifty meaning even further, as explicit statements become dangerous and people seek safety in ambiguity. Worse still, cultural domination can further hone an ear for irony and cynicism, as the denial of alternative voices undercuts the credibility of the government itself.

Is this resistance? Only in the sense that its pool of possibilities includes all kinds of alternatives – resistance, accommodation, and a great deal with no direct political implications at all. Resisting nothing directly is one of the keys to its survival. The temptation to label all complexly indeterminate meaning as cultural resistance risks losing sight of the process through which it might become active resistance, where one interpretation overtakes all the others. It matters, after all, that the Taiping became a huge rebellion while the Eighteen Lords seem to be fading away, in spite of their equally messy and multivocal beginnings, packed with alternative interpretations. Nevertheless, the existence of such alternatives is crucial; they provide the seeds around which new movements may develop. I have thus preferred to talk about potentials for resistance, and reserve the term "resistance" proper for movements born when a single understanding as resistance crystallizes out.

The core of realized resistance lies in that critical moment of rationalization, and the new social relations of interpretation that must accompany it. Even though a resaturation of the Taiping began almost immediately, the central social and ideological innovations of 1850 shaped everything that was to come. While the focus on a surfeit of meaning clarified the important similarities between the early Taiping and the Eighteen Lords, the differences between the two cases have demanded a clearer look at when and how unified interpretations develop. The last few chapters have argued that disorganized interpretation, which typifies Chinese popular religion, has a robust elasticity that allows it to soak up attempts at uniting people in an explicit interpretation. What allowed the Taiping to succeed where the Taiwanese ghosts failed?

Important differences in the social relations of interpretation gave the early Taiping a much stronger potential to resist than the Eighteen Lords. First, the Taiping concentration on God and gods gave it an immediate focus on the heart of politics – the community. When the Taiping destroyed temples or worshiped God, they implicitly offered new definitions of community and gained the possibility of organizing large groups of people. The Eighteen Lords, on the other hand, systematically abandoned community for personal concerns, celebrating competition and individuality at the expense of any form of solidarity. It is difficult to see how such ideas could support strong political organization.

In addition, although both states were weak in their ability to control religious interpretation, the imperial state in 1840s Guangxi was generally feeble in ways that the 1980s Taiwan government was not. The broad breakdown of social order in Guangxi both created a need for effective new social organization and removed major obstacles to innovators. New forms of Taiping social and ideological organization thus found many followers, but brought down only ineffective repression from the weak state. The combination of new and appropriate ideas with the possibility of new forms of social organization to control interpretation (among other things) laid the groundwork for the Taiping transition to resistance. In spite of the sense of crisis in Taiwan in the 1980s, there was no comparable breakdown of social order nor any abdication of the state's power to challenge alternative political organizations. The Eighteen Lords thus offered neither ideas compatible with political organizing nor the possibility of forging new social relations of interpretation with little interference.

In contrast, the pietistic sects in Taiwan have managed to construct new religious and social forms. Like the Taiping, they also deal in gods rather than ghosts, and they have created new institutions to preserve their interpretations. They managed this, however, only by avoiding any possible reading as resistance, and thus avoiding the wrath of the state. Even so, they could only come above ground with the increase of civil liberties in the last decade. Taken together with the Taiping, they reinforce the intimate relationships between symbols and the social organization of interpretation. Yet these are also the exceptions; the vast majority of explicit interpretations simply dissolve back into the whole, unable to construct new institutions of meaning. Looking to the social organization of interpretation clarifies just how difficult and fragile precipitation really is.

# Part IV

## CONCLUSION : TIANANMEN AND BEYOND

# 11

# Institutions of Control, Institutions Beyond Control

While both the cases I have discussed so far involve Chinese religion, the general processes are neither necessarily Chinese nor necessarily religious. Under the right circumstances anywhere, meaning develops a life cycle of its own. Tumultuous times encourage a profusion of new and complex possibilities that elbow their way in among the old taken-for-granted ideas. Both the early God Worshipers and the Taiwanese ghost cult took part in this process, as did the many cases of non-Chinese spirit possession I have already discussed. So did the Virgin of Guadalupe, symbol of Mexican independence, with her Aztec moon and cloak of roses (Wolf, 1958). And so did Yankee Doodle, who changed from the boorish object of British jeering to a revolutionary symbol. The resulting intertwined profusion of meaning has a strong potential to resist – to foster an interpretation that opposes the status quo – but also harbors many other possible developments.

Occasionally, as the Taiping rebels showed, powerful institutions may be able to squeeze order from such chaos, creating a new form of meaning where interpretations claim to be clear and unified. That transformation can spark social movements, and form the seed for new mechanisms of social control. In some sense, every revolutionary ideology crystallizes out of the mixed ideas that preceded it. Yet every new order itself immediately becomes vulnerable to processes of accumulating meaning that help to undermine its control and sap its power. The successful Taiping seizure of control over meaning in 1850 became riddled with new interpretations (and remnants of old ones) as soon as the rebels left home. Similarly, Taiwan's political loosening of the 1980s showed just how much the official ideology had been built on a foundation of shifting cultural sand. And as I will discuss here, even the great socialist ideologies have far less effective control than initially appears, as cycles of saturation, precipitation and new saturation occur there too.

187

The evidence from Taiping rebels and Taiwanese ghosts implies that official interpretations everywhere are necessarily thin and fragile, no matter whether they come from the established state or a rebellious movement. Modern states (both socialist and capitalist) face this problem with particular pressure, because they have given up most claims to a legitimacy based on transcendent values of tradition or religion. Any attempt to enliven their authority with thicker symbols may offer more convincing power, but immediately opens the door to alternative interpretations. Just as importantly, most people, in their daily lives, remain content with implicit meanings and independent from institutionalized meaning, always leaving room for alternative interpretations by not pushing any explicit interpretation too far. These cases show the grave difficulties of creating interpretive unity, either to cement an official hegemony or to foment resistance.

The People's Republic of China should provide an acid test for this approach. Rarely has any state developed such powerful institutions to impose and foster unified interpretations. Theorists of socialism as totalitarianism have especially clarified how the attempt to institutionalize and universalize interpretation works. Such theories paint an extreme picture of an end never realized in practice, and they have grown less popular lately. Yet they also describe how strongly controlled interpretations might be maintained over the long run, and why cultural domination is so important. As Hannah Arendt put it in one of the earliest such studies: "Totalitarianism is never content to rule by external means, namely, through the state and a machinery of violence; thanks to its peculiar ideology and the role assigned to it in this apparatus of coercion, totalitarianism has discovered a means of dominating and terrorizing human beings from within. In this sense it eliminates the distance between the rulers and the ruled" (Arendt, 1958:325).

The central techniques such theories describe atomize and homogenize individuals. People lose social contact with each other apart from the state, while also denying any divisions among themselves. The only division is between the single People and their external enemy (Lefort, 1986:297). The politics of competing organizations comes to an end, yet everything becomes politicized, explicit and ideological. There are no bystanders, as everything that happens in the world must be interpreted to support doctrine (Zinoviev, 1984:221). All interpretation must be made fully explicit, thinned down to a single layer, and enforced through an institutional apparatus that extends from the mass organizations, to small group discussion meetings, to the details of daily life. At least in theory, no room remains for ambiguities as the state systematically strips away alternative sources of meaning.

Language itself can come to reflect the thin official ideology in an impoverished syntax and lexicon, where even the very means to express alternative meaning may disappear (e.g., Thom, 1989:17–59; Blazek, 1991). "A power of discourse as such is constituted, a power which subjugates its agents, passes through them rather than developing within them, inscribes them in an impersonal knowledge which cuts them off from the experience of others and of things" (Lefort, 1986:316).

Mass criticism meetings during the Cultural Revolution underwent just such a ritualization and formalization of language and structure. The meetings invariably began and ended with one of a small number of acceptable revolutionary songs (where syntax, semantics, and even tone and rhythm are frozen). Between the songs, the audience shouted formulaic threatening slogans while the object of criticism was brought on. After a period of criticism, the victim would be led off, and the audience shouted positive slogans of homage to Mao (Ji, Kuiper and Shu, 1990; Madsen, 1984:80–82). Every stage followed a rigid pattern, where acceptable language allowed for only a few variations on set structures. Such potent restrictions on syntactic and semantic flexibility typify languages of power everywhere (Bloch, 1975), and they attempt to dominate all discourse in totalizing regimes.

No actual societies carry this project out with full success, but one can at least see these processes at work in China and elsewhere. Especially in the realm of culture and ideology, many commentators have seen the mechanisms of control as quite successful. Yet the analysis of the Taiping rebels and Taiwanese ghosts strongly suggests inherent limits on the power of any such official interpretation, and thus limits on totalitarian theory. Indeed, the Chinese government clearly lost control of meaning in the spring of 1989, in spite of their potent and compelling domination of institution and interpretation. Still more significantly, though, the aftermath of Tiananmen showed the frailty of official interpretations even in the midst of a major campaign where all the old political machinery has been brought to bear in a vain attempt to unify China around a single shared interpretation.

This chapter and the next will follow the life cycle of the meaning of those demonstrations in Tiananmen, bringing conclusions based on the Taiping rebels and Taiwanese ghosts to a radically different social situation. Even in the People's Republic, the demonstrations saw a great flood of unorganized interpretation, followed by a powerfully enforced official interpretation of the events, which in turn was undermined with a new and more subtle accretion of uncontrolled meaning.

The events of that spring had been building for some years, with occasional outbursts, especially from students, that died down again fairly quickly.[67] The economic reforms were about a decade old in 1989, and the problems of adding capitalist markets to socialist planning began to grow as clear as the benefits had been a few years earlier. Widespread inflation hurt everyone on a fixed salary, and the government began to backpedal quickly on the reforms, threatening the new entrepreneurs. At the same time, new opportunities and dangers had led to ballooning corruption among government officials and their privileged children. Finally, a relative opening of social relations accompanied by lukewarm campaigns for political orthodoxy encouraged students to push harder at the boundaries that still held them.

This round of protests began when Hu Yaobang, who had been a supporter of intellectual reform before being purged from his post as general secretary of the Party, died on 15 April 1989. Several thousand students in Beijing took to the streets to mourn him, and quickly came up with a list of demands for rehabilitating Hu's reputation, increasing aid to education, and promoting greater political openness. The movement intensified over the next few days, especially after police violently stopped about a thousand noisy students from presenting a wreath at central government offices (Zhongnanhai). By the end of April the movement had escalated dramatically to perhaps a hundred thousand students, with significant involvement from workers and local residents. Several demonstrations brought a million people into Tiananmen Square, in the heart of the capital, and many tens of thousands occupied the square constantly. Comparable movements began to spring up in cities across China.

May brought two obvious opportunities to further invigorate the movement. The first was the anniversary of the May Fourth Movement, the grandfather of the modern student movement in China. That movement had shaken China in 1919, with its strong support for modernization, science and democracy. Science and democracy again became watchwords for the students in 1989. Worried about the possibilities, the government began well publicized meetings with the demonstrators on 3 May.

The media peak came just after the second big opportunity of the month – Gorbachev's visit to China. A large number of students began a hunger strike in Tiananmen Square, capturing the attention of the entire nation. Rejuvenated by the fasting martyrs, the movement brought a million people to the square again on 18 May. Premier Li Peng met with starving student leaders for one last fruitless but riveting round of talks (carried on national television). Zhao Ziyang, the general secretary of the Party, visited the hunger strikers with tears in his eyes. Zhao's sympathetic performance marked the end of government patience (and the end of his own political power before long); Li Peng declared martial law shortly afterward.

The demonstrations began to lose momentum after that, and many students left. Yet even the depleted ranks remaining in the Square constituted a large group, and local crowds always turned back the army's tentative forays toward them. The remaining radical core, and others who had come in recently from the provinces, got new life on 29 May: the Goddess of Democracy, a thirty-foot creation of some Beijing art students, joined them at Tiananmen. At this point, however, both the government and the student leaders were beyond negotiating, and the tragic conclusion on 4 June is well known.

I take up this case more briefly than the other two partly because the details will be much better known to most readers, but also because I intend it primarily to illustrate that the processes I have been discussing thrive even in a very different and apparently unfavorable environment. Culture and meaning under socialism have more complex and mixed roles than appears at first glance, with processes of interpretive integration and disintegration inherent in the structure of the system itself.

## DEATH AND REVOLUTION

For almost the entire time I was living in Nanjing in 1984–1985, the prestigious Nanjing Museum was closed. A sign in front explained that the museum was undergoing renovations, but no one could give a date for the re-opening, and no construction work was visible. As so often happened, the flourishing Chinese grapevine offered a hidden alternative explanation. People explained that the director of the museum, an old cadre from the revolutionary period, had committed suicide after a media campaign accusing him of plagiarism. This was a period when many old cadres felt intense pressure from more educated people with less political background, and the Communist Party was strongly promoting education and skills. The director was a victim of such a struggle, as his well-placed friends apparently could not stop others from making an example of him.

Some early and macabre versions told how he had hanged himself from the museum rafters, and his wife refused to let the body be cut down. Later, the stories settled into a single version. The coffin had been placed in the museum for a final viewing, but the director's family refused to let the body be moved until his name was cleared and he could be buried honorably. The government was embarrassed, but also trapped by having allowed the right to mourn the dead. They resolved the stalemate only after nine months of bickering, with a triumph for the director and his supporters in the government (see also Davenport and Larocque, 1986).

This case of how people can so easily usurp sanctioned mourning offers a minor example of a widespread pattern in China. The most famous case was the large outpouring at Zhou Enlai's death in 1976, where public demonstrations in Tiananmen Square overwhelmed the official funeral plans, and marked the beginning of the end of the Cultural Revolution. Another case occurred in 1988, when demonstrations mourning the murder of a university student at the hands of a street criminal took a political turn. Funerals in China have been subject to much government pressure, and official mourning for fallen cadres is highly formalized in action and explicitly interpreted in eulogies (Whyte, 1988). Yet mourning nevertheless offers a free space, where people have sometimes succeeded in piling new meanings on top of the official version. Recognizing the right to mourn has created a symbolic arena that threatens to escape government control. Indeed, granting the right to mourn often leads to the same accretion of meanings elsewhere. From South Africa to South Korea, funerals have allowed mass demonstrations otherwise impossible.

The 1989 demonstrations in Tiananmen began exactly as such an overenthusiastic funeral that swamped the bounds of government control over interpretation (Esherick and Wasserstrom, 1990:839–

840). By the morning after Hu Yaobang's death on 15 April, students were already stacking new meanings onto the mourning with their own outpouring of wreaths, eulogies and poems of praise (*Ming Pao News*, 1989:4). Both the large white banners they displayed, often featuring the character *dian* ("mourning offering"), and their eulogies fell squarely within accepted funeral traditions. Yet by going beyond the carefully drawn lines of the official ceremony, they also constituted a political usurpation.

Student demands escalated over the next few days, and the movement began to organize. Their guerrilla saturation of the funeral forced the government to upgrade the level of official ceremonies, with a silent tribute by the Central Committee on 17 April, Premier Li Peng's visit to Hu's widow the next day, and a memorial service finally scheduled for 22 April (*Ming Pao News*, 1989:5–7). Yet no amount of official ritual could hold off the students' flinging new meanings onto the thin scaffolding of the government funeral. In attempting to offer an officially approved and politically useful memorial, the state inevitably opened the door to new interpretations. Like any performance large and complex enough to make a powerful statement, official funerals cannot fully control interpretation.

While the issue of Hu Yaobang gradually faded from the scene, the funerary symbolism continued to provide one of the primary stylistic themes throughout the demonstrations. Mourning symbolism in fact extends across East Asian protests, easily recognized by the use of white, the traditional color of death ritual. The theme occurs everywhere, from Japanese anti-nuclear protesters wearing white headbands (a kind of minimal mourning dress) promising death before giving up their cause, to Taiwanese marchers carrying the coffin of slain Democracy, to South Korean students mourning their martyrs. This theme of death began at Tiananmen with the wreaths and funeral eulogies for Hu, and continued with the typical white headbands and white banners of protest later on. The white theme of death and mourning finally culminated in the massive hunger strikes that so ignited both Chinese and foreign audiences. With haggard faces, the hunger strikers wore white headbands and usually white clothes, both mourning for lost ideals and warning of their own impending deaths. When the student leader Wu'er Kaixi appeared on television in pajamas, with an oxygen tube in his nose and almost too weak to stand, the image of a hospital death bed was palpable. Funerals make powerful demonstrations because they easily carry many levels of meaning, always including the official line but never limited to it.

A quite different theme – this one red – also flowed through the demonstrations alongside the white theme. Red in China has always been the color of joy and luck: newborns and brides wear red, red verses are pasted over the door at New Year's, and cash gifts come in red envelopes. In addition, of course, red in the People's Republic of China is also the color of the revolution. The large marches where various work units paraded together under red banners in the spring of 1989 have a history that goes back through the revolution to the May Fourth movement of 1919 (Strand, 1990). Students also picked up a great deal of other Communist and patriotic symbolism. They waved red national flags in Tiananmen Square, held portraits of Mao as they marched, and sang the Internationale as they waited for tanks. One telling incident occurred on 23 May, when three men defaced the gigantic portrait of Mao that hangs in the square by throwing paint and eggs on it. The demonstrators were reportedly furious about this, caught the hooligans, and turned them in to the police (*New York Times*, 24 May 1989: A10).[68]

Both the white and red themes pose typical problems of interpretation. Was Hu's death simply a cover for a purely political confrontation? Were all the declarations of patriotism just a disguise? How, for example, should we understand the Beijing University protest banner that read, "We firmly support the correct leadership of the Communist Party" (*New York Times*, 7 May 1989: I15)? When the correspondent asked students what they meant, he got a combination of tactics and sincerity. When he asked whether they preferred capitalism to socialism, he found little thought had been given to the question. The implications suggest a genuine ambiguity of interpretation, a typically overloaded situation where many meanings are available and no mechanism yet exists to foster a single, unified version. While the government would later claim a shared hidden agenda among the protesters (as they claimed that religion was a mere disguise for Hong Xiuquan's revolutionary agenda), and while some people may well have had such thoughts, their actual actions and statements were inherently multivocalic. Making wreaths and waving flags genuinely show mourning and patriotism, whatever lies in the heart of the actor.

Both the white and red themes held many meanings, and their close cohabitation in Tiananmen Square further mixed the pile of possible interpretations. These demonstrations began and lasted as long as they did because they included politically acceptable meanings along with all their others. The Goddess of Democracy statue that the students erected toward the end further mixed the irresolvable blend of possible interpretations. Clearly referring to the American Statue of Liberty (as the government would emphatically point out), in the Chinese context the statue also evoked images both of socialist realist sculpture and of Guanyin, the popular Bodhisattva of Mercy (Esherick and Wasserstrom, 1990:841). She combined the pro-Western possibilities of an American symbol, the typical socialist labor iconography of muscular women holding torches, and a mothering Chinese goddess. As with most of its symbols, the movement itself would never sort out these various possibilities, and much of its appeal rested on the multiplicity of available meaning.

Even the explicitly stated goals of the movement formed an inconsistent mix. "Democracy" came up over and over, but the concept remained very difficult to pin down in practice. The vague generalities typically floated allowed for much more freedom of interpretation than specific policies would have. In some cases actions spoke louder than words, as the student leaders undercut their own discussions of democracy by emulating the vanguard privileges of the Communist Party. Access to the leadership rested on the same kinds of personal networks that characterized the official bureaucracy; they created a standing committee, liaison offices and a propaganda department; and they surrounded their offices with their own guards (Lubman, 1989).

Even after the tragedy of 4 June, the exile movement recreated many of the same contradictions. Acting just like a vanguard party, the leadership answered accusations of crony-based elitism with the claim that creating an elite group of leaders was more crucial than developing a mass membership organization (Chan and Kwong, 1990:560). The reformist *World Economic Herald* similarly showed a powerful technocratic elitism underlying broader claims (Li and White, 1991). Indeed, student attitudes as traditional Chinese intellectuals bred a sense of their moral duty and privileged right to speak to the state, a special position placing them above the rest of society. Such attitudes greatly limited the possible development of the movement (Perry, 1991).

Quite different issues also rose to the surface as a broader range of people joined the protests. While democracy remained the fuzzy but predominant rallying cry of the students, official corruption and the unaccustomed inflation of the period loomed much larger for the rest of the city's population. Corruption was a very general complaint, greatly exacerbated by the economic half-reforms of the past few years (Meaney, 1991; Oi, 1991). Yet a number of the student participants were themselves children of high cadres, and all at these elite universities had hopes of living lives of relative privilege. The inflation issue was even worse. Even though it clearly rankled anyone on a fixed salary, the students hesitated to bring it up for fear of jeopardizing the reforms themselves. They also thought of themselves occupying the moral high ground, above simple pocketbook issues, as opposed to the strictly materialistic hopes of the workers (Perry, 1991:135).

While more detailed studies of these demonstrations continue, even the short sketch here strongly indicates that Tiananmen in 1989 fits the broad pattern I have been discussing for the Taiping and Taiwan. Far from sharing a unified agenda, the participants piled all kinds of interpretations on a few core symbols – democracy and corruption, death and revolution. They left a mass of unresolved ambiguities and inconsistencies, with plenty of room for alternatives or for no explicit interpretation at all.[69] While some commentators have seen this as a failing of the movement, the multivocality of the symbols was in fact as central to the initial success in Tiananmen as it had been to the early organization of the God Worshipers or to the Eighteen Lords. Indeterminate meaning makes long-term organization very difficult, but provides a powerful core for potential social movements. No "true meaning" could be agreed upon until a means to control interpretation developed. In the end, only the government would develop such an institutionalized interpretation.

## TRUE MEANING REVEALED AND ENFORCED

I have argued for the Taiping that precipitating and institutionalizing a new interpretation can be a key catalyst for resistance. The brutal and tragic ending in Tiananmen on 4 June 1989 meant that the demonstrators would never manage such a transformation to a more stable organization. Yet the state itself eagerly played the same role by revealing a single, rationalized, explicit and very thin interpretation of the events in Tiananmen. Unlike the Taiping, they had no need to create new institutions to impose their reading. At least since their revolutionary days in Yen'an, the Communists had developed a sophisticated and pervasive set of institutions to ensure unity around official interpretations. Rarely has an ideology formed on a better prepared social ground.

The initial move occurred in the *People's Daily* on 26 April, where a major editorial hit the themes that would characterize the government line throughout:

> An extremely small number of people were not involved in mourning Comrade Hu Yaobang, were not trying to promote socialist democracy in China, and were not just a bit unhappy and letting off steam. Under the banner of democracy, they were trying to destroy the democratic legal system. Their goal was to poison people's minds, to create chaos throughout the country, to destroy political stability and unity. This was a planned conspiracy, a riot (*Renmin Ribao*, 26 April 1989; translation revised from Han, 1990:84).

These themes would remain at the core of the official precipitation from then on. A tiny group of "black hands" had misled the students in a vain attempt to destroy the country. The conspiracy theory offers a hidden meaning beneath everything that was said, a meaning that fooled the common people. Only the state was able to pierce the disguise and reveal the true interpretation.[70]

In addition, consistent use of the word *luan* ("chaos") brought up all the old official battles against uncontrollable public events that I have already discussed for Taiwan. The events in Tiananmen were "hot and noisy" by any popular standard, with the constant flood of parades, speeches, hunger strikes, photographers, and occasional musical interludes. The People's Republic strongly echoed both the Republican and imperial states by damning all this as chaos, in the standard official condemnation of popular saturation.

At the time, this was only one voice among many, although it was a very powerful one. The state was still using only one means to propagate its message – the tightly controlled news media. Even official reporting, however, still seemed to hold a mixed message, as extensive coverage of the hunger strike and the students' interviews with top leaders surprised everyone. The *People's Daily* version only fully monopolized discourse after 4 June. Deng Xiaoping finalized the official version in a speech on 9 June that reiterated the *People's Daily* themes. Within a few days, all the media began systematically blasting the so-called counter-revolutionary conspirators in a uni-

vocal drone that still continues (*New York Times*, 15 June 1989; A16).
All the thick possibilities of the spring had been reduced to the
simple themes of chaos and conspiracy.

As the literature on totalitarianism implied, mechanisms to
enforce an interpretation in China go far beyond incessant media
campaigns. The entire population is organized into small political
study groups, whose primary purpose is to settle on a unified and
rationalized mass line (often dictated from above in practice), and
then to enforce commitment to it (Whyte, 1974:18–35). In regular
meetings at their workplaces, these small groups discuss current
events and important policies. During campaigns, people are
expected to criticize both their own failings and those of others,
ostensibly leading everyone to see the light. In principle, at least, the
goal is enthusiastic devotion, and not just simple obedience. By mid-
June, all of this machinery had been focussed on the official
interpretation of the demonstrations. Many of the old Cultural
Revolution techniques were also revived, as the state pulled out all
the stops. Public humiliation met all accused wrong-doers, who often
appeared on television with heads bowed, hair shaved, and wearing
placards describing their crimes (*New York Times*, 18 June 1989: IV1).

The initial campaigns hit college campuses especially hard. Small
group meetings became much more frequent, with Deng's speech as
one of the major texts for study. Students and faculty were also
expected to make full confessions of their errors, and to turn each
other in. Beijing University freshmen took military training instead
of starting school. While this was partially a punishment, and
partially an attempt at more controlled indoctrination, it also fit
with a powerful pro-military theme that dominated the first few
months of the campaign.

The top leaders held an enormous congratulatory meeting for the
military on 29 June, under the banner "The People's Army is
Faithful to the Party" (*Renmin Ribao*, 30 June 1989). Through much
of July, the campaign centered on learning from the lives of ten
soldiers, whom Deng had apotheosized as martyred "Guardians of
the Republic" (*Renmin Ribao*, 6 July 1989; 19 July 1989). Shanghai
residents found themselves celebrating the fortieth anniversary of
the People's Liberation Army entering the city, and an officially
sanctioned slogan for China's independence day celebrated the
glorious victory over counter-revolution (*Renmin Ribao*, 23 July
1989; 10 September 1989).

The campaign broadened in the months that followed, as the government pushed people to "sweep away the yellow." Yellow refers to pornography and other sources of spiritual pollution, and the concept clearly extended to any undesired cultural influences, including especially bourgeois values. Going far beyond a glorification of the military, this new direction brought inner thoughts under scrutiny, and allowed the apparatus for promoting official interpretations its full play in the widest public sphere. Small groups took initial responsibility for identifying and sweeping away yellow wherever it appeared. Here the campaign went well beyond justifying the repression of the demonstrations and trying to restore the reputation of the military. It had expanded into all aspects of daily life and thought.

At the same time, the government began to promote a campaign of nostalgia for old revolutionary heroes and values. While Jiang Zemin urged China to remember the Yen'an spirit and continue to rely on it, the thoughts of Mao Zedong gained new life in the media and even in military study groups (*Renmin Ribao*, 15 September 1989; *Shijie Ribao*, 26 June 1991). Grizzled revolutionary veterans were trotted out to share their spirit with students (*Renmin Ribao* overseas edition, 24 June 1991). Newspapers explained the need for proper respect of the flag, and the 150th anniversary of the Opium War saw a campaign for patriotic education (*Renmin Ribao*, 23 September 1989; 31 March 1990). Capping off the patriotism theme, a proper socialist statue of a worker, a peasant, a soldier and an intellectual, working together rose up on the spot where the Goddess of Democracy had once stood (*New York Times*, 22 September 1989: A4). The officially true interpretation of Tiananmen was clear to everyone.

Most strikingly of all, the government urged everyone to emulate various heroes who had given their young lives in their dedication to a true socialist life. The sudden reemergence of the ghost of Lei Feng at the end of 1989 surprised many observers. Lei Feng was a young soldier who had died in 1962, a sort of super Boy Scout, whose gleaming socialist spirit caused him to help people everywhere. He had been one of the ideological underpinnings of Cultural Revolution campaigns, and his return during a period that generally defined itself in contrast to the Cultural Revolution spoke both to the urgency of this campaign and to the dominance of nostalgia as a theme.

A more contemporary, but very similar, hero named Lai Ning has
become a core model to emulate for middle and elementary school
students. Lai Ning was "a classic example of the new man of the
'four haves' [have ideals, morals, civilization, and discipline]"
(*Renmin Ribao*, 14 October 1990). These martyrs' heartfelt dedication
to socialist ideals far outweighed their particular actions in most
standard descriptions. They always appear as prototypes for a new
kind of human being. The point of such a campaign is to remake
people down to the smallest details of their daily lives, rather than to
promote any specific behaviors. Identity itself is at stake. Discussion
meetings of such models would thus ideally leave no corner of the
human soul unswept, bringing every aspect of thought and behavior under official scrutiny.[71]

## SOCIALIST FREE SPACE

While the Taiping had to change heaven and earth to institutionalize, rationalize and control its ideology, the entire mechanism
already stood ready to use in the People's Republic. Yet just like
the other attempts to precipitate I have discussed, even this most
powerful effort left enormous space for resaturation. While unambiguous resistance occurred only rarely after 4 June, a combination
of irony, cynicism and anomie has undermined any straightforward
loyalty to the official line.

Evidence from other socialist societies, especially now that the
changes in Eastern Europe have led to a flood of new literature,
clarifies how certain areas manage to divert the power of officially
institutionalized meaning. While by no means discarding theories of
totalitarianism, these studies add a view of how socialist mechanisms of control, in an ironic dialectic, create their own contradictions. Both the theoretical and empirical evidence supports authors
arguing for the fundamental internal weakness of what had
appeared to be strong socialist states (e.g., Verdery, 1991).

The rest of this chapter addresses how socialist institutions of
control everywhere have created as a byproduct social relations
beyond their control. These free spaces defuse thin official interpretations into many alternative sources of meaning, even though
they remain firmly embedded in the system itself. The alternative
interpretations are themselves weakly organized and inconsistent,
but such complex and ambiguous features allow them to survive

and to coopt official discourse. They resemble Daoist parables of water: hit it and it moves away unscathed; pull your hand back and it returns immediately, placid as ever.

The impossibility of controlling every single institutional context forces a crucial limitation on the state's ability to impose an interpretation, as socialist systems themselves spawn institutional ties outside of their control. This process has been most clearly documented for socialist economics. The lack of genuine competition encourages firms and bureaucrats to hoard resources of all kinds, both by amassing more goods and by disguising what they already have (e.g., Verdery, 1991:422; Shue, 1988:110). In consequence, shortages characterize all levels of the society, leading both consumers and managers to try getting goods outside the official economy, in a "second economy" that may be more or less officially sanctioned (Verdery, 1991:422).

Even when legally sanctioned (as in Hungary in the 1980s or in China now), "second economy units simply could not prosper without having recourse to illegal means in obtaining the necessary inputs. This led to the establishment of an extensive system of corruption sanctioned by custom" (Gábor, 1991:6). The term "corruption," in fact, limits the concept too severely. What people needed above all was a set of personal relationships (*guanxi* in Chinese) on which they could call. Such ties allowed consumers to learn when the first tomatoes of the season would hit the stands, just as they allowed large enterprise managers to get cement when official channels had dried up. While the system can easily deteriorate into bribe-taking, it rests just as much on a kind of generalized reciprocity, where long-term mutual back-scratching combines friendship and utility. With the legal expansion of China's second economy during the reforms of the last decade, such ties have become even more important. One study of reciprocity in a rural village of Heilongjiang estimated that the average family spent 20 percent of their income on gift-giving to establish strong personal networks (Yan, 1991).

"Millionaire" Chen provided one of the star attractions when I joined a group of foreigners taken to visit Fengyang County in Anhui Province, a showcase county for China's economic reforms. Chen had begun his capital accumulation by contracting a lot of land when the new responsibility system first allowed such a retreat from communal farming. With several adult sons, he could farm a lot of land, and turned a healthy profit for several years running. He made his real fortune, though, by using his capital to buy large mats, woven by local peasants out of native reeds. He sold the mats in Manchuria to provide temporary grain storage during the bumper harvests up there.

When we asked how he had come to make such a connection, involving scarce rail links to a very distant market, he explained with a series of particularistic, completely unofficial ties. Chen himself was a low-level Party member, who had gone to visit his son in Manchuria. When he learned that Manchuria needed just the kind of mats he could supply, he used his Party and personal connections to make contact with appropriate cadres. He had sold an entire boxcar full of mats before he left for home. While he showed keen entrepreneurial instinct, someone without his personal network could never have done the same thing. No one considered this illegal or corrupt; he told it to us proudly and openly. He had simply tapped the informal network that anyone must develop to thrive in such a society. Going through the back door, as the Chinese idiom runs, is a way of life.

The increasing commodity economy of the last decade has encouraged the instrumental side of personal connections (Gold, 1985). Nevertheless, the element of apparent reciprocity has always been critical. These are not simply financial transactions, but long-term personal relationships. The goal is to create mutual social debt, rather than to repay a monetary debt. Underneath the anonymous bureaucracy of official society, China is riddled with personal networks, constantly reinforced in daily interactions. While the socialist system unconsciously creates such ties against its own will, so to speak, those ties in turn create alternatives to the system. They substitute a relational ethic for the universalism of official language; they evade the atomization of individuals by creating new ties; and they may challenge official hierarchy as gifts from below leave superiors in debt to underlings (Yang, 1989:50–51).

Huang Shu-min's study of a village near Xiamen City offers many examples of the local brigade leader's reliance on personal ties to fulfill his responsibilities (Huang, 1989:143–150). This leader clearly saw his personal network, with roots especially in the Four Cleanups campaign on the eve of the Cultural Revolution, as his greatest political asset. On one occasion, for example, he approached an old friend in the Xiamen Traffic Control Office to try to get his brigade a contract for constructing steel fences. In the course of their discussions, the brigade head learned that the Traffic Control Office wanted better access to imported cigarettes. He then drew on another connection to the manager of the import store in the Special Economic Zone, who could get cigarettes with low customs duties. By orchestrating a deal between his two friends, the brigade leader won the contract (Huang, 1989:145). These are hardly the mechanisms of economic order that the socialist system strives for, but they are prerequisites to success. No graft took place here, as each party to the deal worked for the benefit of his larger unit. Yet the entire system of reciprocity cross-cut and undermined the neat lines of socialist bureaucratic authority.

None of this constitutes direct resistance, but it guarantees that alternative sources of meaning lurk just below the official order on the surface. Official institutions of interpretation have no control over these areas, which themselves develop as a reflex of the system. "Rather than being merely official corruption bolstering official power, the tactics and ethics of the gift provide, at the same time, a challenge to the principle of state distribution" (Yang, 1989:52).[72]

The family provides another free space where full control remains impossible. Outside of a few short-lived experiments, China has never challenged the primary role of the family in socialization, consumption, and old age care. With the economic reforms of the 1980s, families have also grown increasingly important as productive units, just as they had been before collectivization. The state, of course, still tries to penetrate the family in its campaigns. The Lei Feng and Lai Ning education program in elementary schools partially intends to invade the family through the children. The well publicized case of the sister who allegedly turned in her brother for his part in the Tiananmen demonstrations showed the family as the government would like it to work. Yet for the vast majority of families, the powerful personal ties of socialization, mutual care, and joint economies overwhelm the direct ties between individual and state.

Even political study small groups, a primary mechanism of direct ideological control in the front line of any campaign, may themselves foster alternative institutions. The intensive social interaction they encourage among classmates and co-workers intends to bring the campaign down to the level of daily life. Yet it also creates a group whose solidarity may outweigh the campaign. Chen Jo-hsi offers a poignant fictional account of such an interaction during the Cultural Revolution, when a mother hears that her little son has said "Chairman Mao is a rotten egg" to a playmate (Chen, 1978). After spending several days in petrified fear that the story will spread beyond the playmate's mother, she finally learns that the other little boy appears to be the guilty party instead. Yet neither mother turned in the other, in spite of the enormous pressures at the time, and both ended up as fast friends. The system of control created a solidarity beyond its control.[73]

Similar kinds of interactions appeared frequently during the post-Tiananmen campaigns. One cadre reported that in political study sessions he visited in Guangdong, "No one says a word; they just read the [required] newspaper articles out loud, and count that as having studied" (Shi, 1990:19). Nicholas Kristof documented several more such cases in the *New York Times*. For example, co-workers at a hospital stymied police attempts to find who had raised a banner praising the Rumanian uprising of 1989. Everyone knew the guilty party, but no one would inform. In another incident, an official at a cadre school protected participants in the Tiananmen demonstrations because he himself had taken part. Like the mothers of the children who spoke too freely, his particularistic connections outweighed his official duty. In one final example, a Beijing University professor would not write a self-criticism about Tiananmen, even though the local Party branch secretary kept pushing him. Somehow gaining access to his file and expecting the worst, the professor discovered the secretary had put a note in the file saying the case was closed and the professor was appropriately contrite (*New York Times*, 24 January 1990).

If everyone in the small group cooperates, they can easily defuse the campaign by going through the motions without the substance – mutual self-criticism with a wink. The existence of social and economic networks beyond direct government control ensures that alternative interpretations, or at least free space to escape official interpretation, will always thrive. The official institutions of control breed reactions inherently beyond their control.

# 12

# Irony, Cynicism, and Potential Resistance

Both recent theories of socialism and the evidence from China thus suggest that totalizing institutions never have complete control. The resulting free space has always been there, but has grown increasingly obvious in China over the last decade, as the reforms have encouraged departures from strict state control. Such alternative social relations guarantee that cultural domination can never be total, because the institutions of official interpretation themselves have inherent limits. This chapter will follow how the space created by reciprocal ties, family life, and even political small groups has fostered ambiguous interpretations and refusals to interpret that deflect and deform the campaign for a unified, official reading of Tiananmen.

## LANGUAGE AND CULTURAL DOMINATION

Official socialist language rests on claims of science; it is impersonal, passive, universalizing and explicit. It offers History, not histories (Lefort, 1986:222). Such thin interpretation is far easier to control than overloaded symbolism, but it is also far less powerful. In addition, it leaves itself open to question in ways that messier meaning does not. As any real bureaucrat knows, there is safety in ambiguity, no matter what the Weberian pressures to rationalize. Clear statements allow for clear criticisms.

Thin, official language immediately generates its own problems. Real social experience, after all, creates many histories that can never fully match History. The anonymous and universal truth of science also contradicts the real divisions in the society, especially between the leadership and the masses. Individuals thus experience an abstract discourse about the identity of all the People, yet also place the origins of such language in the centers of real power that the discourse itself denies (Lefort, 1986:220–222).[74] In practice, the system has created a deep distrust of official language, and a reaction that undercuts the goals of official interpretation. The reaction does not directly oppose the line – censorship largely prevents alternative precipitations that would constitute open resistance. Instead, it overloads meaning in a constant search for alternative messages, or a refusal to see any explicit message. As people themselves feel the need to communicate between the lines, they begin to read all language the same way, with a cynical view toward the hidden significances. Seeing ostensibly scientific discourse as allegory immediately vitiates its power.

Distrust of the thin discourse of control, for example, leads people to personalize all information according to the trustworthiness of the source, and thus undercuts its claimed anonymity (Schöpflin, 1991:13). Schöpflin argues further that eastern European samizdat literature developed techniques of inference and allegory to the point that genuine communication suffered: "Intended to side-step the problem of censorship and self-censorship in the Kádár period, the language of the Hungarian opposition was as convoluted as that of officialdom. Czech and Polish patterns were not that different" (Schöpflin, 1991:8). These convolutions were crucially important, because they pushed all reading toward the search for multiple meanings, sapping the strength of any official language.

In Poland in the 1980s, where the split between people and state had torn wide apart, official language underwent a systematic but subtle transformation in unofficial talk, forming what Wierzbicka calls an anti-totalitarian language (Wierzbicka, 1990). Uninflected acronyms in official language grew inflections and sometimes changed gender in popular discourse. Bits of Russian – a language that everyone studied but no one learned – also appeared in ironically altered forms in daily speech (Wierzbicka, 1990:6). Nothing directly resisted, but the added nuances undermined the dominating simplicity of official, controlled discourse.

Thom sees a similar process leading to a refusal of all interpretation in the Soviet Union. What she calls the "wooden language" of Soviet officialdom provoked a general distrust of all language. "This instinctive rejection of the deceitful word is the origin of what one might call 'lyrical consciousness.' The search for a reality beyond words involves an act of empathy towards things, especially towards nature. Often it takes the form of a longing for friendly speechless human contacts" (Thom, 1989:144). Here the reaction repudiates all explicit interpretation.

This process typifies repressive language anywhere; it responds to cultural domination generally, rather than to socialism in particular. Such uses of irony and allegory simply carry to an extreme the fate of the official language in Taiwan that I have already discussed. Studies of non-socialist authoritarian or Fascist regimes show very similar developments. In Fascist Italy, "One can detect, in the absence of freedom of expression, an increased propensity to grasp double meanings. One need only scan the newspapers of the Fascist period to note the recurrence of so-called puns – plainly silly and almost meaningless remarks which suggest that the general repression had turned everything into a laughing matter" (Passerini, 1987:86).

Two retired textile workers related a comparable story from Portugal under Salazar, where the Minister of Education had been speaking to a crowd of workers. As he was promising all the wonders that the government would do for the workers, someone loudly sighed in the back, "Oh, if only it were so!" The offender was hustled out of the meeting, but not before his comment had brought the entire ceremony to a grinding end (Ingerson, 1984:7). Typical irony, the statement allowed multiple interpretations. Even many years after the fact, the two old workers still could not agree on an interpretation. One insisted on a reading as sarcasm, but the other felt it could have been sympathy (Ingerson, 1984:7–8). Multivocality is key to surviving censorship. While the inherent ambiguities of saturation make for only ambiguous resistance, they also perform the crucial function of forcing all official language to be read for its own ambiguities, ironies, and multiple meanings. As irony becomes the way of writing, cynicism becomes the way of reading. The dominating power of thin, official, "rational" discourse thus finds itself undercut from the beginning, even in the absence of any direct resistance.

Anthropologists dedicated to fieldwork tend to scoff at China watchers who read entire political movements out of which official stands where in photographs of a public ceremony. My attitude toward such data changed, however, when I lived in China and realized that many Chinese were staring at those same photographs and drawing the same kinds of conclusions from them. China had always valued messages delivered between the lines, but life under the current regime has perfected the art. All official language claims to be transparently thin, yet all of it is combed for hidden possibilities. Perhaps only in China could a historical play (*Hai*

*Rui Dismissed from Office*) have touched off the Cultural Revolution, with arguments raging over its proper allegorical reading as a possible criticism of Mao.[75]

More than forty years of Chinese experience with mercurially changing political winds have deepened the cynicism greeting any new campaign. Especially after the Cultural Revolution, people have perfected strategies for survival. They know exactly how to manipulate small group sessions to minimize damage.[76] The result has been an array of irony, cynicism and anomie that has powerfully deflected the current campaign without ever resisting it directly. The transparence and frailty of official Chinese language, like all very controlled discourse, make it vulnerable to the accretion of new meanings where institutional domination is weaker.

The very nature of this process, however, makes evidence problematic and difficult to interpret. Successful irony, like sighing "if only it were so," always leaves one unsure of actual intention. After so many decades of campaigns, Chinese are quick studies of the new line, and will speak it immediately. People certainly offer a great deal of surface cooperation to the current post-Tiananmen campaigns. Suggestions of alternatives come primarily in the dissident and foreign press, which generally promote readings as resistance whenever possible. Nevertheless, a great deal of evidence suggests the very marginal success of this campaign, in spite of superficial appearances. Unofficial levels of meaning churn beneath the surface, although very little actually boils up as identifiable resistance.

In the least successful such cases, a hidden alternative meaning clearly constitutes resistance. The best known example in China recently was the poem that appeared in the overseas edition of the *People's Daily* (20 March 1991). It appeared to be a wistful and sentimental bit of patriotic nostalgia, penned by an overseas student longing for his homeland. Word quickly spread, however, that the Chinese characters could also be read along the diagonal to render up a denunciation of Li Peng. Such secret messages are neither ironic nor really saturated. For those who know the trick, the true meaning can be identified in a moment. The government, of course, could also identify the true meaning, and fired the responsible editor (*New York Times*, 30 April 1991).

A more subtle attempt at subversion occurred on national television during the demonstrations themselves. The official news readers on CCTV read the announcement of martial law dressed in black, and spoke as if delivering a funeral eulogy for a fallen leader (Esherick and Wasserstrom, 1990:841). Here again the death symbolism allowed many strands of interpretation, from mourning for Hu Yaobang, to sympathy for the students, to protest against martial law. Or perhaps it was just a coincidence that they wore black that day. Yet once again, the government found the irony not subtle enough. Apparently feeling that the performance veiled a hidden message of protest, the government fired the two news readers (*New York Times*, 18 November 1990: A23).

More successful attempts would have to be more difficult to interpret. Newspaper headlines, even in the ultimately official *People's Daily*, offered several good examples. For instance, on 22 May 1989, just two days after martial law had been declared, the paper carried a front page report on the prime minister of Hungary, who said troops should never be used to solve a political crisis, and criticized Stalin for using troops for internal political suppression (Yi and Thompson, 1989:139). A few days after the bloody end of the demonstrations, the overseas edition of the *People's Daily* reported Kim Dae-jung's comments on the Kwangju uprising in Korea under the headline, "Punish by Law the Arch-Criminals Who Have Suppressed the People's Uprising" (Yi and Thompson, 1989:140). A few days later, the national edition similarly carried a headline reading "The North Korea Labor News Criticizes Roh Tai Woo's Fascist Regime, Which Indiscriminately Kills Innocent Students and Bystanders" (*New York Times*, 22 June 1989: A10). These are perfectly correct, politically acceptable stories for the official press, and I know of no heads that rolled on their account. Yet given the timing, no one needed secret instructions about diagonal readings to wonder if extra meanings might lie beneath the surface. The ambiguity was total; no one will ever determine the "true" meaning of these headlines.

Even apparently clear acts of resistance could grow muddled enough to avoid retribution. An old peasant in a suburban Beijing commune disabled a tank that got stuck in the mud. When security officers later tracked him down, villagers claimed the man was somewhat mentally retarded, and he was finally released (Chance and Engst, 1991:181). Stupidity has always been a good veil for passive workplace resistance, and served its function just as well here. Perhaps, after all, he really was retarded.

Music and the other arts provided ample opportunities for multiple interpretations, not always intended by the artist. In

Kunming, for example, the audience was watching a historical movie about the revolutionary period, which fit the campaign of nostalgia for old cadres. Yet the first time Jiang Jieshi [Chiang Kai-shek], the old arch-enemy, appeared on the screen, the crowd broke into spontaneous applause (*New York Times*, 22 September 1989: A4).

In quite another use of film, a large group of students at a Fuzhou university tramped around their campus late one night in 1990, banging on pots and pans and singing a lyric from the film *Red Sorghum* at the top of their lungs: "Little sister, boldly go forward, go forward! Don't turn back!" (Shang, 1990:104). This performance left several interpretations open. Perhaps the students were just singing a song they liked. The lyrics sounded officially acceptable, but perhaps they referred to the Tiananmen demonstrators. The Carnivalesque fanfare overwhelmed official performance, but no proper interpretation was clear.

Another musical case centered on a Beijing man who played funeral dirges – the sort of thing heard on the radio when a top leader dies – as loud as his stereo could manage. The neighbors yelled out the windows, asking who died, and the man answered "Not Deng Xiaoping, and not Li Peng either! Just a distant grand-uncle." The police came to investigate, and the man insisted he just liked dirges the way other people like pop music. He kept playing his record, every day (Yu, 1991). Here was still more overloaded funeral saturation. Like the other cases, it contained too many possible meanings, which the government found impossible to sort out.

The most famous musical case is Cui Jian, a sort of unofficial poet of the student movement. His song "The Last Gunshot" never mentions the events of 4 June, but audiences draw their own conclusions. During a performance of the song in Guangzhou, many members of the audience lit and waved cigarette lighters. Audiences also wave red cloth during another song, "A Piece of Red Cloth" (Xian, 1991), reminiscent of the tangled possibilities of the red flags at Tiananmen. While most of his audiences might argue that the interpretation as protest is clear in context, enough official meaning still remains for Cui Jian's lyrics consistently to evade the censors as he releases new recordings (Peters, 1991).

Rather than proposing alternative meanings, people can denature official meanings through too much enthusiasm. This has been a problem for the current nostalgia campaign, as a recent T-shirt craze showed. Some T-shirts bore radical Maoist slogans from the

Cultural Revolution days. Quotes from Mao included "Never forget class struggle," "A single spark can start a prairie fire," and "Sweep away all vermin" (*South China Morning Post*, 2 July 1991; Barone, 1991). Strongly recalling the days when Lei Feng first became an official campaign, the sudden resurgence of Mao seems meekly appropriate. Yet both the unorthodox medium and the current context encourage alternative readings as either ridicule of the campaign or as calls to resistance. Again, the students wearing these shirts may intend protest, but the explicit form always allows them to deny any such intent.

In a similarly two-edged memory of the Cultural Revolution, middle-aged urban workers and cadres have been returning in droves to the rural villages they lived in when they were sent down to the countryside during the campaigns of twenty years ago (Ouyang, 1990). At the same time, cassettes of Cultural Revolution songs set to a pop beat have become runaway best-sellers (*New York Times*, 2 June 1992). Nothing here indicates resistance to the government, yet the shirts, the village visits, and the music entail entirely too much cooperation in nostalgia, commemorating the wrong things. By using the exact language of previous campaigns, the T-shirts especially called all slogans and all campaigns into question.

Rather than smothering the campaign with too much cooperative meaning, one can also suffocate it with a lack of any interpretation. Like a work-to-rule labor action, where minimal compliance to the absolute letter of the law disrupts work, campaigns can be met with great ennui underneath a surface of minimal cooperation. Other T-shirts show this pattern, with a kind of celebration of apathy: "Really exhausted," "I'm depressed! Leave me alone!", "Bored" (*South China Morning Post*, 2 July 1991). In a hopeless attempt to stop this sort of thing, the government has made "unhealthy" slogans on T-shirts illegal (*New York Times*, 29 July 1991: A4). In practice, however, they simply cannot control every medium for expressing inappropriate messages. A similar craze for signs on dormitory doors swept college campuses at the same time. They ranged from "Love Nest" to "Hall of Boredom" to "Small Appliances Repaired" (Wang, 1991).

This is less irony than a refusal to engage in the first place. Anomie, in fact, seems to be the most widespread response to the entire situation. Purely pro forma mutual self-criticism now makes political study groups a matter of bored routine, even in the military (e.g., Shi, 1990:19; Li, 1990). A questionnaire administered by Beijing University's graduate student association to their members showed a consistent depressed boredom with everything. When asked what feelings were on campus, a plurality answered that no one felt like doing anything; the next most popular answer described everyone as depressed. The plurality said the greatest current interest on campus was fun, without regard to the consequences. The only enthusiasm at all was for finding a way to go abroad. A majority even claimed that they just would not care if a new student movement began ("Beijing...", 1990).

Such an attitude refuses to embrace any kind of interpretation. It poses no alternatives to the official version of things, but it makes equally clear that acceptance of the official version is only for convenience. The dissident press, from which many of these examples come, often sees them as evidence of resistance. Beneath the ennui or the nostalgic returns to the countryside, they imply, lies a counter-ideology awaiting its opportunity to come above ground. Yet such a view, like seeing Taiwanese pigs as champions of ethnicity, forces an explicit interpretation where none exists for most people.

Aside from the rare acrostic poem or actual act of sabotage, the official campaign falters not against a rock of resistance, but by drowning in a sea of wider meanings. People accept the campaign, conduct their political study, and perform self-criticisms. Yet they also manipulate the system for their own survival, and sit quietly by as others do the same. By recycling bits of old campaigns in T-shirt slogans, trips to the old Cultural Revolution countryside, and loud funeral music, people also add a questioning subtext to the claims of the new campaign. The universal socialist truths claimed in the latest campaign stumble across the detritus of old ones, never quite sufficiently forgotten. Anomie itself undercuts official meaning, which requires enthusiastic participation from everyone, not just passive acceptance. None of this constitutes an explicit oppositional ideology. If such a reading ever becomes clear enough, it will be crushed, as happened to the fired newspaper editor and news readers. The anomie is real; so is the nostalgia, and so, for that matter, is the obedient following of the campaign.

The language of official meaning is always explicit, orderly and rationalized. Yet every time language approaches such a stiff monotone, a new process of accretion adds meaning outside the institutions of control. The very transparency of official language encourages questioning its motives and claims of universality. Just such a process transformed many Taiping leaders' view of Yang Xiuqing from the voice of God, who had to be followed, to a self-aggrandizing fake, who had to be killed. Yang's monopoly on power at the end allowed new interpretations to undermine his claim to divine inspiration. Similarly, official ideology in Taiwan faded fast after the political relaxation of the mid-1980s. Exactly the same disintegration of meaning is occurring with the current campaign in the People's Republic, in spite of the powerful institutions of interpretation. The form of official language itself creates its own reaction.

## IDENTITY AND THE SELFLESS SELF

The system of campaigns and small group political study in part tries to accomplish the atomization of individuals that totalitarian theory expects, linking each unit directly to the state as a cog in the machine of the People as a whole. Campaigns starring heroes like Lei Feng and Lai Ning particularly aim to create a proper sense of the selfless self, dedicated to the common good over any personal or personalistic interests. The People as state leave no room for separate institutions of civil society, at least in principle. Yet in practice, as we have seen, socialist society leaves enormous territories of free space, and issues of identity become especially problematic.

Several studies of socialist and fascist states have shown how the effort to atomize individuals and to create institutions of control can rebound against its intended purposes. István Rév, for example, wrote about the advantages of being atomized in socialist Hungary:

> Since complete coercion can be maintained only by granting power to individuals at all points of the system, the individuals are not completely powerless ... Although the individual's power is but part of the structure of the system – it was delegated to him in order to guard the existing power relations – and there is no other ground of resistance but the ground created by the same system, still, resistance even on the terms of the system may be fateful for the political structure (Rév, 1987:347).

Writing two years before the velvet revolution, he would soon be proved right. An analysis of Italian fascism similarly concluded that the very organizations intended to suppress class conflict forced the regime to respond to public opinion (De Grazia, 1981:226, 233).

The challenge to socialist identity shows up clearly in images of the body. Lefort describes the totalitarian body as a series of synecdoches where the head represents and merges with the body as a whole. The proletariat is the head of the whole people and stands for the people as a whole. In just the same way, the Party heads the proletariat, the leadership heads the Party, and the "egocrat" heads the leadership as the ultimate embodiment of the people (Lefort, 1986:299). Every individual both reproduces and constitutes the body of the People, each contributing to its health anonymously and identically. This kind of attempt in China peaked during the Cultural Revolution, when Mao embodied the People. Presentation of self became a monotone, not because a uniform was required, but because socialist workers have a certain look. Their clothes are cheap but durable, their haircuts are practical, and their eyes shine with enthusiasm. They have no interest in creating themselves as unique individuals or members of other groups through makeup or unique dress; they are dedicated to the common cause of the People. The Lei Feng campaign tried to epitomize and enforce this selfless self during the Cultural Revolution. His revitalization now indicates how far the state feels identity in practice has escaped from its control.

Even during the Cultural Revolution, none of this fully worked. One heard, for example, that looking at the feet let you distinguish rank even when cadres wore the same workers' clothes as everyone else. The quality of the shoes indicated the importance of the wearer. While alternative versions of identity always snuck through the cracks, the economic reforms of the 1980s consciously brought a great relaxation in direct attempts to control personal identity, as long as no clear threats to the state appeared. Household decoration in the 1980s, for example, increasingly abandoned state symbolism like portraits of Mao in favor of the traces of family history. The furnishings reflected family structure and interests, and the dominant decorations were photographs of children, important family occasions, and recent ancestors (Davis, 1989:95–96).

Dress and personal decoration have emphasized the new freedom to express a self apart from the body of the whole People. Dress had become strikingly more varied by 1985 than it had been in 1980. Far more than just a reaction to more easily available consumer goods, dress has become a vehicle to show a self beyond Lei Feng. Young women now often prefer frilly dresses and curled hair. The image of the proletarian is gone, even for actual workers. Many women now transform their faces through a cosmetics fad (*New York Times*, 6 May 1990, I:16); young men do the same with sunglasses. Raised heels, equally popular with men and women, change how people move. Clothing for children particularly expresses both individuality and conspicuous consumption. They gleam with bright colors and cute hats; children still unable to walk often wear leather shoes that their parents cannot afford for themselves. Clothing and personal decoration have opened up an enormous new range for the expression of new kinds of identity, from eccentric individuality to affiliation with new kinds of groups. All depart from the uniformity of the totalitarian body.

Names and titles form another quick marker of identity that has been in flux. In naming babies, for example, the old politically correct names have given way to new kinds of identity. Names in the People's Republic have typically denoted the baby as a carrier of socialist political value; for instance, the most common character in Cultural Revolution names was Hong (red). In the last decade, however, names have grown far less political, often speaking to values of wealth or cultural sophistication (*New York Times*, 30 November 1990: A1). Names no longer mark dedication to the shared ideals of the single People.

Titles of address have undergone an even clearer transformation. Since the Revolution, "comrade" has supported the official leveling of everyone: the term is anonymous, egalitarian, and appropriate to everyone on any occasion. In the early years, other terms clearly marked workers (the true "people") from the less desirable bourgeoisie. *Shifu* (master craftsman) marked even more respect than "comrade," but could only be used for workers and peasants (Ju, 1991). The bourgeoisie were stuck with the old terms, suddenly seen as embarrassing in the first years after the revolution: *xiansheng* (literally, first-born) for men and *xiaojie* (literally, little elder sister) for women. By the time of the Cultural Revolution, the division had become less relevant; anyone could be a "master craftsman" and no one had to be a *xiansheng*.

By the time I lived in China in the mid-1980s, however, all of this was in flux. "Comrade" had become a slightly rude way of getting attention from a stranger on the street. Its only other regular use was the formulaic address of top leaders, like calling Deng "Comrade Xiaoping." Its slow death has continued since, as any sense of the totalitarian body it really addressed has decreased. By 1990, even official television newscasters had abandoned the standard opening of "comrades, hello" for "viewers, hello" (*New York Times*, 18 November 1990: A23). While "master craftsman" still holds its own as a more polite alternative to "comrade," especially for people like servants or janitors, the strongest trend has been toward a revival of the prerevolutionary usage still thriving in Hong Kong and Taiwan. *Xiansheng* and *xiaojie*, along with other terms for older people, distinguish gender, age and rank in ways that "comrade" had attempted to dissolve. Of course, those distinctions had continued to exist all along – socialist China is very hierarchical under the surface. Yet the change in address terms indicates an undermining of that official ideology of the totalitarian body. Without ever denying the official line, all of these changes in identity created a host of new possibilities.

The current *qigong* exercise craze offers a striking alternative to the totalitarian body. *Qigong* develops techniques for manipulating the body's flow of *qi*, the vital force that motivates the entire world. *Qi* flows through everything in its various forms. We can see it most easily flowing in the sinuous mountain ranges and sudden peaks that Chinese landscape artists love, and in the old, twisted trees and rocks that may become objects of popular worship. Daoist meditation manipulated *qi* within the body to form a healthy balance, and the soft forms of martial arts relied on *qi* to create power. *Qigong* exercise routines resemble the slow movements of *taijiquan*, but without the martial aspects. Groups typically exercise under the guidance of a master, sometimes filling large sports stadiums every morning.

Chinese authorities estimate about 60 million regular followers now (*New York Times*, 4 September 1990; Ouyang, 1990). Adepts can direct their flow of *qi* through the hands to accomplish feats like lighting light bulbs or emitting heat rays. Beyond general exercise and health, the most important function is curing by laying on of hands. The sessions can become quite dramatic. When the exercises begin to take effect and the flow of *qi* in the body suddenly changes, new adepts may *fa qi* (release *qi*), writhing or shaking in uncontrollable fits strongly reminiscent of spirit possession. Here a sort of Daoist body has replaced the totalitarian body, overwhelming it with its tangible demonstration of power in curing and released *qi*, much as the initial God Worshiper curings and mass possessions had demonstrated their power. This body is a microcosm of the forces that make up the entire universe, not just the body politic. It also allows the possibility of tremendous individual power to anyone, inherent in their own bodies, and very different from the single body of the People. *Qigong* challenges the state's power to mold identity, and the state has moved to discourage it.[77]

The enormous resurgence of religion in the last decade also suggests a relocation of identity. While the great interest in Christianity still affects only a small portion of the population, the revitalization of Chinese popular religion strikes one everywhere. I arrived in Guiping County to work on the Taiping on Guanyin's birthday. A major local temple to Guanyin, rebuilt after the Cultural Revolution, stood on a hill near the county seat. Worshipers covered the hill, and incense and paper money adorned every tree and rock on the path up to the temple. I have already mentioned the local cadres' tales of powerful spirit mediums. Even more striking were the numbers of newly constructed neighborhood Earth God (She Gong, called Tudi Gong in other areas) temples everywhere. Such temples are by far the most common new religious construction throughout south China. As I rode the bus through the countryside on the annual grave-sweeping day (Qingming), I could see people everywhere taking care of their ancestors. Ancestor worship at home has also again grown commonplace. The fastest growing sides of popular ritual thus appear to be the most local (Earth Gods) and the most family-oriented. Worship of higher gods, with their implied bureaucratic hierarchy and national loyalties, lags behind. The revival of religion not only slaps at official scientific socialism, but it highlights strictly local and family loyalties at the expense of the state. The revival clearly ties most closely to those economic, social, and kinship institutions that avoid total control (Anagnost, 1987).

Mao himself has been one of the liveliest figures in the renewal of popular ritual. Areas of central China flooded in 1991 suddenly sold out of more than 100,000 copies of Mao's portrait just before the lunar new year in 1992. People were pasting him to their front doors, just as they used to put up a new image of the Wealth God each year in the old days (*South China Morning Post*, 7 February 1992). Little Maos also hang from rear-view mirrors in cars all over China, much as amulets from the Eighteen Lords temple do in Taiwan (*New York Times*, 2 June 1992). This usurpation of the rights to Mao's legacy forms part of the new revival of religion, and also part of the nostalgia craze that both follows and abuses the government's official campaigns.

While I have argued that all of these reactions lie inherent in the nature of cultural control in China, the state has also allowed them to become far more openly expressed in the last decade by promising people more personal space. Yet the government has also been surprised and dismayed by the result. Even before the Tiananmen events, the government had been trying to reassert cultural control through a campaign against spiritual pollution, a socialist education campaign, and less systematic attacks on particularly upsetting changes. Along the same lines, they have banned "unhealthy" T-shirts, placed limits on *qigong* assemblies and accused some masters of just taking money from the gullible (identical to their attacks on spirit mediums), and lobbied for the use of "comrade" (*New York Times*, 4 September 1990, 18 November 1990). A self-proclaimed Buddha of the future in central Guangxi, leading his followers to the new age, had been executed for fomenting rebellion shortly before I got to Guangxi.[78] Yet none of this has had much effect, because too many institutions out of their control provide a free space for alternatives to the old drone of Lei Feng and his selfless self, and their ambiguous messages never resist explicitly.

## ORGANIZATION AND RESISTANCE

Let me again pose my usual question: in what sense is any of this resistance? The actual demonstrations and demands in Tiananmen in 1989 clearly constituted the beginnings of resistance. For a few weeks, at least, the head ceased to stand for the entire body, and instead stood opposed to the body. In spite of their ambiguities and inconsistencies, the demonstrators still shared a demand for change. The general saturation left the type of change completely unclear – some implied revolution, others evolution, and others simply patchwork reforms. The broad symbolism of white mourning and red revolution left room for all kinds of interpretation. Like the early God Worshipers, the very messiness of interpretation widened and empowered the appeal of the movement. Unlike the Taiping, however, they were crushed before they could develop the lasting institutions that might have created long-term pressure to change.

The situation is far less clear for the kinds of ironic language and shifting identity that characterized the period after that eventful spring. The literature on socialism tends to show the usual splits between people who see mostly cultural domination and those who instead see mostly cultural resistance, just as I have discussed for other contexts. Some emphasize the absolute hegemony of the official discourse, and treat the messy ambiguities of anything else as evidence for the success of cultural control (e.g., Thom, 1989; Schöpflin, 1991). Others instead find a hidden but fully fledged discourse of resistance in such language (e.g., Wierzbicka, 1990). Much the same argument has taken place over the religious revival in China. Some emphasize religion as anti-hegemonic resistance, while others see the revival primarily as "new interpretations of tradition under the powerful influence of the Marxist state" (Siu, 1989a:11; see also Anagnost, 1987; Siu, 1989b:135 no.3).

The arguments, as usual, have no resolution because they stem from an insistence on reading a single, clear interpretation as resistance or acquiescence where none need exist. The potential to develop organized and explicit resistance clearly lies within the multiple possibilities of these ironies, ambiguities, and refusals to interpret. The key questions for resistance lie less in finding some deeper level of meaning, than in understanding the chances for forging that critical combination of institution and interpretation that might support an active movement. The Taiping succeeded in this project, Taiwanese ghosts will probably never manage it, and Tiananmen was crushed before the process went very far.

Classic totalitarian theory was very pessimistic about the possibilities for internal change of such systems. They saw the mechanisms of cultural control as ultimately effective: "the population of a Communist country is on balance inclined to fight for its unfreedom against those who wish to free it" (Zinoviev, 1984:257). Hannah Arendt wrote in a largely similar tone about totalitarianism, although she left a small opening for external change in the anti-social nature of such regimes (Arendt, 1958:478). Yet the obvious evidence from eastern Europe in 1989 clarified just how shallow totalizing control can be. External changes in the Soviet Union may have been a necessary precursor to the east European changes, but they can never explain the speed and power of the flight from socialism.

I have argued that the totalizing project never succeeds completely. Through its own action it creates personal networks, family ties, and social organizations that lie outside of its direct power. The question for internal resistance centers on how much these institutions can organize new kinds of interpretations as opposition. In some cases, religion has been the natural organ, where states allowed it to continue for tactical reasons. The Catholic Church played such a role in Poland, and the Protestant churches to a lesser extent in East Germany. Islam under the tightly controlling (but not at all socialist) regime of the Shah of Iran played a similar role, offering a free space for alternative interpretations which eventually crystallized into direct opposition. The union movement also took on such a role in Poland, against all odds. In many non-socialist regimes that nevertheless exerted powerful pressures toward cultural domination, the relative independence of the economic sector has allowed organization toward reform to thrive – the recent examples of Argentina, Chile and Taiwan come to mind, along with many others.

Yet China resembles Czechoslovakia or Hungary much more than it does Poland. It has neither a Solidarity nor an independently organized Church. Unlike Christianity in Europe, Chinese popular religion has never had nation-wide or even regional organization that could make it an obvious political actor. China has been scrupulous in crushing or coopting every kind of competing organization on any large scale. Only the very local and weakly organized phenomena I have been discussing remain – neighborhood and family religion, unofficial linguistic usage, overly solidary small groups, new signs of personal identity, and so on. Yet these mini-institutions in fact riddle the apparently omnipotent structure of control with holes lying beyond its control. The denial of histories for History, the hiding of real distinctions as shared identity, the empowerment of individuals and small groups by setting them to watch each other, and even the very transparency of official language conspire to create these gaps. The bits of alternative social structure deflect cultural domination by offering free spaces away from official interpretation.

The Chinese state has successfully inhibited any developments that might have fostered the precipitation of an organized ideology of resistance. The initial shock of the Tiananmen demonstrations, after all, was that the government allowed them to develop as far as they did. Yet far from cementing their ideological dominance, the system of control has instead created an overloaded quicksand. The omnipresent pockets of free space nourish all kinds of alternative interpretations, and also protect the possibility of no interpretation, which so many people express through the growing anomie. The state prevents any newly organized alternative interpretation from thriving, but the same mechanisms prevent it from successfully propagating its own.

The disorganized indeterminacy of these areas beyond direct control determines both their greatest weakness and their greatest strength. Their ambiguous interpretation and organizational weakness make it very difficult to imagine how they could develop the institutional base to become straightforward resistance. In addition, if the opportunity to develop something new ever comes, they will find it very difficult to come to any quick agreement on what to do. The events in Tiananmen showed the dangers, as unanimous positions became increasingly untenable. Much of the current political crisis in east Europe similarly rests on the impossibility of developing any unity, beyond a shared sense of opposition, under the old regime.

Yet these areas also manage both to defuse attempts at official control and to breed a bounty of new possibilities. As in Czechoslovakia or Hungary, they make the cultural base of the regime far weaker than at first appears. Their disorganization and ambiguity prevent them from becoming targets; irony survives censorship precisely because meaning cannot be pinned down. They form islands of potential creativity, ready to yield up their treasures when the opportunity comes.

## CONCLUSION

Post-structuralist theory has honed the tools to deconstruct systematic structures of interpretation, shaking them to bits along hidden fault lines, and leaving behind tangled scraps of inconsistent meaning. Its vision of surplus meaning hiding everywhere in the cracks of ideology, ready to burst things asunder, has allowed important reconsideration of canons of all sorts (including post-structuralism itself, at least in more sophisticated hands). By challenging the right of both internal authorities and external analysts to claim a true and final reading, it has also sparked the questions of resistance and interpretation that inform this book.

Yet by tearing meaning from its social contexts, such an approach risks losing sight of the real social power of interpretation. Meaning in actual social life is not homogeneously messy, in spite of our facile ability to deconstruct any claim of systematic meaning. In practice, some areas of life indeed allow people to revel in multiple, inconsistent, half-interpreted meanings. Other areas, however, are dominated by strict rationality and explicit control over a single truth. Most crucially, real institutions back up these claims, creating the social mechanisms to propagate and enforce them. Under certain social relations of interpretation people thus do, in fact, share single meanings. It matters very little that an intellectual somewhere can yank the facade away, exposing the hidden illusions and blemishes of the ideas. The institutional structure of power itself has to be challenged before such an exposure makes much difference.

A broad tension between claims to a single true interpretation and the uncontrolled multiplication of interpretive possibility characterizes each of the cases I have discussed, and surely runs through much of social life anywhere. Organizations like the state work to consolidate their areas of interpretive control, and even individuals at times feel a push to rationalize. Hong Xiuquan was clearly such a thinker, and much of Max Weber's work on the beginnings of capitalism concerns the point at which large groups felt an internal drive to precipitate new sets of explicit meanings, ranging from how they dealt with God to how they kept track of their money. Yet at the same time, other areas rest in a free space away from institutional attempts to control interpretation, and may actively push on official meaning, deflecting its thin interpretations and adding fresh complications.

The interaction between these two ways of making meaning bears crucial consequences for resistance movements. Saturation allows a potential to resist, but only along with many other potential interpretations. The mass spirit possessions of the early God Worshipers, the complicated possibilities of the Eighteen Lords, and the refusal of interpretation in China's current epidemic of anomie allowed for many kinds of interpretation. Just as those Taiwanese pigs that started this book could suddenly become patriotic icons, collaborative interpretations sit alongside the possibilities for explicit resistance. Of the cases I have discussed here, only the Taiping, at least so far, managed to unify and institutionalize an ideology of resistance.

The rich ambiguities of meaning in these free spaces resist only in the sense that they skew and divert official interpretation. Analysis that reduces all such space either to clear cultural resistance or to a mere restatement of dominant culture, misses both the power and weakness of indeterminate meaning. It guarantees a creative fund of possible innovation and change, resilient against even thorough attempts at control. Yet it also undercuts any form of organization that might actively promote change. The chaotic mass spirit possessions of the God Worshipers nearly destroyed the movement before it began, just as the multivocality of the Eighteen Lords and the ironies and apathies of the People's Republic pose serious obstacles to organized movements for change.

Resistance in the stronger sense of self-consciously trying to change the system must be wrenched from the hoard of potential interpretations. That act in itself creates a new, increasingly systematic set of ideas, realized through a new social organization of meaning. The Taiping genius was in achieving that transformation around 1850. The depth and difficulty of their social metamorphosis, along with the failure to achieve anything similar in the other two cases I have discussed, indicates just how challenging the process is. In an irony of its own, saturated space becomes explicit resistance only by losing its indeterminacy, and the free spaces that so effectively evaded official institutional control must themselves try to impose an interpretation. The Taiping thus recreated many features of the state they fought against, and the Tiananmen demonstrators had taken steps in the same direction.

The genesis of the Taiping Rebellion after 1849, like the creation of socialist institutions of interpretation a century later, expanded the explicitly and officially organized realm of Chinese society. Yet no case of interpretive domination completely succeeds. Taiping ideas were increasingly compromised as the movement wore on, and none of the attempts to unify a meaning of Taiwanese ghosts ever made much headway. Even the totalizing institutions of the People's Republic leave enormous gaps, as they create alternative social organizations of meaning through their own action. The drone of the thin and repressive discourse of control breeds resentment, cynicism and irony, as people always have other sources of meaning. Saturated space alone will overthrow no oppression, but it also keeps oppression from succeeding entirely.

Attempts at control everywhere have engendered their own reactions. In early modern Europe, for example, state suppression of alternate interpretation created a system of dissimulation "so extensive that it was like a submerged continent in . . . religious, intellectual and social life" (Zagorin, 1990:14). The interplay between saturation and precipitation never allows the final victory of one form of interpretation over the other.

It is tempting to concentrate analysis on explicit meaning, where a clear underlying interpretation can unite the complexities of actual speech and symbol. We tend to belittle the chaotic excesses of the possessed God Worshipers, to dismiss the apparently frivolous incoherence of Taiwanese ghosts in the face of real change, and to deplore the inconsistencies and ambiguities of the students demonstrating in Tiananmen Square. The process of what Weber called "rationalization" indeed vitalizes change, as ideas become explicitly worked out calls to action. Yet it also demands a social organization of interpretation that can maintain such a precipitated meaning. Both active resistance movements and institutions of control must rely on similar mobilizations of power over meaning.

At the same time, the opposite process of complicating and confusing meaning continues to play a crucial role. The God Worshipers expanded so quickly because Hong's original ideas disintegrated into the local mix, making them both innovative and locally intelligible, instead of just crazy. Both Taiwanese ghosts and Tiananmen democracy benefited from a similar multiplicity of meaning. Above all, that free space that always presses against rationalized meaning harbors a cache of possible alternatives that may someday come to light. While it undercuts organization of any type, that messy pile of inconsistent meanings holds a well of creativity, sapping any form of interpretive domination and control without resisting any official interpretation directly.

# Notes

1. "Taiwanese" here refers to the majority population in Taiwan, primarily ethnic Hakka and Hokkien Chinese, most of whose ancestors emigrated to the island in the seventeenth and eighteenth centuries. "Mainlanders" are people who came after the end of the Japanese occupation in 1945, and especially after the Communist victory on the mainland in 1949. The mainlanders controlled the bulk of military and political power, and relations between the two groups were still uneasy in the 1970s.
2. See Cohen (1982) for a critique of theories that totalize the underlying system.
3. The idea comes originally from Raymond Williams (1977:133–134).
4. Ingerson (1984:26–30) includes a fuller discussion on the role of potentials.
5. I take the term 'free space' very loosely from David Martin (personal communication), who uses it to describe how evangelical Protestantism in Latin America shields followers from many of the usual demands and expectations of their social world.
6. Most secondary sources refer to the God Worshiping Society before the Taiping was declared, but the movement itself apparently never organized as a formal association of any kind, and just spoke of themselves as people who worshiped God (Mao, 1981:727–729).
7. The Taiping described the system in detail in the "Tianchao Tianmu Zhidu" (Michael, 1966–1971, II:309–320). Where possible, I cite Taiping documents in the Michael translation. Volume I of the work also provides the best English language summary of the movement.
8. Clarke and Gregory (1982) reprint many such examples from contemporary Western reports.
9. The account matches in many details Hong Rengan's confession after the rebellion (in Michael, 1966–1971, III:1511–1530) and probably accurately reflects Hong Rengan's version of events.
10. For more information on Hong's early life see Hamberg (1854:3–8) and Zhong (1984b:1–9).
11. Wagner (1982:17–21) pieces together various versions of the vision. The most extended Taiping version is in the *Taiping Tianri* (in Michael, 1966–1971, II:52–76). Wagner gives the most detailed analysis of the dream, seeing much of the rebellion as a playing out of its hermeneutics, in contrast to my emphasis on reinterpretation and institution. The various Taiping versions of the dream show the historical reworking of Hong's vision, not just the hermeneutic working through of what is already there. Most striking (but not yet available when Wagner was writing) are spirit possession transcripts of Hong asking Jesus to remind him of what actually happened in the dream as the Taiping

prepared the text of the *Taiping Tianri*, showing how the content of the dream itself could change (Wang, 1985:213).

12. This argument that the motives of Hong and the early God Worshipers were primarily religious remains controversial, going against what had been a standard argument among Chinese scholars of the Taiping in the 1950s and 1960s. I follow instead more recent scholars who argue for a fundamentally religious orientation until at least 1847 or 1848, after the movement was already well established in Guangxi (Li, 1981; Wang, 1981). Part of the argument centers around the dating of some rebellious poems; Li Feiran (1981:134–135) makes a strong argument for a much later date than the standard 1837 (Hamberg, 1854:12–13).

13. "Elderhood" in Cantonese parts of China is a recognized male status marked by a rite of passage.

14. This is a fairly new village. The original settlement from the Taiping period was flooded when the river was dammed at Jintian, and the inhabitants were resettled at a new site.

15. I have been tentative in phrasing these events because the evidence is not really adequate. Much of the case comes from oral histories conducted over a century after the fact, at a time when peasants were rehearsing their own histories of exploitation by landlords, and when local historians were looking for just such evidence. Nevertheless, the evidence is there and seems to fit broader trends. Other evidence for institutional breakdown is much clearer.

16. There is some further evidence for increased land concentration in the oral histories conducted in the 1950s. A single landlord, for example, owned most of the land around Thistle Mountain by 1850 (Guangxi..., 1962:1–2).

17. Su Fengwen (1889a) gives extensive lists of bandit gangs, later compiled by Xie (1950).

18. Buddhist-based groups like the White Lotus, organizationally and ideologically quite different from the Triads, began to appear commonly in Guangxi only slightly after the Taiping.

19. Hamberg calls him "Fall large head," apparently misreading a near homophone.

20. I will discuss this in more detail in the following chapter.

21. See Seaman (1978:114) for a Taiwanese example.

22. The usual term for Earth Gods in Taiwan is Tho Te Kong. The term also appears in Guangxi, but only for a very low deity who usually guards bridges, crossroads and other dangerous areas. In spite of the different terms, the functions of Guangxi's She Gong and Taiwan's Tho Te Kong temples appear identical.

23. Both Daoist and Buddhist clergy included long and preaching texts in their rituals, but these were usually sung in a way that made them incomprehensible to onlookers, and often performed with the public banned. In addition, local worthies sometimes lectured villagers on upright behavior, although these were not religious occasions and they certainly did not expound on ritual detail.

24. The state cult had other intents too, as a religion for bureaucrats themselves, and as a way of ensuring cosmic harmony.

25. The Thistle Mountain region temples they remembered were at Daxuanxu, Sanjiang (the largest), Caicun, Anzhong in Jintian, Mushan, and Pingtian.

26. The name of the temple, however, does suggest an alternate reading. Sanjie can also be translated as the Three Worlds, a common religious term referring to Heaven, Earth, and Man. On such a reading, the temple does fit a very standard bit of national religious culture. Like so much, it left many interpretations open.

27. This information is based on interviews at Thistle Mountain, 9 April 1985.

28. The texts were *Panwang Liuluo Shu* and *Panwang Dajiao*.

29. Personal communication, Zhong Wendian, Department of History, Guangxi Normal University.

30. Both temples were described by informants at Thistle Mountain.

31. Hamberg does not specifically date the poem, but seems to imply a later date of 1847, in contrast to the 1844 in other documents. I use 1844 here, since it is generally agreed upon and the exact date does not affect my argument. 1847, however, would fit far better with other activities of the group, since temple attacks were very rare in 1844–1845, and really only became common in 1847.

32. This was a possessed healer at an outdoor meeting of the Cihui Tang.

33. The mention of sorcerors with flowers and swords refers to Maoshan Daoism, which is frequently cited as part of the problem. Maoshan Daoists dressed in female clothes and specialized in exorcistic ritual.

34. Yang Qingxiu is only known from this one case; some indirect evidence suggests he may have been related to Yang Xiuqing (Michael, 1966–1971:5n.). There is no way to find a sure date for the episode, but Hong Rengan mentions it while discussing some other events of 1847 (in Michael, 1966–1971:4–5). It is the only possession event he describes in the document, which might also imply its particular importance as the first of its kind. This is rather thin evidence, but Yang Qingxiu's case probably typified the early possessions, even if it was not the first.

35. Wang Qingcheng (1985) describes two important new sources he discovered in British archives: a volume of *Tianfu Shengzhi* (Imperial Decrees of the Heavenly Father) and two volumes of *Tianxiong Shengzhi* (Imperial Decrees of the Heavenly Older Brother). These report many more possessions of Yang Xiuqing as God and Xiao Chaogui as Jesus than were previously known. The other major sources are well known (*Tianfu Xiafan Zhaoshu* in two parts, and *Tianming Zhaozhi Shu*, in Michael, 1966–1971:86–110, 197–220).

36. Emily Martin [Ahern] describes a nearly identical form of mediumship in Taiwan (Ahern, 1973:228–235). Such performances, however, are nearly unknown now in Taiwan, and she had to make special arrangements to have it done for her.

37. The ceremony appears to be a combination of Yao Daoism with an earlier tradition of possession (see also Strickmann, 1982:24–45).

38. There could also have been other Gods and other Christs at the time. Taiping records do not mention any, but they do frequently speak of possession by imps and devils. Defeated claimants to the voices of God

and Jesus would most likely have been branded in just such language, although the imps and devils could equally well be more traditional spirits who might have possessed people before the God Worshipers arrived.

39. See Overmyer (1974) for a description of the cult.
40. Some, however, were more equal than others. We are all children of God, but later in the Taiping, in Hong's annotations to the New Testament, we learn that only a select few are children of God's first wife: "The Elder Brother [Jesus] and myself and the Eastern King [Yang Xiuqing] – we were originally born out of the belly of God's first wife," that is, the Heavenly Mother, before heaven and earth existed (in Michael, 1966–1971:236).
41. Xing Fenglin (personal communication) has suggested that Xiao Chaogui may have been Yao. Xiao had his mother's natal surname, which is consistent with occasional Yao uxorilocal agreements, although it can occur with Han Chinese as well. His mother's name (Xiao Panshi) also implies a Yao connection with the inclusion of the character Pan (as in Pangu), and a tablet to his father has been found in a Yao area. Chinese and other ethnic groups could also be assimilated to the Yao, and Yao (at least in Thailand) frequently purchased children from other groups, bringing them up to be Yao (Kandre, 1976). Quite plausibly, ethnic distinctions were simply not so strongly drawn then as they are now that the government has so strongly marked ethnic group membership.
42. The only evidence for these flag-raising ceremonies is oral history gathered in the 1950s (Guangxi..., 1962:61,70,77).
43. Many other cults underwent very similar developments where too many cooks had spoiled the broth. The New Guinea Taro Cult, for instance, which I have already cited, quickly tore into a number of separate sects, especially as alternate leaders constantly founded competing sects based on new possessing spirits (Worsley, 1968:68–74).
44. These include, to give just a few examples, the Kalabari of Nigeria (Horton, 1969:26–27), the Korekore Shona of the Zambesi valley (Garbett, 1969; Lewis, 1971:136–139), and the Tikopia (Firth, 1967:309).
45. This was the man named Wang, whom I mentioned in the preceding chapter.
46. This incident also reinforces other references to star spirits. After Jesus announced the names of the three generals, he said: "Hong Xiuquan, my blood brother, you are the sun and your wife is the moon. Feng Yunshan is made of three stars, and Yang Xiuqing also has three stars; Xiao Chaogui has two stars. Yang Xiuqing and Xiao Chaogui are the twin breezes facing the sun. The foreign nations also have a general." Hong asked the name of this foreign general and learned that his surname was Cai and he was still in foreign lands (Wang, 1985:193).
47. I will pursue this point further for socialist control in the final chapters.
48. While both Buddhism and Daoism share in this growth, quite a different pattern prevails for Christian sects, which grew most rapidly immediately after 1945, and have slowed in the last few decades, especially among the Han Chinese (see Qu and Yao, 1986).

49. In addition, Ann Anagnost has provided sophisticated analyses of religion as popular resistance in the People's Republic of China (e.g., Anagnost, 1989).
50. The Co Su Kong temple in Sanxia, which I discuss in most detail here, has closed off the central hall with an ornate wooden fence. They did this primarily to protect the delicate carvings inside, but it also has the effect of marking the center as more of a sacred space than most temples.
51. See Weller (1987c:107–108) for more detail on charms.
52. The introductory essays of Watson and Rawski's *Death Ritual in Late Imperial and Modern China* provide contrasting views about the importance of orthodoxy versus orthopraxis in Chinese religion (Watson and Rawski, 1988:3–34). Individuals, of course, may develop an intense interest in interpretation, sometimes by apprenticing themselves to masters or sometimes by working through their own interpretations.
53. Workers often refuse to destroy temples, and one of the government's difficulties in controlling illegal temples is trying to find work crews willing to dismantle them.
54. This is the right side of the temple from the spirits' point of view, but the left as you face the temple. Taiwanese always use the spirits' viewpoint out of respect to them.
55. See Weller (1987c:60–74) for a fuller analysis. On other occasions, including worship at small ghost shrines, individual worshipers do use a combined incense pot.
56. I am grateful to Meir Shahar for pointing this out to me. The three temples are the Eighteen Lords temple in Kaohsiung (no relation to this one), Huaizhong Ci in Changhua, and the Nineteen Lords of Loyalty and Justice in Peikang. The Nineteen Lords include eighteen dead people and a dog (Qiu, 1979:323).
57. See Seaman (1981) for a discussion of the funeral ritual that can save mothers from this fate.
58. Cigarettes may take on other connotations elsewhere, as in their use at formal banquets for gods in Penghu (James Wilkerson, personal communication).
59. Personal communication, Meir Shahar.
60. Personal communication, James L. Watson.
61. There are a great many variations on the theme. For details, see Qu (1987:21–31).
62. A fourth, public television network recently began broadcasting, but still has no station of its own, and takes time from the other three.
63. I have not seen the soap opera. This account is based on what other people told me, plus description in the weekly viewers' magazine published by CTS, *Huashi Zonghe Zhoukan* (Nos. 712–716).
64. The explanation is arguable even for his own cases, where the people had been colonized for centuries and the contrast between use-value and exchange-value tends to simplify and idealize the contrast between wage labor and other labor processes. Nevertheless, Taussig clearly has a case of close ties between economic and cultural change. Crain (1991) traces similar devil imagery back more historically.

65. He also went around giving an inspirational public talk called "How to Have a Beautiful Life."
66. Jordan and Overmyer document several cases of factionalism and fission (e.g., Jordan and Overmyer, 1986:79–88, 89–91, 131–134, 218–221).
67. *Ming Pao News* (1989) has a detailed chronology.
68. There have been suggestions that the incident was manufactured by the authorities to discredit the students (e.g., *Ming Pao News* 1989:112).
69. My analysis clearly owes a debt to culturally informed approaches to Tiananmen like Esherick and Wasserstrom (1990) and Strand (1990). Both those essays emphasize how the demonstrations followed a kind of cultural script. This is an important point, but should not disguise either the improvization and innovation in any such demonstration, or the inherent ambiguities. See also Wassertrom's discussion of state (and other) narratives of Tiananmen as myth (Wasserstrom, 1992:259–261).
70. The claim of hidden agendas of a few leaders who maneuver the blind masses at will typifies a common view of history in the People's Republic, in spite of their socialist commitment to people's history. Studies of the Taiping, for instance, usually see Hong's religion as only a trick he used to create a following, not something he actually believed (see Weller, 1987a).
71. For examples see *Renmin Ribao*, 22 December 1989; 30 December 1989; 27 February 1990; 5 March 1990; 6 March 1990; also *New York Times*, 27 February 1990: A4.
72. Localist interests may similarly provide an institutional space relatively sheltered from official manipulation. Vivienne Shue, for example, argues that collectivism may have strengthened some forms of traditional particularism, and that local cadres had to protect their local domains to survive (Shue, 1988:65,139).
73. Similar effects may occur within schools. Perry Link (1989) shows how hand-copied entertainment fiction flooded through high schools even during the most repressive periods of the Cultural Revolution. Campaigns against it could never uncover any leaders, as the material diffused too formlessly and quickly to stamp out.
74. See Anagnost (1989) for an important analysis of China that similarly uses Lefort to show the internal contradictions created by the totalizing project of the state.
75. I have discussed comparable allegorical readings in Taiping historiography elsewhere (Weller, 1987a).
76. Whyte (1974) has many examples of this, as does Chen (1980) in a fictionalized autobiography that roots this sort of cynical manipulation in the early days of the People's Republic.
77. "*Qigong* deviation" even became an official psychiatric disorder in 1989 (Chen, 1992).
78. See Anagnost (1987, 1989) for more cases of government campaigns against religion.

# Character List

*Note*: **Mandarin and Hokkien terms appear together here. I assume readers who know Chinese will feel no confusion.**

| | |
|---|---|
| Bai Shangdi Ren | 拜上帝人 |
| biao che | 飙车 |
| bu | 补 |
| Budai Heshang | 布袋和尚 |
| Cihui Tang | 慈慧堂 |
| Co Su Kong | 祖师公 |
| Dai Wansheng | 戴万生 |
| dajia le | 大家乐 |
| Daxuanxu | 大宣墟 |
| dian | 奠 |
| dian xue | 点穴 |
| die xian | 碟仙 |
| fa qi | 发气 |
| Feng Yunshan | 冯云山 |
| fu | 福 |
| fumu guan | 父母官 |
| Gan Wang | 甘王 |
| Guan Gong | 关公 |
| Guangxi | 广西 |
| guanxi | 关系 |
| Guanyin | 观音 |
| Gui | 贵 |
| Guiping | 桂平 |

| | |
|---|---|
| guipo | 鬼婆 |
| guniang | 姑娘 |
| Guomindang | 国民党 |
| guqin | 古琴 |
| hoat-su | 法师 |
| Hong Rengan | 洪仁玕 |
| Hong Xiuquan | 洪秀全 |
| hu-a | 符仔 |
| Huang Ermei | 黄二妹 |
| Hu Yiguang | 胡以胱 |
| Iu Ieng Kong | 有应公 |
| iu kiu pit ieng | 有求必应 |
| Jiang Gong | 蒋公 |
| jiao | 醮 |
| Jintian | 金田 |
| jitong | 乩童 |
| kanluan jieyue | 戡乱节约 |
| kui | 鬼 |
| lai | 来 |
| Lang | 朗 |
| Langguang | 朗广 |
| lauziat | 闹热 |
| Leigong | 雷公 |
| Lian | 练 |
| Liang A-fa | 梁阿发 |
| Liao Tianding | 廖添丁 |
| ling | 灵 |
| Lin Shuangwen | 林爽文 |

| | |
|---|---|
| Liu Dagupo | 刘大姑婆 |
| Liuwu | 六乌 |
| luan | 乱 |
| luanyen | 乱言 |
| Luo Dagang | 罗大纲 |
| luotong | 落童 |
| mayou ji | 麻油鸡 |
| Mazu | 妈祖 |
| mifan zhu | 米饭主 |
| Pangu | 盘古 |
| Panhu | 槃瓠 |
| Panwang | 盘王 |
| Panwang Dajiao | 盘王打醮 |
| Panwang Liuluo Shu | 盘王流落书 |
| piancai | 偏财 |
| Pingnan | 平南 |
| qi | 气 |
| Qiansa | 阡陌 |
| qigong | 气功 |
| Qing | 清 |
| Qingming | 清明 |
| Quanshi Liangyen | 劝世良言 |
| renao | 热闹 |
| Sanjie | 三界 |
| Sanxia | 三峡 |
| She Gong | 社公 |
| sheng ku | 圣库 |
| Shi Dakai | 石达开 |

| | |
|---|---|
| Shiba Wanggong | 十八王公 |
| shifu | 师傅 |
| Sigu | 斯谷 |
| siu hun | 收魂 |
| taijiquan | 太极拳 |
| Taiping | 太平 |
| Taiping Tianguo | 太平天国 |
| tang-ki | 童乩 |
| Tho Te Kong | 土地公 |
| Tiananmen | 天安门 |
| Tiandi Hui | 天地会 |
| Tian Hou | 天后 |
| Tianjing | 天京 |
| tianwai you tian | 天外有天 |
| tiao | 跳 |
| tiao gui | 跳鬼 |
| tu | 土 |
| Tudi Gong | 土地公 |
| Wang Zuoxin | 王作新 |
| wansui | 万岁 |
| Wei Changhui | 韦昌辉 |
| Wenchang | 文昌 |
| Xiangzhou | 象州 |

| | |
|---|---|
| xiansheng | 先生 |
| Xiao Chaogui | 萧朝贵 |
| xiaojie | 小姐 |
| Xiao Panshi | 萧盘氏 |
| xie | 邪 |
| Xinxu | 新圩 |
| xiucai | 秀才 |
| Xunzhou | 浔州 |
| yang | 阳 |
| Yang Qingxiu | 杨庆修 |
| Yang Xiuqing | 杨秀清 |
| Yao | 瑶 |
| Yaochi Jinmu | 瑶池金母 |
| Yiguan Dao | 一贯道 |
| yin | 阴 |
| Yiquan | 义犬 |
| Yongan | 永安 |
| Zhuang | 僮 |
| Zijing Shan | 紫荆山 |
| zutou | 组头 |

# Bibliography

Abu-Lughod, Lila, 1990 "The Romance of Resistance: Tracing Transformations of Power Through Bedouin Women," *American Ethnologist*, 17(1): 41–55.

Adas, Michael, 1979 *Prophets of Rebellion: Millenarian Protest Movements Against the European Colonial Order*, Chapel Hill: University of North Carolina Press.

Ahern, Emily M., 1973 *The Cult of the Dead in a Chinese Village*, Stanford: Stanford University Press.

———— 1975 "The Power and Pollution of Chinese Women," in Margery Wolf and Roxane Witke (eds), *Women in Chinese Society*: 193–214, Stanford: Stanford University Press.

———— 1981a *Chinese Ritual and Politics*, New York: Cambridge University Press.

———— 1981b "The Thai Ti Kong Festival," in Emily Martin Ahern and Hill Gates (eds), *The Anthropology of Taiwanese Society*: 397–425, Stanford: Stanford University Press.

Anagnost, Ann S., 1987 "Politics and Magic in Contemporary China," *Modern China* 13(1): 40–61.

———— 1989 "Imagining Community: The 'Civilized Village' Campaign and the 'Return' of Popular Religion in Post-Mao China," paper presented at the Conference on "Communities in Question: Religion and Authority in East and Southeast Asia," Hoa Hin, Thailand.

Arendt, Hannah, 1958 *The Origins of Totalitarianism*, 2nd edn, Cleveland: World Publishing Company, Meridian.

Aron, Raymond, 1977 [1957] *The Opium of the Intellectuals*, trans. Terence Kilmartin, Westport, Conn: Greenwood Press.

Bakhtin, Mikhail, 1984 [1965] *Rabelais and His World*, trans. Hélène Iswolsky, Bloomington: Indiana University Press.

Banwo Jushi, 1874 *Yuekou Qishi Jishi* [Record of the Cantonese Bandit Uprising].

Barone, Michael, 1991 "Washington Whispers," *US News and World Report*, 8 July: 14.

Barthes, Roland, 1975 [1973] *The Pleasure of the Text*, trans. Richard Miller, New York: Noonday Press.

"Beijing Daxue Xuesheng Sixiang Diaocha Baogao [Report on a Study of the Thought of Beijing University Students]," 1990, *Kaifang Zazhi*, September: 55.

Bellah, Robert N., 1965 "Epilogue: Religion and Progress in Modern Asia," in Robert N. Bellah (ed.), *Religion and Progress in Modern Asia*: 168–229, New York: Free Press.

Berger, Peter L., 1988 "An East Asian Development Model?" in Peter L. Berger and Hsin-Huang Michael Hsiao (eds), *In Search of an East Asian Development Model*: 3–11, New Brunswick, NJ: Transaction Books.

Blazek, Bohuslav, 1991 "In Lieu of Marxism: Black Hole," paper presented at the Conference on "Obstacles to the Transformation of Soviet-type Societies in Eastern Europe," Vienna, photocopy.

Bloch, Maurice, 1975 "Introduction," in Maurice Bloch (ed.), *Political Language and Oratory in Traditional Society*: 1–28, London: Academic Press.

Bodde, Derk, 1961 "Myths of Ancient China," in Samuel N. Kramer (ed.), *Mythologies of the Ancient World*, New York: Doubleday.

Bourdieu, Pierre, 1977 *Outline of a Theory of Practice*, trans. Richard Nice, *Cambridge Studies in Social Anthropology*, Vol. 16, Cambridge: Cambridge University Press.

Bradbury, R. E., 1966 "Father, Elders, and Ghosts in Edo Religion," in Michael Banton (ed.), *Anthropological Approaches to the Study of Religion*: 127–153, London: Tavistock.

Brandes, Stanley, 1988, *Power and Persuasion: Fiestas and Social Control in Rural Mexico*, Philadelphia: University of Pennsylvania Press.

"Brief Introduction to the Tsu Shih Temple," 1990, n.p., photocopy.

Cai Fang and Xiao Tian, 1985 "Shiba Wanggong Daojile [The Eighteen Lords Have Arrived]," *Huashi Zonghe Zhoukan*, No. 714, 24 June: 34–36.

Cai Shaoqing, 1987 *Zhongguo Jindai Huidangshi Yanjiu* [Research Into the History of Chinese Secret Societies], Beijing: Zhonghua Shuju.

Chan Yuen Ying, and Kwong, Peter, 1990 "Trashing the Hopes of Tiananmen," *The Nation*, 23 April 1990: 545, 560–64.

Chance, Norman A. and Engst, Fred, 1991 "A Decade of Change," in Norman A. Chance, *China's Urban Villagers*, 2nd edn: 161–87, Fort Worth: Holt, Rinehart & Winston.

Chang, K. C., 1983 *Art, Myth, and Ritual: The Path to Political Authority in Ancient China*, Cambridge, MA: Harvard University Press.

Chen Jo-hsi, 1978 "'Chairman Mao is a Rotten Egg'" in *The Execution of Mayor Yin and Other Stories from the Great Proletarian Cultural Revolution*: 37–66, Bloomington: Indiana University Press.

Chen, Nancy N., 1992 "Deviation and the State: Psychiatry and Popular Practice in Contemporary Urban China," paper presented at the annual meeting of the Association for Asian Studies, Washington, DC.

Chen Tianhui, 1985 "Shiba Wanggong Shi Yingxiong [The Eighteen Lords Are Heros]," *Huashi Zonghe Zhoukan*, No. 713, 17 June: 30–31.

Chen Yuan-tsung, 1980 *The Dragon's Village*, New York: Penguin.

Clarke, Prescott and Gregory, J. S., 1982 *Western Reports on the Taiping: A Selection of Documents*, Honolulu: University Press of Hawaii.

Cohen, Jean L., 1982 *Class and Civil Society: The Limits of Marxian Critical Theory*, Amherst: University of Massachusetts Press.

Cohn, Norman, 1957 *The Pursuit of the Millennium*, London: Secker & Warburg.

Comaroff, Jean, 1985 *Body of Power, Spirit of Resistance: The Culture and History of a South African People*, Chicago: University of Chicago Press.

Crain, Mary M., 1991 "Poetics and Politics in the Ecuadorean Andes: Women's Narratives of Death and Devil Possession," *American Ethnologist*, 18(1): 67–89.

Davenport, Alice and Larocque, Alain, 1986 "The Fall and Rise of an Errant Museum Curator," *Far Eastern Economic Review*, 6 February: 43–45.

Davis, Deborah, 1989 "My Mother's House," in Perry Link, Richard Madsen, and Paul Pickowicz (eds), *Unofficial China: Popular Culture and Thought in the People's Republic*: 88–100, Boulder: Westview.

Davis, Winston, 1980 *Dojo: Magic and Exorcism in Modern Japan*, Stanford: Stanford University Press.

De Grazia, Victoria, 1981 *The Culture of Consent: Mass Organization of Leisure in Fascist Italy*, Cambridge: Cambridge University Press.

Desroche, Henri, 1971 *The American Shakers: From Neo-Christianity to Presocialism*, Amherst: University of Massachusetts Press.

Dodds, E. R., 1951 *The Greeks and the Irrational*, Berkeley: University of California Press.

Douglas, Mary, 1978 [1969] *Purity and Danger: An Analysis of Concepts of Pollution and Taboo*, London: Routledge & Kegan Paul.

Duara, Prasenjit, 1991 "Knowledge and Power in the Discourse of Modernity: The Campaigns Against Popular Religion in Early Twentieth-century China," *Journal of Asian Studies*, 50(1): 67–83.

Dumont, Louis, 1980 *Homo Hierarchicus: The Caste System and Its Implications*, trans. Mark Sainsbury, Louis Dumont and Baisa Gulati, Chicago: University of Chicago Press.

Eco, Umberto, 1984 "The Frames of Comic 'Freedom' " in Thomas A. Sebeok (ed.), *Carnival!*: 1–9, *Approaches to Semiotics*, No. 64, Berlin: Mouton.

Elliott, Peter, 1990 "Call for Hard Work," *Financial Times*, 10 October: 15.

Esherick, Joseph W. and Wasserstrom, Jeffrey N., 1990 "Acting Out Democracy: Political Theater in Modern China," *Journal of Asian Studies*, 49(4): 835–865.

Feuchtwang, Stephan, 1974 "Domestic and Communal Worship in Taiwan," in Arthur P. Wolf (ed.), *Religion and Ritual in Chinese Society*: 105–129, Stanford: Stanford University Press.

———— 1977 "School-temple and City God," in G. William Skinner (ed.), *The City in Late Imperial China*: 581–608, Stanford: Stanford University Press.

———— 1992 *The Imperial Metaphor: Popular Religion in China*, London: Routledge.

Fields, Karen E., 1982 "Charismatic Religion as Popular Protest: The Ordinary and Extraordinary in Social Movements," *Theory and Society*, 11: 321–361.

Firth, Raymond, 1967 *Tikopia Ritual and Belief*, Boston: Beacon.

Fish, Stanley, 1980 *Is There a Text in This Class? The Authority of Interpretive Communities*, Cambridge, MA: Harvard University Press.

Freedman, Maurice, 1966 *Chinese Lineage and Society: Fukien and Kwangtung*, London School of Economics Monographs in Social Anthropology, No. 33, London: Athlone.

Friedland, Jonathan and Kaye, Lincoln, 1990 "Pennies from Heaven," *Far Eastern Economic Review*, 25, January: 54–56.

Gábor, István R., 1991 "Modernity or a New Kind of Duality? Second Thoughts on the 'Second Economy'," paper presented at Conference on the "Obstacles to the Transfomation of Soviet-type Societies in Eastern Europe," Vienna, photocopy.

Garbett, G. Kingsley, 1969 "Spirit Mediums as Mediators in Valley Korekore Society," in John Beattie and John Middleton (eds), *Spirit Mediumship and Society in Africa*, New York: Africana.

Gates, Hill, 1987 "Money for the Gods," *Modern China*, 13: 259–277.

Geertz, Clifford, 1973a [1963] "The Integrative Revolution: Primordial Sentiments and Civil Politics in the New States," in *The Interpretation of Cultures*: 255–310, New York: Basic.

———— 1973b *The Interpretation of Cultures: Selected Essays*, New York: Basic.

Gilmore, David D., 1984 *Aggression and Community: Paradoxes of Andalusian Culture*, New Haven: Yale University Press.

Ginzburg, Carlo, 1980 [1976] *The Cheese and the Worms: The Cosmos of a Sixteenth-century Miller*, trans. John Tedeschi and Anne Tedeschi, Baltimore: Johns Hopkins University Press.

Gluckman, Max, 1960 "Rituals of Rebellion in South-east Africa," in Max Gluckman (ed.), *Order and Rebellion in Tribal Africa*: 110–136, Glencoe, IL: Free Press.

Gold, Thomas B., 1985 "After Comradeship: Personal Relations in China Since the Cultural Revolution," *China Quarterly*, No. 104, December: 657–675.

Goodman, Felicitas D., 1973 "Apostolics of Yucatan: A Case Study of a Religious Movement," in Erika Bourguignon (ed.), *Religion, Altered States of Consciousness, and Social Change*, Columbus, OH: Ohio State University Press.

Gould-Martin, Katherine, 1976 *Women Asking Women: An Ethnography of Health Care in Rural Taiwan*, dissertation submitted to Rutgers University.

Gramsci, Antonio, 1971 *Selections from the Prison Notebooks*, ed. and trans. Quintin Hoare and Geoffrey Nowel Smith, London: Lawrence & Wishart.

Guangxi Shifan Xueyuan Shidixi 72 Ji, 1981 "Taiping Tianguo Qiyi Jige Wenti de Diaocha [Investigation Into Several Questions Concerning the Taiping Heavenly Kingdom Uprising]," in *Taiping Tianguoshi Yanjiu Wenxuan* [Selected Research on the History of the Taiping Heavenly Kingdom], ed. Guangxi Taiping Tianguoshi Yanjiuhui: 271–290, Nanning: Guangxi Renmin Chubanshe.

*Guangxi Tongzhi* [Complete Gazetteer of Guangxi], 1891 Local Gazetteer, Hu Qian (ed.).

Guangxi Zhuangzu Zizhiqu Tongzhiguan, comp., 1962 *Taiping Tianguo Geming Zai Guangxi Diaocha Ziliao Huipian* [Compiled Materials from the Investigation of the Taiping Heavenly Kingdom Revolution in Guangxi], Nanning: Guangxi Zhuangzu Zizhiqu Renmin Chubanshe.

Guangxisheng Taiping Tianguo Wenshi Diaochatuan (ed.), 1956 *Taiping Tianguo Qiyi Diaocha Baogao* [Report on Investigations into the Taiping Heavenly Kingdom Uprising], Beijing: Sanlian Shudian.

*Guiping Xianzhi* [Guiping County Gazetteer], 1920 Local Gazetteer.

*Guixian Zhi* [Gui County Gazetteer], 1893 Local Gazetteer, comp. Liang Jixiang.

Hamberg, Theodore, 1854 *The Visions of Hung-siu-tshuen and the Origin of the Kwang-si Insurrection*, Hong Kong: China Mail.

Han Minzhu (ed.), 1990 *Cries for Democracy: Writing and Speeches from the 1989 Chinese Democracy Movement*, Princeton: Princeton University Press.

Hansen, Valerie, 1990 *Changing Gods in Medieval China, 1127–1276*, Princeton: Princeton University Press.

Harrell, C. Stevan, 1974 "When a Ghost Becomes a God," in Arthur P. Wolf (ed.), *Religion and Ritual in Chinese Society*: 193–206, Stanford: Stanford University Press.

Horton, Robin, 1969 "Types of Spirit Possession in Kalabari Religion," in John Beattie and John Middleton (eds), *Spirit Mediumship and Society in Africa*: 14–49, New York: Africana.

Hsu Wen-hsiung, 1980 "Frontier Social Organization and Social Disorder in Ch'ing Taiwan," in Ronald G. Knapp (ed.), *China's Island Frontier: Studies in the Historical Geography of Taiwan*: 87–105, Honolulu: University Press of Hawaii.

Hu T'ai-li, 1986 "Shen, Gui yu Dutu: Dajia Le Duxi Fanying zhi Minsu Xinyang [Gods, Ghosts and Gamblers: The Influence of Popular Beliefs on the Everybody's Happy Lottery]," paper presented at the Second International Conference on Sinology, Academia Sinica, Taipei.

Huang, Philip C. C., 1990 *The Peasant Family and Rural Development in the Yangzi Delta, 1350–1988*, Stanford: Stanford University Press.

Huang Shu-min, 1989 *The Spiral Road: Change in a Chinese Village Through the Eyes of a Communist Party Leader*, Boulder: Westview.

Ingerson, Alice E., 1984 *Corporatism and Class Consciousness in Northwestern Portugal*, Ph.D dissertation submitted to the Johns Hopkins University.

Ji Feng Yuan, Kuiper, Koenraad and Shu Shaogu, 1990 "Language and Revolution: Formulae of the Cultural Revolution," *Language in Society* 19: 61–79.

Jian Youwen [Jen Yu-wen], 1958 *Taiping Tianguo Dianzhi Tongkao* [Research into the Institutions of the Taiping Heavenly Kingdom], Hong Kong: Mengjin Shuwu.

———— 1973 *The Taiping Revolutionary Movement*, New Haven: Yale University Press.

Jiang Renxiu, 1987 *Dajia Le Dubuo Zhi Yanjiu* [Research Into Everybody's Happy Gambling], Taichung: Taiwan Taizhong Difang Fayuan Jianchachu.

Jordan, David K., 1972 *Gods, Ghosts, and Ancestors: The Folk Religion of a Taiwanese Village*, Berkeley: University of California Press.

Jordan, David K. and Overmyer, Daniel L., 1986 *The Flying Phoenix: Aspects of Chinese Sectarianism in Taiwan*, Princeton: Princeton University Press.

Ju Zhucheng, 1991 "The 'Depreciation' and 'Appreciation' of Some Address Terms in China," *Language in Society*, 20: 87–90.

Kaminsky, Howard, 1962 "The Free Spirit in the Hussite Revolution," in Sylvia L. Thrupp (ed.), *Millenial Dreams in Action: Essays in Comparative Study*, The Hague: Mouton.

Kandre, Peter K., 1976 "Yao (Iu Mien) Supernaturalism, Language, and Ethnicity," in David J. Banks (ed.), *Changing Identities in Modern Southeast Asia*: 171–197, The Hague: Mouton.

Kojima Shinji, 1983 "Shilun Baishangdijiao, Baishangdihui yu Kejiaren de Guanxi [On the Relation Between the God Worshiping Religion, the God Worshiping Society and Hakkas]," in *Taiping Tianguoshi Yizong* [Selections on the History of the Taiping Heavenly Kingdom], Vol. 2, ed. Taiping Tianguo Lishi Yanjiuhui, Beijing: Zhonghua Shuju.

Kuhn, Philip A., 1977 "Origins of the Taiping Vision: Cross-cultural Dimensions of a Chinese Rebellion," *Comparative Studies in Society and History*, 19: 350–366.

Lefort, Claude, 1986 *The Political Forms of Modern Society: Bureaucracy, Democracy, Totalitarianism*, ed. John B. Thompson, Cambridge, MA: MIT Press.

Leonard, Anne P., 1973 "Spirit Mediums in Palau: Transformations in a Traditional System," in Erika Bourguignon (ed.), *Religion, Altered States of Consciousness, and Social Change*, Columbus, OH: Ohio State University Press.

Le Roy Ladurie, Emmanuel, 1979 *Carnival in Romans*, trans. Mary Feeney, New York: G. Brazillier.

Lévi-Strauss, Claude, 1970 *Introduction to a Science of Mythology*, trans. John Weightman and Doreen Weightman, Vol. 1, *The Raw and the Cooked*, New York: Harper & Row, Harper Torchbooks.

Lewis, Ioan M., 1971 *Ecstatic Religion: An Anthropological Study of Spirit Possession and Shamanism*, Harmondsworth: Penguin.

Li Cheng and White, Lynn T. III, 1991 "China's Technocratic Movement and the World Economic Herald," *Modern China*, 17(3): 342–388.

Li Da, 1990 "Qingnian Junguan Dizhi Yang Bobing [Young Officers Oppose Yang Bobing]," *Dangdai Shishi Zhoukan*, 20 October: 14.

Li Feiran, 1981 "Hong Xiuquan Zaoqi Sixiang Pouxi [Analysis of Hong Xiuquan's Early Thought]," in *Taiping Tianguoshi Yanjiu Wenxuan* [Selected Research Articles on the History of the Taiping Heavenly Kingdom], ed. Guangxi Taiping Tianguoshi Yanjiuhui: 120–146, Nanning: Guangxi Renmin Chubanshe.

Li Feiran, Deng Jiezhang, Zhu Zhefang and Peng Dayong, 1982 "Taiping Tianguo Qiyi de Guangxi Shehui [Guangxi Society in the Taiping Heavenly Kingdom Uprising]," in *Taiping Tianguoshi Xintan* [New Analysis of the History of the Taiping Heavenly Kingdom], Nanjing Daxue Lishixi Taiping Tianguoshi Yanjiushi: 147–173, Suzhou: Jiangsu Renmin Chubanshe.

Li Wenhai and LiuYangdong, 1989 *Taiping Tianguo Shehui Fengqing* [Social Customs of the Taiping Heavenly Kingdom], Beijing: Zhongguo Renmin Daxue Chubanshe.

Li Yih-yuan, 1988 "Taiwan Minjian Zongjiao de Xiandai Qushi: Dui Peter Berger Jiaoshou Dongya Fazhan Wenhua Yinsu Lun de Huiying [The Modern Tendencies of Taiwan's Popular Religion: A Response to Professor Peter Berger's Theory of Cultural Factors in East Asian Development]," unpublished paper, photocopy.

Lian Shilun and Lian Huijin, 1985 *Shiba Wanggong de Youlai (shang)* [The Origin of the Eighteen Lords (part 1)], Tanshui: privately printed.

Liang Renbao, 1981 [1957] "Taiping Tianguo he Kuanggong [The Taiping Heavenly Kingdom and Miners]," in *Taiping Tianguoshi Yanjiu Wenxuan* [Selected Research on the History of the Taiping Heavenly Kingdom], ed. Guangxi Taiping Tianguoshi Yanjiuhui: 50–64, Nanning: Guangxi Renmin Chubanshe.

Limón, José, 1989 "*Carne, Carnales*, and the Carnivalesque: Bakhtinian *Batos*, Disorder, and Narrative Discourses," *American Ethnologist*, 16(3): 471–486.

Link, Perry, 1989 "Hand-copied Entertainment Fiction from the Cultural Revolution," in Perry Link, Richard Madsen, and Paul Pickowicz (eds), *Unofficial China: Popular Culture and Thought in the People's Republic*: 17–36, Boulder: Westview.

Liu Jie, 1963 "Taiping Tianguo zai Guangxi Qiyi de Zhuyao Yuanyin [Major Causes of the Guangxi Uprising of the Taiping Heavenly Kingdom]," *Guangxi Zhuangzu Zizhiqu Lishi Xuehui Yuekan*, 1963(1).

Lü Simian, 1982 *Lü Simian Dushi Zhaji* [Lü Simian's Notes on Reading History], Shanghai: Shanghai Guji Chubanshe.

Lu Yangyuan, 1982 "Taiping Tianguo Qiyi Qian de Tudi Wenti [Land Problems Before the Taiping Heavenly Kingdom Uprising]," *Guangxi Shehuikexueyuan Lunwenxuan Lishi Zhuanji* 1982: 1–11.

Lubman, Sarah, 1989 "The Myth of Tiananmen Square: The Students Talked Democracy But They Didn't Practice It," *Washington Post*, 30 July: C5.

Madsen, Richard, 1984 *Morality and Power in a Chinese Village*, Berkeley: University of California Press.

Malinowski, Bronislaw, 1935 *Coral Gardens and Their Magic*, Vol. 2, London: George Allen & Unwin.

Mao Jiaqi, 1981 "Taiping Tianguo Lishishang Jige Wenti de Zhiyi [Doubts About Several Questions Concerning the History of the Taiping Heavenly Kingdom]," in *Taiping Tianguo Shixueshu Taolunhui Lunwen Xuanji* [Collected Essays from the Symposium on Historical Studies of the Taiping Heavenly Kingdom], ed. Zhonghua Shuju Jindaishi Bianjishi, Vol. 3: 727–746, Beijing: Zhonghua Shuju.

————— 1989 "'Tianxiong Xiafan Shengzhi' He Taiping Tianguo Zaoqi Lishi de Jige Wenti [Several Problems Concerning the 'Sacred Orders of the Heavenly Elder Brother on Earth' and the Early History of the Taiping Heavenly Kingdom]," in *Taiping Tianguo Shi Yanjiu, Erji* [Research into the History of the Taiping Heavenly Kingdom, Vol. 2], ed. Mao Jiaqi: 23–39, Nanjing: Nanjing University Press.

Mao Jiaqi, Fang Zhiguang and Dong Guanghua (eds), 1980 *Taiping Tianguo Xingwangshi* [History of the Rise and Fall of the Taiping Heavenly Kingdom], Shanghai: Shanghai Renmin Chubanshe.

Martin, David, 1990 *Tongues of Fire: The Explosion of Protestantism in Latin America*, Oxford: Blackwell.

Martin, Emily, 1988 "Gender and Ideological Differences in Representations of Life and Death," in James L. Watson and Evelyn S. Rawski (eds), *Death Ritual in Late Imperial and Modern China*: 164–179, Berkeley: University of California Press.

Meaney, Connie Squires, 1991 "Market Reform and Disintegrative Corruption in Urban China," in Richard Baum (ed.), *Reform and Reaction in Post-Mao China: The Road to Tiananmen*: 124–142, New York: Routledge.

Meskill, Johanna Menzel, 1979 *A Chinese Pioneer Family: The Lins of Wu-feng, Taiwan, 1729–1895*, Princeton: Princeton University Press.

Michael, Franz, 1966–1971 *The Taiping Rebellion: History and Documents*, in collaboration with Chang Chung-li, Seattle: University of Washington Press, 3 vols.

Migdal, Joel S. 1982 "Capitalist Penetration in the Nineteenth Century: Creating Conditions for New Patterns of Social Control," in Robert P.

Weller and Scott E. Guggenheim (eds), *Power and Protest in the Countryside: Studies in Rural Unrest in Asia, Europe and Latin America*: 57–74, Durham: Duke University Press.

Ming Pao News Staff, 1989 *June Four: A Chronicle of the Chinese Democratic Uprising*, trans. Zi Jin and Qin Zhou, Fayetteville: University of Arkansas Press.

Myers, Ramon H., 1980 *The Chinese Economy: Past and Present*, Belmont, California: Wadsworth.

*New York Times*, New York, newspaper; articles by Nicholas Kristof and Sheryl WuDunn.

Oi, Jean, 1991 "Partial Market Reform and Corruption in Rural China," in Richard Baum (ed.), *Reform and Reaction in Post-Mao China: The Road to Tiananmen*: 143–161, New York: Routledge.

Ouyang Ming, 1990 "'Ni Re Wo Ye Re [Your Fads and Mine]," *Kaifang Zazhi*, September: 21.

Overmyer, Daniel L., 1974 "The Tz'u-hui T'ang: A Contemporary Religious Sect on Taiwan," paper presented at the Annual Meeting of the Canadian Society for Asian Studies, Toronto.

————— 1989 "Attitudes Toward Popular Religion in Ritual Texts of the Chinese State: *The Collected Statutes of the Great Ming*," unpublished paper, n.p., photocopy.

Paige, Jeffrey M., 1975 *Agrarian Revolution: Social Movements and Export Agriculture in the Underdeveloped World*, New York: Free Press.

Passerini, Luisa, 1987 *Fascism in Popular Memory: The Cultural Experience of the Turin Working Class*, Cambridge: Cambridge University Press.

Perry, Elizabeth J., 1991 "Intellectuals and Tiananmen: Historical Perspective on an Aborted Revolution," in Daniel Chirot (ed.), *The Crisis of Leninism and the Decline of the Left: The Revolutions of 1989*: 129–146, Seattle: University of Washington.

Peters, Matt, 1991 "Rock 'n' Revolt," *Far Eastern Economic Review*, 28 March: 30–31.

*Pingnan Xianzhi* [Pingnan County Gazetteer], 1883 Local Gazetteer, comp. Qiu Bin.

Polanyi, Karl, 1944 *The Great Transformation*, New York: Rinehart.

Qiu Dezai, 1979 *Taiwan Miaoshen Zhuan* [The Story of Taiwan's Temples and Gods], Taipei: Xintong Shuju.

Qu Haiyuan, 1987 "*Dajia Le*" *Xianxiang zhi Chengyin yu Yingxiang zhi Yanjiu* [Research Into the Origins and Influence of the "Everybody's Happy" Phenomenon], Taipei: Xingzhengyuan Yanjiu Fazhan Kaohehui.

Qu Haiyuan and Yao Lixiang, 1986 "Taiwan Diqu Zongjiao Bianqian zhi Tantao [Discussion of Religious Changes in the Taiwan Area]," *Bulletin of the Institute of Ethnology, Academia Sinica*, 75: 655–685.

Rabelais, François, 1955 *Gargantua and Pantagruel*, ed. J.M. Cohen, Harmondsworth: Penguin.

*Raozhi* [Stopping the Cycle], 1978 Kaohsiung: Raozhi Zazhishe.

*Renmin Ribao* [People's Daily], Beijing, newspaper.

Rév, István, 1987 "The Advantages of Being Atomized: How Hungarian Peasants Coped with Collectivization," *Dissent*, 34(3): 335–350.

Rohsenow, Hill Gates, 1973 *Prosperity Settlement: The Politics of Paipai in Taipei, Taiwan*, dissertation submitted to the University of Michigan.

Sangren, P. Steven, 1987 *History and Magical Power in a Chinese Community*, Stanford: Stanford University Press.

Schöpflin, George, 1991 "Conservative Politics and Factors of Conservatism in Post-Communist Polities," paper presented to the Conference on the "Obstacles to the Transformation of Soviet-Type Societies in Eastern Europe," Vienna, photocopy.

Scott, James C., 1976 *The Moral Economy of the Peasant: Rebellion and Subsistence in Southeast Asia*, New Haven: Yale University Press.

———— 1985 *Weapons of the Weak: Everyday Forms of Peasant Resistance*, New Haven: Yale University Press.

Seaman, Gary, 1978 *Temple Organization in a Chinese Village. Asian Folkore and Social Life Monographs*, Vol. 101, Taipei: Orient Cultural Service.

———— 1981 "The Sexual Politics of Karmic Retribution," in Emily Martin Ahern and Hill Gates (eds), *The Anthropology of Taiwanese Society*: 381–396, Stanford: Stanford University Press.

Shahar, Meir, 1991 "Lucky Dog," *Free China Review*, July: 64–69.

Shang Tong, 1990 "Yi Ge Nande de Xiqing Jieri: Fuzhou Laiqu Jianwen [A Rare Holiday: A Trip to Fuzhou]," *Jiushi Niandai Yuekan*, February: 104–105.

Shepherd, John, 1984 "Sinicized Siraya Worship of A-li-tsu," *Bulletin of the Institute of Ethnology, Academia Sinica*, 58: 1–81.

Shi Ming, 1990 "Dalu Mimi Xing [A Secret Visit to the Mainland]," *Minzhu Zhongguo Yuekan*, February: 17–23.

*Shiba Wanggong Chuanqi* [The Strange Tale of the Eighteen Lords], 1985, television series, Director Song Wenzhong, Zhonghua Dianshitai.

*Shiba Wanggong* [The Eighteen Lords], 1985, film, Yonghuai Gongsi.

*Shijie Ribao*, Hong Kong, newspaper.

Shue, Vivienne, 1988 *The Reach of the State: Sketches of the Chinese Body Politic*, Stanford: Stanford University Press.

Siu, Helen F., 1989a *Agents and Victims in South China: Accomplices in Rural Revolution*, New Haven: Yale University Press.

———— 1989b "Recycling Rituals: Politics and Popular Culture in Contemporary Rural China," in Perry Link, Richard Madsen, and Paul Pickowicz (eds), *Unofficial China: Popular Culture and Thought in the People's Republic*: 121–137, Boulder: Westview.

Skocpol, Theda, 1979 *States and Social Revolutions: A Comparative Analysis of France, Russia, and China*, New York: Cambridge University Press.

*South China Morning Post*, Hong Kong, newspaper.

Speidel, William M., 1976 "The Administrative and Fiscal Reforms of Liu Ming-ch'uan in Taiwan, 1884–1891: Foundations of Self-strengthening," *Journal of Asian Studies*, 35(3): 441–459.

Strand, David, 1990 "'Civil Society' and 'Public Sphere' in Modern China: A Perspective on Popular Movements in Beijing, 1919–1989," *Duke Working Papers in Asian/Pacific Studies*, Durham: Duke University Press.

Strickmann, Michel, 1982 "The Tao Among the Yao: Taoism and the Sinification of South China," in *Rekishi Ni Okeru Minshu to Bunka*, 23–30, Tokyo.

Su Fengwen, 1889a "Gufei Zonglu [Compilation of Sectarian Bandits]," in *Guangxi Tongzhi Jiyao* [Summary of Guangxi Gazetteers], ed. Su Zongjing, rev. Yang Fuli.
———— 1889b "Pinggui Jilue [Record of Pacifying Guangxi]," in *Guangxi Tongzhi Jiyao* [Summary of Guangxi Gazetteers], ed. Su Zongjing, rev. Yang Fuli.
*Taiwansheng Tongzhi* [Gazetteer of Taiwan Province], 1980 comp. Taiwansheng Wenxian Weiyuanhui, Taipei: Zhongwen.
Tambiah, S. J., 1970 *Buddhism and the Spirit Cults in North-east Thailand*, Cambridge Studies in Social Anthropology, No. 2, Cambridge: Cambridge University Press.
Taussig, Michael T., 1980 *The Devil and Commodity Fetishism in South America*, Chapel Hill: University of North Carolina Press.
Thom, Françoise, 1989 *Newspeak: The Language of Soviet Communism*, trans. Ken Connelly, London: Claridge Press.
Thompson, E. P., 1971 "The Moral Economy of the English Crowd in the Eighteenth Century," *Past and Present*, 50: 76–136.
Thrupp, Sylvia L., 1962 "Millennial Dreams in Action: A Report on the Conference Discussion," in Sylvia L. Thrupp (ed.), *Millennial Dreams in Action*, The Hague: Mouton.
Tilly, Charles, 1982 "Routine Conflicts and Peasant Rebellions in Seventeenth-century France," in Robert P. Weller and Scott E. Guggenheim (eds), *Power and Protest in the Countryside: Rural Unrest in Asia, Europe, and Latin America*: 13–41, Durham: Duke University Press.
Topley, Marjorie, 1975 "Marriage Resistance in Rural Kwangtung," in Margery Wolf and Roxane Witke (eds), *Women in Chinese Society*: 67–88, Stanford: Stanford University Press.
Turner, Victor, 1967 *Forest of Symbols: Aspects of Ndembu Ritual*, Ithaca: Cornell University Press.
———— 1969 *The Ritual Process: Structure and Anti-structure*. Symbol, Myth, and Ritual Series, Ithaca: Cornell University Press.
———— 1974 *Dramas, Fields, and Metaphors: Symbolic Action in Human Society*, Ithaca: Cornell University Press.
Verdery, Katherine, 1991 "Theorizing Socialism: A Prologue to the 'Transition'," *American Ethnologist* 18(3): 419–439.
Wagner, Rudolf G., 1982 *Reenacting the Heavenly Vision: The Role of Religion in the Taiping Rebellion*. China Research Monograph, No. 25, Berkeley: Institute of East Asian Studies, University of California, Berkeley.
Wakeman, Frederic, 1966 *Strangers at the Gate: Social Disorder in South China, 1839–1861*, Berkeley: University of California Press.
Wallace, Anthony F. C., 1956 "Revitalization Movements," *American Anthropologist*, 58: 264–281.
Wang Qingcheng, 1981 "Lun Hong Xiuquan de Zaoqi Sixiang ji Qi Fazhan [On the Early Thought of Hong Xiuquan and Its Development]," in *Taiping Tianguoshi Xueshu Taolunhui Lunwen Xuanji* [Selected Articles from the Conference on the History of the Taiping Heavenly Kingdom], ed. Zhonghua Shuju Jindaishi Bianjiwu: 243–280, Beijing: Zhonghua Shuju.

————— 1985 " 'Tianfu Shengzhi,' 'Tianxiong Shengzhi' he Taiping Tianguo Lishi ['Holy Writs of the Heavenly Father,' 'Holy Writs of the Heavenly Elder Brother' and the History of the Taiping Heavenly Kingdom]," *Jindaishi Yanjiu*: 191–239.

Wang Shilang, 1980 *Riben Zhimindi Tizhi Xia de Taiwan* [Taiwan Under the Japanese Colonial System], Taipei: Zhongwen Tushu Gongsi.

Wang Xiyou, 1991 "Beijing Dangan [Beijing File]," *Jiushi Niandai Yuekan*, July: 52–53.

Wasserstrom, Jeffrey N., 1992 "Afterword: History, Myth, and the Tales of Tiananmen," in Jeffrey N. Wasserstrom and Elizabeth J. Perry (eds), *Popular Protest and Political Culture in Modern China*: 244–280, Boulder, CO: Westview Press.

Watson, James L., 1985 "Standardizing the Gods: The Promotion of T'ien Hou ('Empress of Heaven') Along the South China Coast, 960–1960," in David Johnson, Andrew J. Nathan, and Evelyn S. Rawski (eds), *Popular Culture in Late Imperial China*: 292–324, Berkeley: University of California Press.

Watson, James L. and Rawski, Evelyn S. eds, 1988, *Death Ritual in Late Imperial and Modern China*, Berkeley: University of California Press.

Weber, Max, 1946 "The Protestant Sects and the Spirit of Capitalism," in H. H. Gerth and C. Wright Mills (eds), *From Max Weber: Essays in Sociology*: 302–322, New York: Oxford University Press.

————— 1958 *The Protestant Ethic and the Spirit of Capitalism*, trans. Talcott Parsons, Foreword by R. H. Tawney, New York: Scribner's.

————— 1978 [1956] *Economy and Society: An Outline of Interpretive Sociology*, eds Guenther Roth and Claus Wittich, Berkeley: University of California Press.

Weller, Robert P., 1984 "Ideology, Organization and Rebellion in Chinese Sectarian Religion," in Janos M. Bak and Gerhard Benecke (eds), *Religion and Rural Revolt*: 390–406, Manchester: Manchester University Press.

————— 1985 "Bandits, Beggars and Ghosts: The Failure of State Control Over Religious Interpretation in Taiwan," *American Ethnologist* 12(1): 46–61.

————— 1987a "Historians and Consciousness: The Modern Politics of the Taiping Heavenly Kingdom," *Social Research*, 54(4): 731–755.

————— 1987b "The Politics of Ritual Disguise: Repression and Response in Taiwanese Religion," *Modern China*, 13: 17–39.

————— 1987c *Unities and Diversities in Chinese Religion*, Seattle: University of Washington.

Whyte, Martin K., 1974 *Small Groups and Political Rituals in China*, Berkeley: University of California Press.

————— 1988 "Death in the People's Republic of China," in James L. Watson and Evelyn S. Rawski (eds), *Death Ritual in Late Imperial and Modern China*: 289–316, Berkeley: University of California Press.

Wierzbicka, Anna, 1990 "Antitotalitarian Language in Poland: Some Mechanisms of Linguistic Self-defense," *Language in Society*, 19: 1–59.

Williams, Raymond, 1977 *Marxism and Literature*, Oxford: Oxford University Press.

Winn, Jane Kaufman, 1991 "Banking and Finance in Taiwan: The Prospects for Internationalization in the 1990s," unpublished paper.

Wolf, Arthur P. 1974 "Gods, Ghosts, and Ancestors," in Arthur P. Wolf (ed.), *Religion and Ritual in Chinese Society*: 131–82, Stanford: Stanford University Press.

Wolf, Eric R., 1958 "The Virgin of Guadalupe: A Mexican National Symbol," *Journal of American Folklore*, 71: 34–39.

———— 1969 *Peasant Wars of the Twentieth Century*, New York: Harper & Row.

Worsley, Peter, 1968 *The Trumpet Shall Sound: A Study of "Cargo" Cults in Melanesia*, 2nd edn, New York: Schocken.

*Wuxuan Xianzhi* [Wuxuan County Gazetteer], 1914 Local Gazetteer, Tang Chaosheng (ed.).

Xian Xiang, 1991 "Zai Guangzhou Kan Cui Jian Yanchanghui [Watching Cui Jian's Concert in Guangzhou]," *Jiushi Niandai Yuekan*, March: 60–61.

Xie Xingyao, 1950 *Taiping Tianguo Qianhou Guangxi de Fan Qing Yundong* [Anti-Qing Movements in Guangxi Around the Taiping Heavenly Kingdom], Beijing: Renmin Chubanshe.

Xing Fenglin, 1981 "Guanyu Yang Xiuqing Jiatuo Tianfu Fushen Chuanyan de Ruogan Wenti [On Several Questions Concerning Yang Xiuqing's False Possessions by the Heavenly Father]," in *Taiping Tianguoshi Yanjiu Wenxuan* [Selected Research on the History of the Taiping Heavenly Kingdom], ed. Guangxi Taiping Tianguoshi Yanjiuhui. Nanning: Guangxi Renmin Chubanshe.

*Xinsheng Bao* [New Life], Newspaper, Taipei.

*Xunzhou Fuzhi* [Xunzhou Prefecture Gazetteer], 1897 Local Gazetteer, comp. Xia Jingyi.

Yan, Yunxiang, 1991 "Factors of Stability and Instability in Rural China: A View from a Heilongjiang Village," paper presented at Fairbank Center for East Asian Research, Harvard University.

Yan Zhengji, 1962 [1854] "Lun Yuexi Zei Qingbing Shi Shimo [All About the Guangxi Bandits and the Qing Army]," in *Taiping Tianguo Shiliao Zongpian Jianji*, Vol. 2 [Selected Historical Sources on the Taiping Heavenly Kingdom], comp. Taiping Tianguo Lishi Bowuguan, Beijing: Zhonghua Shuju.

Yang, Mayfair Mei-Hui, 1989 "The Gift Economy and State Power in China," *Comparative Studies in Society and History* 31(1): 25–54.

Yao Ying, 1867 *Zhongfutang Quanji* [Collected Works from the Zhongfu Hall], Nanjing University Library, microfilm.

———— 1957, *Dongcha Jilue* [Sketch of My Assignment to Taiwan], Taipei: Taiwan Yinhang.

Yi Mu, and Thompson, Mark V., 1989 *Crisis at Tiananmen: Reform and Reality in Modern China*, San Francisco: China Books.

Yu Gan, 1991 "'Wo Ai Ting Aiyue' ['I Like Listening to Dirges']," *Zhengming*, May: 21.

Yu Kuang-hong, 1990 "Making a Malefactor a Benefactor: Ghost Worship in Taiwan," *Bulletin of the Institute of Ethnology, Academia Sinica*, 70: 39–66.

"Yueni Jilüe [Record of the Cantonese Rebels]," n.d., in *Taiping Tianguo Shiliao Zongpian* [Collected Historical Sources on the Taiping Heavenly

Kingdom], ed. Taiping Tianguo Lishi Bowuguan, Vol. 2, Beijing: Zhon-
ghua Shuju, 1962.
Zagorin, Perez, 1990 *Ways of Lying: Dissimulation, Persecution, and Conformity
in Early Modern Europe*, Cambridge MA: Harvard University Press.
Zhang Zongrong, 1985 *Shiba Wanggong Chuanqi* [The Strange Tale of the
Eighteen Lords], in collaboration with Li Liqing, Taipei: Yiqun.
Zhong Wendian, 1984a " 'Mifan Zhu' Sanlun [Some Thoughts on 'Rice
Lords']," paper presented at Jindai Zhongguo Huitang Wenti Xueshu
Taolunhui.
———— 1984b *Taiping Tianguo Renwu* [Personalities of the Taiping Hea-
venly Kingdom], Nanning: Guangxi Renmin Chubanshe.
Zinoviev, Alexander, 1984 *The Reality of Communism*, ed. Charles Janson,
New York: Schocken.

# Index

*Note:* Most references are to China, unless otherwise stated.

accommodation: and
  resistance  116–17, 167–8
address, titles of  215–16
Ahern, Emily  7, 52, 116
ambiguity  181–2
amoral marginal cults  87–8
ancestor worship  217
Ang Gong  171–2
anomie  211–12
Apollonian cult (Greece)  87
Apostolics (Yucatan)  89–90
architecture
  Eighteen Lords temple  132–4
  Taiwanese temples  119–22
Arendt, Hannah  188, 219
arts: and subversion  209–10
Asia, Southeast: class culture  10

Bakhtin, Mikhail  11, 17–18, 22
bandits  43–5, 58, 98–9
  recruitment to Taiping  44–5
baptism: of money  11, 166
Barthes, Roland  18–19, 22
Beijing: Forbidden City  119
Berger, Peter  152
Big-head Goat (Zhang Zhao)  44,
  45
boundaries, social: and spirit
  possession  79–82
Bourdieu, Pierre  20
Brandes, Stanley  12
Budai Heshang (Cloth-bag
  Monk)  138–9

campaigns, government, post-
  Tiananmen  198–200, 204, 208,
  210–11, 212, 217–18
capitalism
  and rural unrest  41–3
  and Taiwanese religion  148–52,
  166–7
Carnival  11, 12–13, 25
Catholic Church  90

chaos  12–13, 197
  and control  169–76
charcoal  42
chemistry: saturation  23
Chen Jo-hsi  203–4
Chen, Millionaire  201–2
Christianity
  and Hong Xiuquan  36–40, 72
  and Taiping  34–5, 50–1, 60–4
chromaticism  16
cigarettes: as offerings  136,
  137–9
class: tacit resistance  9–15
Cloth-bag Monk (Budai
  Heshang)  138–9
Co Su Kong  171
  ritual  7, 172–3
  temples  120, 121
collecting the souls (*siu hun*)  156–7
Colombia  144
  baptism of money  11, 166
  devil worship  3, 149–50, 166
communitas  26
Confucius
  birthday ritual  172
  destruction of tablets  38–9, 61
control
  and institutions  187–204
  and language  205–13
  limits of  169–83
  religious: by elites  55–6, 172–4;
    by government  54–5,
    169–72, 176–80; in
    sects  174–6
  of saturation  26–7
  of spirit possession  72, 90–4,
    175
  of Taiping  94–110, 182–3
corruption: and Tiananmen  195–6
criminals: exposure by
  mediums  98–9
  *see also* bandits; pirates
Cui Jian  210

249

cults
amoral marginal 87–8
official state 54–5
organization of 87–94
*see also* possession, spirit; Taiping
Cultural Revolution 207–8
and identity 214
mass criticism meetings 189
nostalgia campaign 199, 210–11, 217–18
curing, magical 87, 106
and Taiping 64–8

Daoism
magical curing 65
ritual 122–3
Daoist Association 156
death: and revolution 191–5
*see also* funerals; mourning
decoration: Taiwanese temples 120–1
Delphic oracle (Greece) 91–2
democracy: and Tiananmen 195
Deng Xiaoping 197
*die xian* (bowl spirit) 137
difference: and resistance 25–6
Dionysian cult (Greece) 87
dog worship 47, 58–9
in Eighteen Lords temple 134–5
domination *see* control
doxa 20
dress: and identity 214–15

Earth Gods 52–3
She Gong temples 217
temple destruction 62
Tho Te Kong 5, 131, 132–3
Eco, Umberto 12
economy
commodity 11, 202; and ghosts 144–5
and rural unrest 41–3
second 201–2
and Taiwanese religion 148–52, 166–7
Edo (West Africa) 143
education: exam system 36
Eighteen Lords temple
academic readings 165–8

anomalies of 131–9
booklet 164–5
copies of 155–7
failed precipitations 154–68
and lotteries 139–42
movie 150, 157–61
rise in popularity 124–8
television soap opera 161–4
elites: religious control 55–6, 172–4
England: class culture 10
ethnic boundaries: and spirit possession 79–81
ethnic composition
of Taiping 79–80
of Xunzhou Prefecture 46–8
Everybody's Happy
(*dajia le*) 139–42, 178–9
examination system 36

families
free space 203
Taiping on 99–100
fascism: and identity 213–18
Feng family 56–7
Feng Yunshan 37, 79, 82, 98
in Guangxi 50
imprisonment 64, 95
temple destruction 61, 62
Fish, Stanley 21–2
free space 26–8
mourning as 191–3
religious 51–6
and rural unrest 40–9
socialist 200–4
and Taiping 40–9, 51–60
funerals 144–5, 191–4

Gan Wang 57–8, 63
Gates, H. 116
Geertz, Clifford 6
gender relations: Taiping 33
Germany, East 220
ghost(s)
festivals 170–1
and lotteries 141–2
worship 3–4, 28, 129–31, 147–8; and financial rewards 143–5

ghost(s) (*cont.*)
  *see also* Eighteen Lords temple
Ginzburg, Carlo 10–11
God Worshipers (Bai Shangdi Ren)
  *see* Taiping
gods
  Chinese 51–6; and
    Taiping 60–4
  magical curing 65
  in Taiwan 146–7
  of Xunzhou Prefecture 56–60
  *see also under specific names*
Good Words to Admonish the Age 36,
  37, 38
government
  and control 188–204
  and identity 213–18
  and interpretative
    communities 176–80
  official language 205–13
  and religious control 54–5,
    169–72, 176–80
  and saturation 26–7
  and spirit possession 72, 175
  use of mediums 92
Gramsci, Antonio 9, 10
Grandaunt Liu (Liu Dagupuo) 59
Guan Gong 51
Guangxi 34
  free space 40–9, 50–1, 56–60
  magical curing 65–7
  spirit possession 70–2, 103–4
*guanxi* (personal networks) 201–3
Guanyin 82–3, 217
Guiping 59, 70–1, 217
*guniang* temples 59
Guoyu 92

Hakkas
  in Taiping 79–80
  in Xunzhou Prefecture 46, 47,
    48
Hamberg, Theodore 34, 39, 45, 63,
  72–3, 74
Hansen, V. 54
heat and noise (*lauziat*)
  control of 169–76
  in Eighteen Lords temple 127–8
  in Taiwanese temples 118–24

heterodoxy 20
Hong Rengan 34, 37, 38, 66, 69
Hong Xiuquan 34, 35, 50, 79, 105
  ideology 50–1, 60–4, 82–3, 84
  magical curing 64, 65–6
  move to politics 96–7
  spirit possession 73, 94–5
  vision 36–40, 72
Hu T'ai-li 141, 142
Hu Yaobang: funeral 190, 192–3
Hu Yiguang 46
Hua County: Hong Xiuquan
  in 36–9
Huang Ermei 97
Huang Shu-min 202–3
Hungary 213

identity: in totalitarian
  states 213–18
ideology
  state control of 187–204
  Taiping 33–5
illness *see* curing, magical
incense 5–6
  cigarettes as substitute for 136,
    137–9
indigo 42–3
institutions: and control 187–204
  *see also* government
intellectuals: as leaders 40
interpretation
  and control 181–3
  of Eighteen Lords temple 152–3
  and language 205–13
  of religion 5–9, 19–20, 117–18,
    123–4
  of resistance 3–15
  and saturation 16–29
  social power of 221–4
  and spirit possession 75–6
  and Taiping 86–7, 94–110
  of Tiananmen 192–6; by
    state 196–200
interpretative communities 21–2
  and government 176–80
  in Hua County 38–9
  in religion 53–6
  in Xunzhou Prefecture 84
Iran 220

Italy
  class consciousness 9
  official language 207
Iu Ieng Kong temples 131
  see also Eighteen Lords temple;
    ghost worship

Japan: occupation of Taiwan 114
Jiang Jingguo 115, 178
Jiang Nan 178, 179
jiao 53, 58
journeys, spirit 71–2
jumping (tiao) 77

Kalabari (Nigeria) 87
King Gan (Gan Wang) 57–8, 63
Kristof, Nicholas 204

Lai Ning 200, 203
land reform: Taiping 33
Lang temple 59
language
  anti-totalitarian 206
  and cultural domination 181–2,
    189, 205–13
  saturation of meaning 16–29
  wooden 206
language games 69–70
Lee, Ann 92–3
Lefort, Claude 214
Lei Feng 199, 203
Le Roy Ladurie, E. 25
Lévi-Strauss, Claude:
  mediators 16–17
Li Meishu 121, 172–3
Li Peng 191
Lian family 164–5
Liang A-fa 36, 38
Liao Tianding temple 137, 147
  television soap opera 162–3
literature: post-structural
  theory 20–2
Liuwu temple, Sigu 47, 59, 61–2
lotteries 139–42, 178–9
Luo Dagang 82

Ma Co (Mazu) temples 120
  see also Tian Hou

Mao Zedong 217–18
Martin, E. see Ahern
Mazu see Ma Co; Tian Hou
meaning
  multiplicity of 221–4
  of rituals 5–9, 19–20
  saturation of 16–29
  see also interpretation; language
media
  censorship in Taiwan 177
  and Eighteen Lords temple 150,
    151, 157–65
  interpretation of
    Tiananmen 197–8
  and subversion 208–11
mediators 16–17
mediums 71–3, 77
  authority in Taiping 73–5
  and cult organization 91–2
  exposure of criminals 98–9
  spirit writing 174–5
  in Taiwan 146
  see also possession, spirit
military: after Tiananmen 198
miners, silver 43
mothers, new: and
  pollution 136–7
Mountainstreet village 171–2
mourning
  as free space 191–3
  symbolism 193–4
movements, new: leaders 39–40
movies
  Eighteen Lords temple 150,
    157–61
  and subversion 209–10
music
  and subversion 209–10
  in Taiwanese rituals 122
  Tristan chord 16–17

names: and identity 215
Nanjing: Taiping in 104–5
Nanjing Museum 191–2
networks, personal (guanxi) 201–3
newspapers: and subversion 209
nostalgia campaign 199, 210–11,
  217–18

offerings: in Eighteen Lords
temple 135–9
officials *see* government
Opium War (1839–42) 43
opossums 16
orthodoxy 20, 117
Overmyer, D. L. 169–70

Palau Modekngei 81, 90
Pangu 47, 58–9
peasant culture 10–12
*see also* working class
*People's Daily* 197, 208, 209
*piancai* 148–9
pigs: in rituals 6, 7–8, 19
pirates, river 43, 44
Poland 220
official language 206
Polanyi, K. 149
pollution: of new mothers 136–7
Portugal: official language 207
possession, spirit 34
emotional power of 75–9
faking 105
mass 77, 89–90
and organization of cults 87–94
power of 72–85
problems of 103–4
and social boundaries 79–82
of Taiping 69–75, 78–81, 82–5,
97–8, 103–4
in Taiwan 141, 146
in Xunzhou Prefecture 69–72
post-structuralism 221
and meaning 20–2
precipitation 26–9
in Eighteen Lords
temple 154–68
and saturation 180–3
of Taiping 35, 86–110
priests, Daoist 123
publications
Eighteen Lords booklet 164–5
of Taiping 100–1

Qiansa temple 59
*qigong* exercise 216–17

Rabelais, François 11, 17–18

rainbows 16
rationalization 22–3, 106–7
reciprocity: in socialist
systems 201–3
religion
and capitalism 148–52, 166–7
in China 51–6
control of 54–6, 169–80
and government 169–72,
176–80
and Hong Xiuquan 36–40, 72
and lotteries 139–42
and resistance 220
resurgence of 217; in
Taiwan 115–16, 146–8
and Taiping 34–5, 50–1, 60–4
in Xunzhou Prefecture 47–8,
56–60
*see also* ghost worship;
possession, spirit; rituals;
temples
Religion of Compassion (Cihui
Tang) 77–8, 82
resistance 180–3
concepts of 3–13
and Eighteen Lords
temple 166–8
and interpretation 13–15, 16–29
and official language 208–13
and organization 218–21
religious activity as 116–18
Rév, István 213–14
reversals: of dominant
order 12–13
revolution: and death 191–5
rice lords (*mifan zhu*) 45–6
Righteous Dog (Yiquan)
temples 135
rituals 76
control of 54–6, 172–4
in Eighteen Lords temple 127,
135–9
meanings of 5–9, 19–20
and possession cults 81–5
and Taiping 63–4
in Taiwanese temples 122–3
*see also* ghost worship
Roberts, Issachar 50, 64, 94
Rohsenow, H. 116

romance of resistance 13
rural unrest
  and free space 40–9
  theories of 41–2

Sangren, Steven 117
Sanjiang 57, 58, 59
Sanxia (Taiwan)
  ghost festival 171
  meanings of rituals 7, 8, 19
  temples 55–6, 119, 121
saturation 180–3
  of meaning 16–29
  in spirit possession 75–6, 83–4
  in Taiping 35, 51–68
  in Taiwanese ghost
    worship 129–53
  in Taiwanese ritual 118–28
Schöpflin, G. 206
Scott, James 10, 11, 14
second economy 201–2
sects 174–6
  *see also under specific names*
sesame oil chicken: as
    offering 136–7
sexuality
  female, threat of 136–7
  unclean 135
Shakers (American) 92–3
Shang oracles 92
Shi Dakai 47, 66, 80, 98
signs 76
silver mines 43
singing, paired 47, 57, 59, 61–2
socialist states
  free space 200–4
  and identity 213–18
  official language 205–6
Soviet Union: official
    language 206
spirits: corrupt 74–5
  *see also* journeys; possession;
    writing
state *see* government
strongmen 45–6
structuralism: and mediators 17
students
  in Tiananmen
    demonstrations 190–6

after Tiananmen
    demonstrations 198
study groups 211–12
  alternative institutions 203–4
  interpretation of
    Tiananmen 198
subversion 13, 208–13
superstition 176
symbolism: in Tiananmen 193–4

T-shirts: as subversion 210–11
Taborite heresy 90–1
Taiping (formerly God
    Worshipers) 3, 13, 28
  background 33–49
  bandit recruitment 44–5
  ethnic composition 79–80
  free space for 40–9, 51–60
  ideology 33–5; religious
    belief 34–5, 50–1, 60–4
  magical curing 64–8
  mediums 73–5
  political organization 86–110
  publications 100–1
  resistance 167–8
  and saturation 50–68
  spirit possession 69–85
  transformation 86–7, 97–103
  women in 82–3
Taiwan
  ghost worship 3–4, 28; and
    cultural domination 169–
    83; precipitations 154–68;
    saturated ritual 129–53
  *guniang* temples 59
  lotteries 139–42, 178–9
  religion: background 113–28;
    and capital 148–52, 166–7;
    control of 176–80;
    resurgence of 115–16, 146–8
  Religion of Compassion 77–8,
    82
  rituals 5–9, 19, 118–24
Taro Cult (New Guinea) 79, 81
Taussig, Michael 3, 11, 149, 166
television
  Eighteen Lords temple soap
    opera 161–4
  subversion 208–9

temples 52–3
    control of ritual 55–6
    destruction by Taiping 61, 62,
        100, 106
    multiple 120
    three wall 131
    in Taiwan 115–16;
        architecture 119–22
    in Xunzhou Prefecture 47–8,
        56–60
    *see also* Eighteen Lords temple
Thailand: ghosts 143–4
Thistle Mountain (Zijing Shan) 41,
    43, 50, 57, 58, 59
Thom, F. 206
Thompson, E. P. 10
Three Generations temples 56–7,
    58, 62, 100
Tian Hou (Mazu) 51, 54, 173–4
    *see also* Ma Co
Tiananmen Square
    demonstrations 4, 28–9
    background 189–91
    interpretations of 192–6; by
        state 196–200
    and resistance 218–21
    television news 208–9
totalitarianism
    and control 188–204
    and identity 213–18
    and resistance 219–21
traitors: exposure by
    mediums 98–9
Triads 44–5, 70, 114
Tristan chord 16–17
Turner, Victor 6
    communitas 26

visions 76
    of Hong Xiuquan 36–40, 72

Wagner, Richard: *Tristan and
    Isolde* 16–17
Wallace, Anthony 40
Wang Qingcheng 101
Wang Zuoxin 95

Watchtower movement
    (Rhodesia) 88–9
Watson, J. L. 54, 55, 173
Way of Unity (Yiguan Dao) 175
Weber, Max 179
    rationalization 22–3, 106–7
Wei Changhui 80, 97, 98
Wierzbicka, A. 206
women
    new mothers and
        pollution 136–7
    and spirit possession 81–3
    in Taiping 82–3
working class: tacit
    resistance 9–15
writing, spirit 174–5

Xiangzhou 57, 63
Xiao Chaogui 80, 82–3
    as Jesus 94, 96, 97–8, 99–100,
        104
    status in Taiping 73–4
Xunzhou Prefecture
    magical curing 65–7
    religion in 56–64
    rural unrest 40–9
    spirit possession 70–2

Yang Qingxiu 69
    status in Taiping 73, 74
Yang Xiuqing 80, 82
    downfall 104–5, 108
    as God 94, 98–100, 103
    magical curing 66–7
Yao 80
    Pangu god 47, 58–9
    spirit journeys 72, 73
    in Xunghou Prefecture 46, 48
Yao Ying 99, 170

Zhang Zhao (Big-head Goat) 44,
    45
Zhao Ziyang 191
Zhou Enlai 192
Zhou Xineng 99
Zhuang 80
    in Xunzhou Prefecture 46, 47